The Cambridge Companion to

John Updike is one of the most prolific and import.
contemporary period, with an acclaimed body of work that spans half a century and is inspired by everything from American exceptionalism to American
popular culture. This Companion joins together a distinguished international
team of contributors to address both the major themes in Updike's writing as
well as the sources of controversy that Updike's writing has often provoked. It
traces the ways in which historical and cultural changes in the second half of
the twentieth century have shaped not just Updike's reassessment of America's
heritage, but his reassessment of the literary devices by which that legacy is
best portrayed. With a chronology and bibliography of Updike's published
writings, this is the only guide students and scholars of Updike will need to
understand this extraordinary writer.

STACEY OLSTER is Professor of English at the State University of New York,
Stony Brook.

THE CAMBRIDGE
COMPANION TO
JOHN UPDIKE

EDITED BY
STACEY OLSTER

CAMBRIDGE
UNIVERSITY PRESS

CAMBRIDGE UNIVERSITY PRESS
Cambridge, New York, Melbourne, Madrid, Cape Town, Singapore, São Paulo

Cambridge University Press
The Edinburgh Building, Cambridge CB2 2RU, UK

Published in the United States of America by Cambridge University Press, New York

www.cambridge.org
Information on this title: www.cambridge.org/9780521607308

© Cambridge University Press 2006

First published 2006

Printed in the United Kingdom at the University Press, Cambridge

A catalogue record for this publication is available from the British Library

ISBN-13 978-0-521-84532-8 hardback
ISBN-10 0-521-84532-7 hardback
ISBN-13 978-0-521-60730-8 paperback
ISBN-10 0-521-60730-2 paperback

CONTENTS

NOTES ON CONTRIBUTORS

Marshall Boswell is the T. K. Young Professor of English at Rhodes College in Memphis, Tennessee. He is the author of *John Updike's Rabbit Tetralogy: Mastered Irony in Motion* (2001) and *Understanding David Foster Wallace* (2003). In addition, he has authored two works of original fiction, the story collection *Trouble With Girls* (2003) and a novel titled *Alternative Atlanta* (2005). He is currently working on a new novel.

John N. Duvall is Professor of English and editor of *MFS: Modern Fiction Studies* at Purdue University, West Lafayette, Indiana. He is the author of *Faulkner's Marginal Couple* (1990) and *The Identifying Fictions of Toni Morrison* (2000), the editor of *Productive Postmodernism: Consuming Histories and Cultural Studies* (2002), and co-editor of *Faulkner and Postmodernism* (2002).

Donald J. Greiner holds the chair of Carolina Distinguished Professor of English at the University of South Carolina, where he also serves as Associate Provost and Dean of Undergraduate Affairs. In addition, he is co-executive editor of the journal *Critique: Studies in Contemporary Fiction*. He is the author of three books and dozens of articles on John Updike, and he has amassed one of the largest private collections of Updike material in the United States.

D. Quentin Miller is Associate Professor of English at Suffolk University, Boston. He is the author of *John Updike and the Cold War: Drawing the Iron Curtain* (2001). He is also the editor of *Prose and Cons: New Essays on Contemporary U.S. Prison Literature* (2005) and of *Re-Viewing James Baldwin: Things Not Seen* (2000). He has published a composition textbook entitled *The Generation of Ideas* (2005) and is one of the editors of the *Heath Anthology of American Literature*. His essays have appeared in journals such as *American Literature*, *American Literary Realism*, and *Legacy: A Journal of American Women Writers*.

Stacey Olster is Professor of English at the State University of New York at Stony Brook. She is the author of *Reminiscence and Re-Creation in Contemporary American Fiction* (1989) and *The Trash Phenomenon: Contemporary Literature, Popular Culture, and the Making of the American Century* (2003). Her articles have appeared in *Critical Inquiry, Modern Fiction Studies, Studies in the Novel, Michigan Quarterly Review*, and *Critique*.

Sanford Pinsker is an Emeritus Professor at Franklin & Marshall College, Lancaster, Pennsylvania. He now lives in south Florida where he continues to write about American literature and culture on cloudy days.

James Plath is Professor of English at Illinois Wesleyan University and the editor of *Conversations with John Updike* (1994). His first work on Updike examined *The Painterly Aspects of John Updike's Fiction*. Essays of his also appear in *Rabbit Tales: Poetry and Politics in John Updike's Rabbit Novels* (1998) and *John Updike and Religion: The Sense of the Sacred and the Motions of Grace* (1999).

Jay Prosser is lecturer in American Literature and Culture at the University of Leeds, England. His essays on American literature have appeared in *PMLA, Modern Fiction Studies, A/B: Auto/Biography Studies*, and *Yearbook of English Studies*, among other places. His most recent book is *Light in the Dark Room: Photography and Loss* (2005).

James A. Schiff, Assistant Professor of English at the University of Cincinnati, has written two books on John Updike: *John Updike Revisited* (1998) and *Updike's Version: Rewriting The Scarlet Letter* (1992). He is also the author of *Understanding Reynolds Price* (1996) and the editor of *Critical Essays on Reynolds Price* (1998).

Edward Vargo has been a professor of English and dean at Divine Word College in Iowa; Fu Jen University in Taipei, Taiwan; and Assumption University in Bangkok, Thailand. He is the author of one of the first full-length studies of Updike's writings, *Rainstorms and Fire: Ritual in the Novels of John Updike* (1973). In addition to his work on Updike, he has also published essays on cross-cultural readings of American literature and on higher education in the New World Order in international journals and collections. He currently lives and writes in Bangkok.

Kathleen Verduin is Professor of English at Hope College, Holland, Michigan. She is the author of articles on American literature and modern fiction. From 1983 to 1998 she served as co-editor of the series Studies in Medievalism and co-organizer of the annual International Conference on

Medievalism. She is at work on a study of Dante's influence on American writers from Emerson to Wharton.

Kristiaan Versluys teaches American literature at Ghent University in Belgium. He was president of the Belgian Luxembourg American Studies Association and secretary of the European Association for American Studies. He is the editor of *Neo-Realism in Contemporary American Literature* (1992) and publishes widely on Jewish-American literature and the literature of New York. He is the director of the Ghent Urban Studies Team (GUST), an interdisciplinary research group that deals with the city as both a physical and cultural phenomenon. He regularly teaches summer school at Columbia University. During the academic year 2004–05 he was a Fellow at the Netherlands Institute for Advanced Study, working on the discursive responses to 9/11.

CHRONOLOGY

1932   John Hoyer Updike is born on 18 March in Reading, Pennsylvania, the only child of Wesley Russell Updike, who later would teach mathematics at Shillington High School, and Linda Grace (Hoyer) Updike, an employee at Pomeroy's Department Store and aspiring writer. Until the age of thirteen, lives in Shillington (later fictionalized as Olinger), a suburb of Reading (later fictionalized as Brewer). For most of this period, lives with both his parents and maternal grandparents in the same house.

1936   Begins Shillington public schools.

1938   Experiences first attack of psoriasis.

1945   First publication, "A Handshake with the Congressman," appears in the Shillington High School *Chatterbox*. Moves with parents and grandparents to a farmhouse, originally owned by the Hoyers, in Plowville on 31 October.

1950   Graduates Shillington High School as senior class president and co-valedictorian. Enters Harvard University on a tuition scholarship, where he eventually majors in English. Begins writing and drawing sketches and cartoons for the *Harvard Lampoon*.

1953   Elected president of the *Harvard Lampoon*. Marries Mary Pennington, a Radcliffe fine arts student and daughter of a Unitarian minister, on 26 June.

1954   Graduates from Harvard *summa cum laude*. Spends 1954–55 academic year at the Ruskin School of Drawing and Fine Art in Oxford, England, on a Knox Fellowship. First poem published in the *New Yorker*, "Duet, with Muffled Brake Drums," appears in 14 August issue, followed by first short story, "Friends from Philadelphia," in 30 October issue. Offered a staff position at the magazine by fiction editor Katharine White.

1955   Daughter Elizabeth born on 1 April. Returns to US and sets up
        house on West 85th Street and Riverside Drive in New York City.
        Becomes a "Talk of the Town" writer for the *New Yorker*.

1957   Son David born on 19 January. Leaves the *New Yorker* and moves
        to Ipswich, Massachusetts (later fictionalized as Tarbox), to
        concentrate on his fiction and poetry.

1958   First poetry collection, *The Carpentered Hen and Other Tame
        Creatures*, published.

1959   First novel, *The Poorhouse Fair*, and first short story collection, *The
        Same Door*, published. Awarded Guggenheim Fellowship to
        support work on *Rabbit, Run*. Immerses himself in writings of
        Søren Kierkegaard and Karl Barth. Son Michael born on 14 May.

1960   *Rabbit, Run*, with alterations to avoid potential obscenity lawsuits,
        published. *The Poorhouse Fair* wins the Rosenthal Foundation
        Award of the National Institute of Arts and Letters. Daughter
        Miranda born on 15 December.

1962   Teaches creative writing at Harvard in July and August, the first of
        two unsatisfying stints as a college instructor.

1963   *The Centaur* published and receives the National Book Award for
        Fiction the following year.

1964   Elected to the National Institute of Arts and Letters. Travels to
        Russia and Eastern Europe as part of the US-USSR Cultural
        Exchange Program.

1965   Awarded Le prix du meilleur livre étranger for *The Centaur*. Elected
        to the American Academy of Arts and Letters. Starts depositing his
        papers in the Houghton Library at Harvard.

1966   "The Bulgarian Poetess" wins First Prize in the O. Henry Prize
        Stories competition.

1967   Expresses support of Vietnam War among responses collected in
        Authors Take Sides on Vietnam. Along with other writers signs
        letter urging Soviet writers to help safeguard Jewish cultural
        institutions.

1968   *Couples* published and remains on the bestseller lists for a year.
        Updike featured on 26 April cover of *Time*. Moves to London for a
        year with his family and begins research into the life of James
        Buchanan, Pennsylvania's only US President.

1969   *Midpoint and Other Poems* published.

1970   Film version of *Rabbit, Run* released.

1971   *Rabbit Redux* published and receives the Signet Society Medal for
        Achievement in the Arts.

1972 Appointed Honorary Consultant in American Letters to the Library of Congress for a three-year term. Wesley Updike dies on 16 April.

1973 Travels to Ghana, Nigeria, Tanzania, Kenya, and Ethiopia as a Fulbright Lincoln Lecturer.

1974 Separates from his wife Mary and moves into an apartment in Boston. Teaches at Boston University in the fall, his last stint as a college instructor.

1975 *A Month of Sundays*, first of three rewritings of *The Scarlet Letter*, published.

1976 Elected to the fifty-member Academy of Arts and Letters. Awarded no-fault divorce in March.

1977 Marries Martha Ruggles Bernhard on 30 September. Lives with her and her three sons in Georgetown, Massachusetts.

1978 Testifies against government support of the arts before House of Representatives Subcommittee on Select Education.

1979 *Too Far to Go: The Maples Stories* published and made into a two-hour television movie.

1981 *Rabbit Is Rich* published and wins the National Book Critics Circle Award, to be followed the next year by the Pulitzer Prize for Fiction and the American National Book Award. Updike receives the Edward MacDowell Medal for literature and is made the subject of a BBC documentary, "What Makes Rabbit Run?"

1982 Appears on 18 October cover of *Time*. Moves to Beverly Farms, Massachusetts, in May.

1984 Receives the National Book Critics Circle Award for Criticism for *Hugging the Shore*.

1987 Receives the Elmer Holmes Bobst Award for Fiction. Movie adaptation of *The Witches of Eastwick* released.

1989 *Self-Consciousness* (memoirs) published. Linda (Hoyer) Updike dies on 10 October. Updike presented with the National Medal of Arts at the White House.

1990 *Rabbit at Rest* published, completing the Rabbit tetralogy, and wins the National Book Critics Circle Award, to be followed the next year by the Pulitzer Prize for Fiction.

1991 Receives First Prize in the O. Henry Prize Stories competition for "A Sandstone Farmhouse" and Italy's Premio Scanno Prize for *Trust Me*.

1992 Travels to Brazil. Awarded an honorary Doctor of Letters degree from Harvard University.

1993 *Collected Poems 1953–1993* published.

1995 Awarded the Howells Medal from the American Academy of Arts
and Letters, given every five years to the best work of fiction
published during that period, for *Rabbit at Rest*. Receives the
French honorary rank of Commandeur de l'Ordre des Arts et des
Lettres. *Rabbit Angstrom: A Tetralogy* published.

1996 *In the Beauty of the Lilies* published and receives the Ambassador
Book Award.

1998 Receives the Harvard Arts First Medal and the National Book
Foundation Medal for Distinguished Contribution to American
Letters.

2000 *Gertrude and Claudius* and *Licks of Love* published.

2003 Presented with the National Medal for the Humanities at the White
House. *The Early Stories, 1953–1975* published.

2004 Receives the PEN/Faulkner Award for Fiction for *The Early Stories,
1953–1975*.

ABBREVIATIONS

All page citations to Updike's works refer to the first editions listed in the Select Bibliography. When, for purposes of clarification, additional information was required, shortened titles appear. Those abbreviations refer to the following texts:

Afterlife	*The Afterlife and Other Stories*
Americana	*Americana and Other Poems*
Assorted	*Assorted Prose*
Back	*Bech Is Back*
Bay	*Bech at Bay: A Quasi-Novel*
Bech	*Bech: A Book*
Brazil	*Brazil*
Buchanan	*Buchanan Dying: A Play*
Carpentered	*The Carpentered Hen and Other Tame Creatures*
Centaur	*The Centaur*
Coup	*The Coup*
Couples	*Couples*
Early	*The Early Stories, 1953–1975*
Farm	*Of the Farm*
Gertrude	*Gertrude and Claudius*
Hugging	*Hugging the Shore: Essays and Criticism*
Licks	*Licks of Love: Short Stories and a Sequel*
Lilies	*In the Beauty of the Lilies*
Looking	*Just Looking: Essays on Art*
Marry	*Marry Me: A Romance*
Memories	*Memories of the Ford Administration: A Novel*
Midpoint	*Midpoint and Other Poems*
Month	*A Month of Sundays*
More	*More Matter: Essays and Criticism*
Museums	*Museums and Women and Other Stories*

Music	*The Music School: Short Stories*
Odd	*Odd Jobs: Essays and Criticism*
Picked-Up	*Picked-Up Pieces*
Pigeon	*Pigeon Feathers and Other Stories*
Poorhouse	*The Poorhouse Fair*
Problems	*Problems and Other Stories*
Redux	*Rabbit Redux*
Rest	*Rabbit at Rest*
Rich	*Rabbit Is Rich*
Roger's	*Roger's Version*
Run	*Rabbit, Run*
S.	*S.*
Same	*The Same Door: Short Stories*
Seek	*Seek My Face*
Self-Consciousness	*Self-Consciousness: Memoirs*
Tetralogy	*Rabbit Angstrom: A Tetralogy*
Tossing	*Tossing and Turning: Poems*
Toward	*Toward the End of Time*
Witches	*The Witches of Eastwick*

INTRODUCTION: "A SORT OF HELPLESSLY 50'S GUY"

STACEY OLSTER

At the beginning of *U and I* (1991), news of Donald Barthelme's death prompts Nicholson Baker to contemplate how "disassembled and undirected and simply bereft" he would feel were he to learn of the demise of the writer he considers his "emotional plenipotentiary": "All I wanted, all I counted on, was Updike's immortality . . . He was, I felt, the model of the twentieth-century American man of letters: for him to die would be for my generation's personal connection with literature to die."[1] Hyperbolic, perhaps, but not inaccurate given the enormously prolific career that John Updike has had since the publication of his first story in 1954: twenty-one novels, fifteen short story collections, seven volumes of poetry, seven essay collections, five children's books, one play, and one memoir. It is no wonder that Baker, who acknowledges having read Updike "very intermittently," still admits to "thinking about him constantly."[2]

Updike's subject, broadly construed, has always been America, where, as the poem "Americana" (2001) states, "beauty is left / to make it on its own, with no directives / from kings or cultural commissars on high" (*Americana*, 5). Indeed, spanning as it does the entire second half of the twentieth century, Updike's writing provides a historical roadmap that traces the changes undergone by the nation since the end of the Second World War: beginning with the regionalism of the autobiographical short stories and the creation of Olinger as a Pennsylvania equivalent of Faulkner's Yoknapatawpha and Anderson's Winesburg, extending to the Cold War whose inception and end frames the epic Rabbit Angstrom tetralogy (1960, 1971, 1981, 1990), and projected forward to a post-holocaust 2020 that is the temporal setting of *Toward the End of Time* (1997). Less obviously, but nevertheless consistently, Updike's subject has also been writing, evidenced first by his reviews of other writers – past (for example, Hawthorne, Melville, Whitman, Wharton, Mencken) as well as present (Bellow, Vonnegut, Le Guin, Tyler, Roth), foreign (Queneau, Calvino, Sōseki, Borges, Soyinka) as well as American – and apparent more and more in the intertextual allusiveness and metafictional devices that permeate his own novels themselves (*A Month of Sundays* [1975], *S.* [1988], *Memories of the Ford Administration* [1992], *Gertrude and Claudius* [2000]). In so doing, he has joined an awareness of contemporary theoretical developments to the modernist influence of those writers – Joyce, Proust, and Nabokov – he most often claims as his literary antecedents.

These concerns are not unique to Updike, of course. Among those contemporaries who emerged during the 1950s and whose works also may be seen as chronicling the past half-century of American history, the names of Norman Mailer, Gore Vidal, and Philip Roth come immediately to mind. But unlike Mailer, who approaches his subject by way of the psychopathic outsider in works like *The Executioner's Song* (1979) and *Oswald's Tale* (1995), or Vidal, who adopts the point of view of the privileged Washington, DC, insider in his "American Chronicle" series, or Roth, who employs the lens of Jewish ethnicity in *American Pastoral* (1997) and *The Plot Against America* (2004), Updike has devoted himself to the transcription of "middleness with all its grits, bumps, and anonymities, in its fullness of satisfaction and mystery" (*Assorted*, 186). Significantly, Updike's relationship to that "middle" has altered over time. In 1968, the year that *Couples* was published, his appearance on the 26 April cover of *Time* that accompanied a feature on "The Adulterous Society" presumed that Updike's perspective typified the American perspective. In 1989, by contrast, the writer who still located his authorial "stock in trade" in "an intuition into the mass consciousness and an identification with our national fortunes" was forced to admit that the liberal political position by which he defined himself "had unfairly gone unfashionable on me" during that same late 1960s period (*Self-Consciousness*, 124, 125). Far from simply – and uncritically – articulating the concerns of an American mainstream, then, Updike's canon tells the more interesting story of a writer, often distinctly out of sync with his culture, grappling with a half-century's worth of change.

Born in 1932, Updike is too young for that "unfashionable" political position to have been the result of what Thomas Hill Schaub has termed the "story of chastened liberalism" that the failure of Soviet Russia to live up to the utopian Marxist dream produced.[3] On the contrary, to the extent that Updike identifies himself as having a political affiliation, it is the result of early exigency: of growing up the son of a Roosevelt Democrat forced to supplement a high school teacher's salary with construction work during the summers and the grandson of a Jacksonian Democrat forced to labor on town highway crews after losing his money in the 1929 Wall Street Crash, of coming from a family, in short, that "had simply *been* poor, and voted Democrat out of crude self-interest" (119). The priorities inscribed in his writing, nonetheless, are fully in keeping with key elements of that 1950s discourse in which a liberalism defined, according to Lionel Trilling, by "an impassioned longing to believe" and betrayed by Soviet practices eventuated:[4] the replacement of ideology with psychology, adherence to a realism of ordinary facts as distinct from the perceived naïveté of 1930s–1940s naturalism and social realism, affirmation of what William Phillips dubbed "new 'Americanism.'"[5] Yet if such confluence between personal and cultural values enabled Updike to claim, in retrospect, "I was happy in the Fifties" – especially after having survived "the khaki-brown Forties and the grit-gray Thirties" (*More*, 25) – the fiction that emerged from that period did not provide the triumphant "yea-saying to the goodness and joy of life" that a 1955 *Life* editorial titled "Wanted: An American Novel" demanded.[6] Reflecting instead his sense of the period as an intermediate "post-war decade," the 1950s in Updike's early work typically figures, in recollection or direct portrayal, as a "middle bulge" (*Coup*, 132), a "climate of time between, of standoff and day-by-day" (*Couples*, 106). As such, the tensions of Cold War standoffs are translated into the tensions of domestic standoffs – what Updike has called the "politico-marital" (*Self-Consciousness*, 134) – and competitive gamesmanship, and an inability to locate viable systems of belief yields endings in which characters remain in suspension.

Nowhere are these qualities more clearly displayed than in *Rabbit, Run* (1960), the "helplessly 50's kind of book written by a sort of helplessly 50's guy," as Updike recalled, that serves in many ways as a template for much of the fiction that follows.[7] Overflowing ashtrays, dust balls beneath radiators, pork chops congealing in grease, and scatter rugs whose corners keep turning under comprise the facts at the forefront of Harry Angstrom's daily life, while in the background Dwight D. Eisenhower and Harold Macmillan begin a series of talks in Gettysburg and Tibetans battle Chinese Communists in Lhasa. Excellence in sports becomes a gauge of excellence in love, as Harry compares his first-rate basketball career with his second-rate marriage. Athletic rivalry translates into erotic rivalry once Harry discovers that a former teammate has slept with his mistress. Perhaps most important, the "crisscrossing mess" of domesticity that "clings to [Harry's] back like a tightening net" is just a localized version of the "red lines and blue lines and stars" that form the "net he is somewhere caught in" that, in turn, forms the map of the country by which he tries to chart his escape at the novel's outset (*Run*, 14, 36). Receiving no answer to the question posed during that aborted attempt – in an America that "from shore to shore" seems identical, "[i]s it just these people I'm outside, or is it all America?" (33) – and confronted by "a paralyzing sense of reality" in which "his child is really dead, his day is really done" (302), he ends the book once again midflight.

And with the final word "runs" that concludes the book, Updike's character joins the many others in postwar American fiction, of quite varying literary predilections, whose vain searches – whether for freedom from responsibility or responsibility to fill the "vast blank" of freedom (50) – leave them, often literally, in transit: John Laskell boarding a train on the last pages of Trilling's *The Middle of the Journey* (1947), the eponymous narrator preparing to emerge from underground in Ralph Ellison's *Invisible Man* (1952), Yossarian going AWOL in Joseph Heller's *Catch-22* (1961), perhaps most ominous, Jake Horner getting into a taxi en route to "Terminal," the final word in John Barth's *The End of the Road* (1958).

It is Updike's devotion to a form of layered realism wherein what is visible suggests what is invisible, both equally constitutive of what should be considered "real," that distinguishes Harry's quest as more than just another 1950s rebellion against a conformist society, however. "Plain realism has never seemed to me enough," he stated when commenting upon his preference for "crotchety modernist magicians" like Joyce and Calvino. "Novel-readers must have a plot, no doubt, and a faithful rendering of the texture of the mundane; but a page of printed prose should bring to its mimesis something extra, a kind of supernatural as it were, to lend everything roundness – a fine excess that corresponds with the intricacy and opacity of the real world" (*Odd*, 869–870). Typically, that roundness in Updike's work is achieved by way of connections among unlike things. As he explained in a 1964 speech titled "Why Write?," drawing on a sheet of paper "an assortment of objects – flowers, animals, stars, toaster, chairs, comic-strip creatures, ghosts, noses" – and connecting them with lines provided a valuable early exercise, for when completed "they all became the fruit of a single impossible tree" (*Picked-Up*, 34). Thus, in *Rabbit, Run*, a basketball hoop endowed with "high perfect hole," "crotch of the rim," and "pretty skirt of net" gains transcendental import when the orgasm that concludes a later amorous act is described as a "falling through" (37, 4, 85). But since the roadmap that Harry follows in his attempt to escape from Brewer is also described as a "net" in which he feels himself trapped, and the image of descent prefigures all those airplane crashes – at Lockerbie, of John F. Kennedy Jr. – that punctuate the later Rabbit works, the sexuality by which the human condition is transcended is complicated by intimations of human mortality that cannot be denied.

In the 1950s those intimations were more than abstract for Updike, whose "inner alarm" at "all the desolating objective evidence of our insignificance and futility and final nonexistence" was only alleviated by the reading of Søren Kierkegaard and Karl Barth (*Odd*, 844). Their works affirmed that God was part of that irrefutable reality that Updike sought to portray.

"'Something beyond which it is impossible to conceive anything greater' must exist in reality as well as in the mind," he paraphrased in a review of Barth's *Anselm: Fides Quaerens Intellectum* (1931), "for if it existed only in the mind, it would not be 'something beyond which it is impossible to conceive anything greater'" (*Assorted*, 275–276). Such a deity has little to do with institutionalized religion – Updike very early in his career dismissed the "more or less watered down Puritan God" worshiped in "nice white church[es]" who "is not very real to me" in favor of "God who throws the lightning bolt" who is "God the Creator"[8] – and everything to do with faith. Indeed, it is faith alone and unaccompanied by the false support of good works that, in Updike's view, distinguished his own Lutheran upbringing from that of other Christian denominations (*Self-Consciousness*, 130). Because this God is not the product of human invention but is "Wholly Other" (*totaliter aliter*), as Updike's reading of Barth makes clear, "We cannot reach Him; only He can reach us" (*Assorted*, 273–274).

Correspondingly, one of the ways in which God reaches humans in Updike's work is through those real things that function as "masks for God."[9] As Clarence Wilmot, one of Updike's clergyman characters, preaches, "We do not worship a God immensely above us, out of human reach, but One Who does not disdain to touch us, to lay even rough hands upon us, . . . and to speak to men in metaphors drawn from their daily lives" (*Lilies*, 50–51). The inarticulate Rabbit, who "has no taste for the dark, tangled, visceral aspect of Christianity" but still believes in an "unseen world" with which his actions constitute transactions (*Run*, 237, 234), thus can see in a golf-ball's trajectory that magical "*it*" that, as Updike later explains, holds out "the hope of perfection, of a perfect weightlessness and consummate ease," ultimately, of "grace" (*Run*, 134; *Rest*, 56). In contrast, Teddy, Clarence's lapsed Christian son, senses the need for faith expressed in his rootless grandson's letter, "[b]ut Teddy had no faith to offer; he had only the facts of daily existence. Weather, family news, local change" (*Lilies*, 412).

As J. D. Salinger's forays into Zen Buddhism, Flannery O'Connor's and Walker Percy's strict Catholicism, Bernard Malamud's Jewish mysticism, and, perhaps most idiosyncratic, Norman Mailer's proposed war between God and the Devil attest, Updike was not alone in his religious inclinations during the 1950s. Nor is he alone in them today: one thinks, for example, of all those quotidian things – ATM machines, illegal pharmaceuticals, supermarkets – that join Don DeLillo's characters in shared systems of belief. With the publication of *Couples* and declaration of "sex as the emergent religion, as the only thing left," however, Updike established his own particular niche.[10] In the "*post-pill paradise*" that is Tarbox, Massachusetts (*Couples*, 52, 91), God presides by way of the "pricking steeple and flashing [weather]cock" that adorn the Congregational Church and wife swapping supports the edifice erected by residents "to keep the night out" (82, 7). As such, what is individualized in *Rabbit, Run* becomes socialized in *Couples*.

To the extent that success in this death-defying venture depends on a mythologizing of women – with nothing less than God located between the legs of one woman and the genitalia of another described as "heavenly" (343, 194) – Updike's theologizing of the adulterous union harks back in American literature to Hawthorne's "instinctive tenet that matter and spirit are inevitably at war" (*Hugging*, 77). Not coincidentally, the city on a hill in Plymouth County that is Tarbox was first settled as a port by Puritans. To the extent that the adulterous husband whose presence hovers over the novel is John F. Kennedy, its theologizing of sex is a specifically post-Second World War phenomenon, the act of upper-middle-class thirtysomethings who move to Tarbox in the 1950s and, living in "an indulgent economy" (105), lose all sense of the Protestant work ethic they have inherited: "The men had stopped having careers and the women had stopped having babies. Liquor and love were left" (12). If Harry Angstrom resists David Reisman's *Lonely Crowd* (1950), these characters are William H. Whyte's *Organization M[e]n* (1956). Frank, a banker, asks his friend Harold's wife Marcia to "sexualize" him because "[w]ith this sloppy marketing running, it's probably the best investment left" (112); Harold, a stockbroker, looks upon Frank's wife Janet as "a bad investor who would buy high and sell after the drop and take everybody she could down with her" (119). Carol reflects upon "what a lot of *work*" goes into the biological creation of each human being (238), and Janet confirms the sentiment when submitting to "the long work" of Harold's second climax (152).

If this depiction of sex as work qualifies the degree to which Updike saw the election of Kennedy as having brought back "the *fun* in being an American" (305), as characters claim – "fun" being the noun most often invoked by Updike characters who attempt to distinguish the 1950s from other decades (*Coup*, 272; *Seek*, 141) – the assassination of Kennedy that occurs at midpoint shatters that myth of happy consensus entirely. In Updike's portrayal, in fact, it did not so much leave "an emptiness [as] revealed one already there," is less "confirmation of chaos" to come as indication that the period through which the characters have been living is "one of those dark ages that visits mankind between millennia, between the death of and rebirth of gods, when there is nothing to steer by but sex and stoicism and the stars" (294, 372). And the novel shows no signs of that darkness abating. The shift of Tarbox from idyllic retreat to suburban sprawl that signals a modernization justified "as part of the national necessity, the overarching honor of an imperial nation" (387), as evidenced by hints of future war in Vietnam, may also signal a nation *"fat and full of pimples and always whining for more candy"* that God *"doesn't love . . . any more"* (200), as evidenced by the apocalyptic burning of the Congregational Church "by God's own lightning" (441). Even worse, it may signal a nation that God has never especially favored above all others: the conflagration turns out to be the result of a fundamental unsoundness in the building's construction. Having already quashed the myth of American consensus, the book ends by querying the myth of American exceptionalism. In so doing, it forms part of that ongoing investigation to which Updike has devoted himself since first posing the question in 1957: "What is it that distinguishes the American Man from his counterparts in other climes; what *is* it that makes him so special?" (*Assorted*, 4).

As Richard H. Pells has argued, that myth formed very much a part of 1950s discourse, particularly after the failure of leftist politics abroad left intellectuals scrambling to differentiate between the United States and Europe.[11] Emerging first by way of contrast – "a political lesser evil" (Leslie A. Fiedler), a republic "fundamentally sounder and stronger than its enemies" (Jacques Barzun), "the distinctly better mousetrap" (John Updike)[12] – America eventuated in a plethora of texts that claimed to have uncovered the source of its uniqueness and the uniqueness of its national character: Henry Nash Smith's *Virgin Land* (1950), Perry Miller's second volume of *The New England Mind* (1953), R. W. B. Lewis's *The American Adam* (1955), John William Ward's *Andrew Jackson: Symbol for an Age* (1955), and Marvin Meyers's *The Jacksonian Persuasion* (1957), to name but a few.[13]

Aware of the imaginative component that infuses all such attempts at national definition, Updike in midcareer conceded: "When a Japanese says 'Japanese,' he is trapped on a little definite racial fact, whereas when we say 'American' it is not a fact, it is an act, of faith, a matter of lines on a map and words on paper, an outline it will take generations and centuries more to fill in" (*Problems*, 45) – the nation not "a face of God," as Harry Angstrom assumes (*Redux*, 47), but another imagined community, to borrow Benedict Anderson's phrasing.[14] At the same time, Updike has always remained aware that the land in which a Shillington boy, by dint of effort, could get a Harvard education, a *New Yorker* staff position, and the chance to practice his craft unencumbered by other obligations was still a "country that had kept its hackneyed promises – life, liberty, pursuit of happiness – to me" (*Self-Consciousness*, 137). Qualification of the actuality in his work is thus offset by celebration of the ideal. A State Department political officer asserts, "I love this crazy, wasteful, self-hating nation in spite of itself" (394) while the Vietnam War still rages in *In the Beauty of the Lilies* (1996). Updike defends his support of the same conflict by praising America as a "great roughly rectangular country severed from Christ by the breadth of the sea"

(*Self-Consciousness*, 103), majestic in size, unique in being providentially ordained, but still separated from Christ by its practices. What changes over time is the balance between acclamation and reservation.

Significantly, it is not the shift in America's fortunes that causes the greatest shift in that balance. The America of the Rabbit novels is in steady decline as the threat that communist aggression poses in the first two books is replaced by the leverage that oil grants the Middle East in the third and the edge that technology affords Japan in the fourth. Yet Harry Angstrom still proclaims American unilateralism at the end of *Rabbit Is Rich* (1981) – "Who needs Afghanistan? Fuck the Russkies. Fuck the Japs, for that matter. We'll go it alone, from sea to shining sea" (465) – while the country is literally and figuratively running out of gas. Alfred Clayton can chart the resignation of Nixon, the non-election of Ford, and the selection of the "not, absolutely, convincing" Carter in *Memories of the Ford Administration* (1992), and affirm "[t]he torch still shines" (352, 79). Rather, it is the erosion in the 1950s of the bipolar politics from which America gained definition that causes that national symbol to dim as the Cold War comes to an end.[15] For, as Michael Rogin correctly recognizes, it is precisely that kind of binarism – whether conceived as Manicheanism, exceptionalism, or, to use his own term, "American political demonology" – that has been crucial in determining the concept of American citizenship from the start.[16] When, politically, "the only difference between the two old superpowers is they sell their trees to Japan in different directions," as Harry quips (*Rest*, 352), and, economically, the personalized rivalry of "good clean dog eat dog" is replaced by "Japan, and technology, and the profit motive" (*Rich*, 24; *Rest*, 272), why *not* wonder, as Harry does, "what's the point of being an American?" (*Rest*, 442–443). Hardly any, when the "frozen far heart . . . of the grand old republic" is as ready to infarct as the one diagnosed as "tired and stiff and full of crud" and, worst of all, "typical" that is accorded Harry in 1989 (442, 166).

This is not to suggest that Updike's admission of American typicality has made his political position any more fashionable than it was in 1989. On the contrary, his representation of American normativity in terms – exclusively, according to detractors – of middle-class white masculinity and apparent denigration of everyone else in terms of racialized, ethnic, and/or gendered otherness has provoked controversy since the start of his career. To be sure, Updike's work often seems to warrant such allegations. The deification of women as mistresses and dismissal of them as wives do combine in *Of the Farm* (1965) into a view of all women as daughters of Eve, indifferent to that "riddle" of death that men seek to solve and "a subspecies, less than equal to Man, a part of the whole" for having originated as part of his body (152, 151). The juxtaposition of black sexuality and Apollo 11 WASP technology in *Rabbit Redux* (1971) does introduce black and white as mirror-image binaries; conversely, the portrait of Africa "look[ing] like the country north of Vegas" in *The Coup* (1978) and ruled by a man as "American as apple pandowdy" can confirm the imaginative limitations of an author whose mirror reflects only a North American white man's visage (206, 173). Likewise, Henry Bech, for all that his "irrepressible Jewish God" contrasts with Updike's own "tenuous and diffident Other" (*Back*, 123, 122), may be more ego than alter: in Bulgaria the mirror "gave him back only himself"; in Jerusalem it gives him back southern California (*Bech*, 70; *Back*, 68). When, with his dying breath, a critic hurls the worst insult he can think of at him, it serves as Updike's wry acknowledgement of how outdated and circumscribed the "[m]iddle-middle" treatment of "[l]a bourgeoisie" to which Bech (and, by implication, Updike himself) has devoted himself has been deemed to be: "You're Fifties!" (*Bech*, 45; *Bay*, 206).

Yet evidence also exists – particularly in Updike's later works – that the ways in which gender, race, and ethnicity are defined may involve more than simple binaries. *The Witches of Eastwick* (1984) and *S.* (1988) open with husbands divorced, deserted, or turned to dust and women whose incantations and attempts at Eastern religion are driven by the same fear of death and desire for transcendence that habitually haunt Updike's men. *Gertrude and Claudius* (2000) presents a queen through whose bloodline the throne passes. *Seek My Face* (2002) defines the human species as "less differentiated by gender than many" and men and women as "both made to run, and to hang on to branches, and to eat nuts and berries" (252, 253). *Brazil* (1994) shows nature confounding all racial difference, as occurs when its hero and heroine exchange colors in the Mato Grosso. *Self-Consciousness* (1989) posits a genealogical inheritance of "mixed blood" and predicts an "ideal colorblind society" flickering at the "edge of the sluggishly evolving one" (164, 195). If nostalgia is indeed, as Updike long ago posited, "love for that part of ourselves which is . . . forever removed from change and corruption" (*Assorted*, 287), the evolution that occurs over his career shows him resisting that unnatural impulse.

By approaching Updike's writing more with respect to recurrent themes than individual texts, and by deliberately incorporating into its discussion those neglected works of the past decade, this volume of essays foregrounds the element of evolution into its very structure. In so doing, it seeks to do justice to Updike's *oeuvre* in a number of ways. First, it facilitates comparisons between Updike and other writers who have dealt with similar subjects over the course of their careers. Second, it juxtaposes earlier and later Updike works against each other – in effect, situates Updike in dialogue with himself – so as to illustrate the ways in which both inform each other. Third, it permits readers to consider the degree to which the evolution of Updike's career has allowed for the possibility of change. The trajectory of the volume, then, proceeds from a consideration of those subjects that form the basis of Updike's work to those subjects that time has forced him to reappraise, with the focus throughout on Updike's fiction, the genre with which readers are most familiar, and any other work (essays, reviews, poems) incorporated as ancillary.

"Part I: Early influences and recurrent concerns" introduces readers to the thematic appropriation of "middleness," the techniques of American neo-realism, and the orthodox brand of theology that underlie Updike's writing as constants. D. Quentin Miller opens this study of Updike's aesthetics by examining those early writings that take place in Olinger, the middle ground on which battles between insulation and stagnation, change and claustrophobia, are habitually waged by Updike's young and artistic alter egos. Kristiaan Versluys distinguishes the realism of Updike's early stories as a contemporary variation of a nineteenth-century original: its devotion to the quotidian indebted to William Dean Howells and Walt Whitman on the one hand, its search for an all-encompassing metaphor or moment of stasis adhering to the poststructuralist interrogation of fixed meaning on the other. Marshall Boswell concludes by discussing the influence that Kierkegaard's and Barth's dialectics have had on Updike's art and aesthetics, in particular on the novel of "moral debate" in which the clash between ethics and inner call to faith eventuates.

"Part II: Controversy and difference" examines the sexual mythologizing of women that derives from Updike's own religious impulse and the eroticizing/exoticizing of blacks and Jews that reflects a canonical American literary tradition. Within this section Kathleen Verduin juxtaposes Updike's reliance on feminine archetypes – earth mother, sexual temptress, and witch – that constrict women against the mundane realities of American life that he depicts as frustrating women. Jay Prosser extends Updike's interest in American slavery, which is to say imperialism at home, to the phenomenon of imperialism abroad and, with Updike's delineation of the chronic psoriasis from which he suffers, to skin as it is related to his most intimate self. Lastly, Sanford Pinsker explores the way in which Updike's cross-dressing as the Jewish Henry Bech, his most famous authorial alter ego, provides Updike with a mouthpiece that is simultaneously him and not him.

"Part III: American chronicles" traces the changes in the second half of the twentieth century that have mandated not just Updike's reassessment of America's heritage, but his reassessment of the literary devices by which that legacy is best portrayed. To that end, Edward Vargo turns his attention to Updike's portrayal of American history and charts the shift from a discourse grounded in naïve facticity to a discourse that, as problematized by postmodern theory, admits to history's tainted indeterminacy. James Plath focuses on Updike's reprise of one classic text of American literary history, *The Scarlet Letter* (1850), and his reconceptualization of infidelity as being as natural, within contemporary times, as fidelity. James A. Schiff explores Updike's depiction of American popular culture, and American movies in particular, as the means through which, in an age in which God would seem to have disappeared, both national and spiritual consolidation have come to be achieved. Finally, Donald J. Greiner surveys that post-Second World War age with respect to the Rabbit tetralogy in order to investigate Updike's portrait of American exceptionalism as the nation ordained by God and forged by Enlightenment principles begins to falter. The end result of such questioning of faith, as John N. Duvall's concluding essay on "U(pdike) & P(ostmodernism)" argues, is Updike's increasing experimentation with those narrative devices – metafiction, deconstruction, parody, pastiche – that refuse readers the comforts of certainty.

With the title of that concluding essay itself parodying the title of Updike's most widely anthologized story, "A & P" (1961), the reappraisal of Updike's writing to which this volume has been dedicated comes to a fitting close. If, as Nicholson Baker claims, Updike is indeed "the model of the twentieth-century man of letters" – not to mention the model of mainstream American literature, as the anthologizing of his work would seem to indicate – then his appropriation of such narrative devices as parody and pastiche might well suggest where that mainstream may now be heading.

NOTES

1. Nicholson Baker, *U and I: A True Story* (New York: Random House, 1991), pp. 13, 63, 13.
2. Ibid., p. 29.
3. Thomas Hill Schaub, *American Fiction in the Cold War* (Madison: University of Wisconsin Press, 1991), p. viii.
4. Lionel Trilling, Introduction (1975), *The Middle of the Journey* (1947; New York: Avon, 1976), p. xviii.
5. William Phillips, "Our Country and Our Culture," *Partisan Review*, September–October 1952, p. 586.
6. "Wanted: An American Novel," *Life*, 12 September 1955, p. 48. I am grateful to Thomas Hill Schaub for bringing this editorial to my attention.
7. John Updike, "Why Rabbit Had to Go," *New York Times Book Review*, 5 August 1990, p. 24.
8. Charles Thomas Samuels, "The Art of Fiction XLIII: John Updike," *Paris Review* 45 (1968), p. 101.

9. Ibid., p. 116.

10. James Plath, ed., *Conversations with John Updike* (Jackson: University Press of Mississippi, 1994), p. 52.

11. Richard H. Pells, *The Liberal Mind in a Conservative Age: American Intellectuals in the 1940s and 1950s* (New York: Harper and Row, 1985), pp. 149–150, 181.

12. Leslie A. Fiedler, "Our Country and Our Culture," *Partisan Review*, May–June 1952, p. 295; Jacques Barzun, "Our Country and Our Culture," *Partisan Review*, July–August 1952, p. 426; John Updike, *Self-Consciousness*, p. 139.

13. Pells, *The Liberal Mind*, pp. 149–150.

14. See Benedict Anderson, *Imagined Communities: Reflections on the Origin and Spread of Nationalism* (London: Verso, 1983).

15. For the most extensive treatment of the impact that the Cold War has had on Updike's writing, see D. Quentin Miller, *John Updike and the Cold War: Drawing the Iron Curtain* (Columbia: University of Missouri Press, 2001).

16. Michael Rogin, *Ronald Reagan, the Movie and Other Episodes in Political Demonology* (Berkeley: University of California Press, 1987), pp. 272–300.

I

EARLY INFLUENCES AND RECURRENT CONCERNS

I

D. QUENTIN MILLER

Updike, middles, and the spell of "subjective geography"

> When I write, I aim in my mind . . . toward a vague spot a little to the east of Kansas.
>
> – John Updike in a 1968 interview with Charles Thomas Samuels

Setting is never merely background in John Updike's fiction. His characters are so intertwined with their settings that their very identities adhere to certain places. Updike's subject matter has ranged considerably across time (in historical works like *In the Beauty of the Lilies* [1996] and futuristic works like *Toward the End of Time* [1997]) and place (Africa in *The Coup* [1978], the Soviet Union in *Bech: A Book* [1970], and Brazil in *Brazil* [1994]). Yet he is often associated with middles, especially the mid-Atlantic region, home to the American middle class. His relationship to his boyhood in small-town Shillington, Pennsylvania, in particular, has had a profound and enduring impact on his development and on his reputation. Shillington is the origin of his conception of "middleness," and this particular setting is linked to his art in tangible ways. In his 1962 memoir "The Dogwood Tree: A Boyhood" he writes, "To transcribe middleness with all its grits, bumps, and anonymities, in its fullness of satisfaction and mystery: is it possible or, in view of the suffering that violently colors the periphery and that at all moments threatens to move into the center, worth doing? Possibly not; but the horse-chestnut trees, the telephone poles, the porches, the green hedges recede to a calm point that in my subjective geography is still the center of the world."[1]

Because of this devotion to the center that is Shillington, Updike's critics have accused him of looking no further than his front door for inspiration. This accusation is especially unfair in the light of the many literary, mythical, and artistic inspirations we find throughout Updike's *oeuvre*. And yet: his uncanny ability to "transcribe middleness" by attending to precise, unvarnished reality, and to rely on his "subjective geography" to locate his work, is part of what solidifies his artistic vision. Details are the core substance of Updike's artistry. It may be a useful analogy to think of the details of his fiction as the home from which he departs into more abstract realms: science, religion, mythology, literature, and visual art. The details of his youth are directly linked to the home from which he departs, and especially in his early

fiction the process of leaving home and returning to it are the catalysts for
his art. To follow through with the analogy, Updike, especially in his early
career, departs from the details of his upbringing into many other universes,
but also returns to those details for inspiration, for ideas, and for a solid
foundation upon which to build his fiction.

In Updike's first two short story collections, *The Same Door* (1959) and
Pigeon Feathers (1962), there is a disparity between his relatively guarded
stories of the present or recent past (usually set in New York, England, or the
North Shore of Massachusetts) and the more evidently personal stories of
the past, set in the fictional Olinger. This disparity is evident not only in the
setting of the stories but in their narration: the Olinger stories are more often
than not first-person narratives. These stories are also categorized by restless
motion, either a character's desire to leave the small-town setting ("The
Happiest I've Been," "Flight," "A Sense of Shelter," "Pigeon Feathers") or
an adult character's unwilling return to his home town ("The Persistence of
Desire," "Home"). Two of Updike's first four novels, *The Centaur* (1963) and
Of the Farm (1965), also follow the pattern of guilty departure and difficult
return, respectively. Taken together, these early Olinger stories and novels
reflect Updike's ambivalence toward the details of the region he regards as
"the center of the world." As he describes in his 1962 memoir, the "suffering
that violently colors the periphery . . . threatens to move into the center,"
and it is natural to want protection against such suffering and violence.
At the same time, this center can be confining, even suffocating, especially
to characters with artistic ambition. The final phrase of the story "Home"
(1960) conveys this ambiguity: "in folds of familiarity the land tightened
around him" (*Pigeon*, 168). At once a blanket and a noose, the land of
Updike's youth is the perfect setting for *nostalgia* translated, according to its
Greek roots, as "the pain of returning home."

The driving force behind much of Updike's early fiction is an attempt to
bridge the gap between the man he has become and the boy he was. Robert
M. Luscher notes of *Pigeon Feathers*, "while some of the younger characters
flee *from* the past, those who have crossed or linger on the threshold between
adolescence and maturity flee *toward* the past, wrestling with its details and
yearning to recapture its mysteries."[2] A good example is the character Clyde
in "The Persistence of Desire" (1959) who "stood crisscrossed by a double
sense of himself, his present identity extending down from Massachusetts to
meet his disconsolate youth in Pennsylvania, projected upward from a distance of years" (12). The double self is created through a double-distancing
here, of time and space, and the act of writing chronicles Updike's attempts to
uncrisscross these disparate facets of his identity. His alter egos who escape
Olinger tend to be either writers or artists; art, as a result, is both a way

to escape the "grits, bumps, and anonymities" of middleness and a way to infuse them with meaning.

At the same time, the theme of expatriation or exile to a region outside of Olinger creates in Updike's protagonists a recurrent portrait of someone conscious of not-belonging, a liminal condition common to the artist who feels at once outside of his surroundings, yet simultaneously involved with them. "The Happiest I've Been" (1959), Updike's first story written as a first-person narrative, embodies both a return to Olinger and a departure from it. The narrator, John Nordholm, has returned from college on winter holiday, yet he leaves Olinger for Chicago to visit a girlfriend during the course of the story, and restlessness and motion are evident throughout. The narrator's surname might be a pun on "not home," for although he is in his home town, he spends the story departing from it. His nickname is "Norseman," which connotes an explorer; yet despite the motion of the story, John, like Harry Angstrom during his attempt at escape in *Rabbit, Run* (1960), does not get far from his house initially. The road trip around which the story revolves is an exercise in delay, and John's state of mind is that of an explorer coming to terms with the happiness of exploration itself. John's friend Neil tries to convince John's parents that the seventeen-hour drive to Chicago will be no different from staying home: "He'll be safer than in his bed," Neil assures Mrs. Nordholm (*Same*, 222). John, overwhelmingly excited by the prospect of flight, takes the opportunity to fix the details of home in his mind: "I embraced my mother and over her shoulder with the camera of my head tried to take a snapshot I could keep of the house, the woods behind it and the sunset behind them, the bench beneath the walnut tree where my grandfather cut apples into skinless bits and fed them to himself, and the ruts in the soft lawn the bakery truck had made that morning" (222).

He invests this look backwards with a good deal of meaning soon after; he and Neil have in common the fact that they live, unglamorously, with their grandparents: "This improved both our backward and forward vistas; we knew about the bedside commodes and midnight coughing fits that awaited most men, and we had a sense of childhoods before 1900, when the farmer ruled the land and America faced west" (223). The "vistas" he refers to are temporal here, but they also apply to the spatial vistas he describes, the details of his home and his thick description of the roads leading out of Olinger. After the chaotic all-night party that precedes his departure, John finds himself on the road and blissful, largely because of the road itself. Yet it is not just departure that explains his near-ecstasy, for he feels "a widespreading pride: Pennsylvania, your state" (242). Just as the act of departure brings his state into focus as something to be proud of, the act of remembering the happiest he has been gives John the ability to articulate the significance of both journey and place.

In other early stories Updike's young protagonists aim their mental cameras not over their mothers' shoulders, but directly at their mothers. The picture that emerges is one of a powerful woman who desires to set her son free, but also to keep control of him. "Flight" (1959) is Updike's second published story written in the first person, and Updike's transition into an author comfortable in that mode is apparent from the story's first sentence: "At the age of seventeen I was poorly dressed and funny-looking, and went around thinking about myself in the third person. 'Allen Dow strode down the street and home.' 'Allen Dow smiled a thin sardonic smile.' Consciousness of a special destiny made me both arrogant and shy" (*Pigeon*, 49). These sentences are laden with significance: Updike's narrator is unusually self-conscious about his appearance, he is aware of his relative lack of wealth, and he is developing the sensibility of a writer. Beyond that, he is burdened by a "special destiny," a role his sharp-tongued mother has bestowed upon him that is a curse as well as a blessing.

Allen's first narrated memory is of his mother climbing a mountain with him and pointing to Olinger below them, a town whose social disparities are evident from that vantage point. Allen's gaze lifts outward so that he can see "the entire county" and his mother, in a decidedly unmaternal gesture, digs her fingernails into his scalp and announces, "'There we all are, and there we'll all be forever.' She hesitated before the word 'forever,' and hesitated again before adding, 'Except you, Allen. You're going to fly'" (50). The image of flight is an appealing one, especially when contrasted with the images of burial that Updike's protagonists associate with the earth (such as Harry Angstrom in *Rabbit, Run* or David Kern in "Pigeon Feathers"). Allen's conflict arises from the tension between his mother's prophecy, which "felt like the clue [he] had been waiting all [his] childhood for" (50), and his inability to fulfill the prophecy while still in Olinger: "I cynically intended to exploit both the privileges of being extraordinary and the pleasures of being ordinary. She feared my wish to be ordinary; once she did respond to my protest that I was learning to fly, by crying with red-faced ferocity, 'You'll never learn, you'll stick and die in the dirt just like I'm doing'" (51).

Such mixed signals from his powerful and difficult-to-please mother partially account for the fact that Allen's flight and his homecoming are as trying as they are necessary. The title "Flight" has many connotations, but it acts in two main ways: the story of Allen's life, following the myth of his youth, is a story of flight from his stultifying home town; yet the story he tells us from a mature perspective is a kind of flight back to his past, even into his ancestral past as he begins with a meditation on generations, especially on his parents and grandparents. His flight into the past yields this observation: "each generation of parents commits atrocities against their children which by God's decree remain invisible to the rest of the world" (53). He studies a photograph of his mother and understands that her desperate prophecy about his "special destiny" may be little more than her own displaced, unfulfilled desire, for he knows that his mother's wish was to live in New York, yet she was unable to disobey her father's command that she stay: "the great moist weight of that forbidding continued to be felt in the house for years, and when I was a child, as one of my mother's endless harangues to my grandfather screamed toward its weeping peak, I could feel it around and above me, like a huge root encountered by an earthworm" (55). The imagery here is still that of mountains and earth, yet Allen is now aware of the enormous impediments to his own flight since he has compared himself to an earthworm. His mother's wishes for his transcendence seem inadequate to the task of transforming him into something that might fly.

Allen is sure that his mother's desire for flight – both his and her own – are related to her fear of marriage, the human force that has the capacity to "destroy" (59). In particular, Allen's mother has determined that she and Allen's grandfather had "been made captive by people better yet less than they," and Allen's father and the ghost of his grandmother "stood to one side, in the shadows but separate from the house's dark core, the inheritance of frustration and folly that had descended from my grandfather to my mother to me, and that I, with a few beats of my grown wings, was destined to reverse and redeem" (59). Such a graceful image contrasts sharply with Allen's self-consciousness, his humiliation at losing a public debate (even being scolded by the principal and booed by the audience), and his insecurity about how to approach sex. His romantic encounter with Molly Bingaman illustrates the damage of his mother's prophecy. His attraction to Molly has something to do with her relative wealth; of the four Olinger debaters, Allen observes, "She was the best dressed" (60), a detail that contrasts with his earlier description of himself as someone who was poorly dressed because his mother insisted on buying small quantities of well-made clothes instead of "a wide variety of cheap clothes" like his classmates wore (55). His special destiny, from the point of view of a self-conscious teenager, is to be the kid who sticks out, and he does not necessarily welcome such attention. When he returns from the debate, wounded by his poor performance but enervated by his encounter with Molly, Allen's mother scorns his behavior and tells him, "Don't go with little women, Allen. It puts you too close to the ground" (65). Since he has bought into her mythology of him as a youth fated to fly from the town in order to succeed, he sabotages his relationship with Molly, and embraces not his mother, but her story of him.

Allen's story becomes even larger than his mother, though she is its source. He uses it to account for his very identity within the Olinger community and feels powerless to act in any way except according to its dictates: "The entire town seemed ensnarled in my mother's myth, that escape was my proper fate. It was as if I were a sport that the ghostly elders of Olinger had segregated from the rest of the livestock and agreed to donate in time to the air; this fitted with the ambiguous sensation I had always had in the town, of being simultaneously flattered and rejected" (67). This "ambiguous sensation," coupled with the pressure to transcend the world around him, develops into anxiety, relief from which can come only through escape, in Allen's mind: "I kept listening for the sounds of my brain snapping, and the image of that gray, infinitely interconnected mass seemed to extend outward, to become my whole world, one dense organic dungeon, and I felt I had to get out; if I could just get out of this, into June, it would be blue sky, and I would be all right for life" (69). The overwhelming pressure preceding high school graduation is not an unusual sensation, but it is telling that Allen imagines the afterworld as "blue sky" since he associates flight with escape. His mother eventually "wins," forcing him to break off his liaison with Molly for good in favor of pursuing a better life beyond Olinger. We do not know for certain what Allen eventually becomes, though it is clear from the trajectory of the story – the development of a boy who thinks of himself in the third person and who tries to fulfill his destiny by reading late at night – that he is poised to become something like a writer. His revenge against his mother's insistence that he fly away, then, is that he flies back, through his memory, in order to tell this story.

The mother's role as liberator and limiter is sometimes played by younger women in Updike's early fiction. These young women offer the possibility for sex or romantic attraction as a transcendent force, yet they also seem stuck in Olinger. William in "A Sense of Shelter" (1960) is a victim of the same "special status" fate accorded to Allen in "Flight." When he declares his love for Mary Landis, she says, "You're going to go on and be a great man" (98). Like Allen's mother in "Flight," Mary sees marriage as the threat to this greatness yet, also like Allen's mother, Mary hates their town, especially their school, which she refers to as "this junky place" (96). William has begun to ascribe tremendous significance to their humble school, more to him than a mere shelter; he envisions it as a castle, himself the king, and Mary the queen. This may be a childish fantasy for someone about to graduate high school, but it coincides with the belief circulating through his town that he will become a "great man." So powerful is his understanding of this mythology that he does not even feel his own failure acutely. After his disastrous encounter with Mary in which he not only fails to convince her to love him, but also insults her, he returns to his obliviousness: "Between now and the happy future predicted for him he had nothing, almost literally nothing, to do" (101). This sentiment absolves him of responsibility; in fact, responsibility may be what makes home more than "a sense of shelter," as Harry Angstrom eventually realizes in *Rabbit, Run*. Part of John Nordholm's elation in "The Happiest I've Been" is due to "blessing irresponsibility" (*Same*, 241), and his story, like William's, is characterized by a "sensation of my being picked up and carried" (224). What "carries" both characters is a sense of separation rather than a sense of shelter. Perhaps their security in the knowledge that they will leave their towns, fulfilling the popular prophecies, is what gives Updike's protagonists like William the luxury to love Olinger while others who are destined to be mired there for life naturally hate it.

In "The Dogwood Tree" Updike writes of "three great secret things": sex, religion, and art.[3] All three offer the possibility for transcendence, and if sex is most prominent in stories like "Flight" and "A Sense of Shelter," set in the Olinger schools, religion dominates his domestic Olinger stories like "Pigeon Feathers" (1961), which stands out among the Olinger stories for its development of metaphor and its elaborate depth. Like the other stories discussed here, "Pigeon Feathers" begins with frantic movement – the protagonist's family's move from Olinger to Firetown – followed by chaos, both the literal disorder of the rural house and the spiritual displacement David feels upon reading a history that denies Jesus Christ's divinity. The safe details of home again serve to protect him from the "suffering that violently colors the periphery," yet he is intrigued by this other world: "The world outside the deep-silled windows – a rutted lawn, a whitewashed barn, a walnut tree frothy with fresh green – seemed a haven from which he was forever sealed off" (*Pigeon*, 119). By reading into the abstract realm of theological doubt, David departs from these comforting details of home.

The details of this home are not always comforting, though, because David Kern's family members are hostile to and demanding of one another: "Strange, out in the country, amid eighty acres, they were crowded together" (121). This sense of crowding – a recurrent motif in the Rabbit novels – is a primary motivator for a character's flight. Fear is another such motivator, and David's fear of death is associated with the earth: he lives in terror of being put in a hole and left there in absolute darkness and anonymity. After an anxious visit to his outhouse during which his fears cause him to run wildly home, David finds comfort not in his family or his house, but in words; he looks up the word "soul" in the dictionary and is relieved to find that "[t]he careful overlapping words shingled a temporary shelter for him" (126). Although he loses this assurance overnight, clearly words have the capacity both to terrify him and to protect him, giving substance to the same qualities he desires from religious belief. He is described as hiding in a newspaper; he also bows his tear-stained eyes to a book to hide from his catechetical teacher, and he seeks knowledge in his grandfather's Bible. If David is poised to fly, printed words are his wings.

David's need to fly from his town is partly attributable to his fear of immobility; when his mother asks him, "don't you ever want to rest?," he replies, "No. Not forever" (136). His mother attempts to convince him that the beautiful details of their quotidian life matter more than the afterlife, but David, led out of his secure home by words, takes no comfort in that idea. As his crisis deepens he loses "his appetite for reading" (141) and feels alone in the deep hole he most fears. His solution is to stay away from his home as much as possible, or to destroy it, with his father's help, in symbolic acts like igniting brush fires and, eventually, shooting pigeons.

Updike's willingness to assign tremendous significance to his childhood home reaches a crescendo in *The Centaur*, a powerful attempt to mythologize the artist's early portrait by returning, as James Joyce did in *A Portrait of the Artist as a Young Man* (1916) and *Ulysses* (1922), to ancient Greek stories. Art, the third great "secret thing," achieves unprecedented prominence in *The Centaur*, and perspective is a notable narrative innovation: Peter Caldwell, Updike's alter ego who has become a painter, occasionally narrates the story in the first person, sometimes conscious of his adult identity and sometimes not. The book is also narrated omnisciently in places, even when Peter is one of the subjects. The shifting perspective in the book as well as the way it straddles the mythical and real worlds are related, significant moments in Updike's development from a largely regional, personal writer into an artist with a vision that transcends time and place while still paying close attention to time and place. As Alice and Kenneth Hamilton write, "The mythological sequences [in *The Centaur*], intriguing and illuminating though they are, serve chiefly to give us insight into Updike's belief that the truth about any landscape does not lie on the surface but is found when observation deepens into vision."[4] In his imagination Updike is becoming Prometheus, the creator, in this novel as his father sacrifices his godly status for him. The mythological content of *The Centaur* is meant to substantiate a central claim that Peter makes while defending his youth to his adult love: "We moved, somehow, on a firm stage, resonant with metaphor" (70). The role of the artist as Updike conceives it at this point in his career is not only to reconstruct this firm stage in acute detail, but to reveal the metaphors that make those details significant.

Through details revealed in his *Self-Consciousness* (1989) memoirs, we can glean that Updike more clearly resembles Peter Caldwell than he resembles his recurrent protagonists Harry Angstrom or Henry Bech. Peter is an artist, though one who is not confident of his abilities; he describes himself as "an authentic second-rate abstract expressionist" (*Centaur*, 102–103). Although Peter is an abstract expressionist, his artistic influences are clearly the early Renaissance realists Jan Vermeer and Albrecht Dürer, to whom he repeatedly alludes in his narrative. Vermeer and Dürer – whose Dutch and German identities connect to Updike's genealogy – are from a tradition that would ally them with Updike's writing style more clearly than with Peter's painting style: these are visual artists who convert minute detail into breathtaking beauty. James Plath, writing of the Updike-Vermeer relationship, argues, "it *is* enough to find radiance in the commonplace, because [Updike's] characters find in such moments a means of elevating the quality of their otherwise ordinary lives, and in the process they experience a reaffirmation of life itself by noticing, as did Vermeer, how light brings substance to life."[5] Art functions as an escape from Peter's home town, especially from "the children in the land around us"; describing the 4-H club, he writes:

> The dull innocence of some and the viciously detailed knowingness of others struck me as equally savage and remote from my highly civilized aspirations. We met in the church basement, and after an hour of slides illuminating cattle diseases and corn pests, I would sweat with claustrophobia, and swim into the cold air and plunge at home into my book of Vermeer reproductions like a close-to-drowned man clinging to the beach. (74)

Vermeer clearly represents to him the possibility that there is another world beyond the confines of his town, a world better suited to his sensibilities; he later writes of "the cities, where I hoped my life would take me" and prepares for exile by aspiring to become Vermeer: "That Vermeer himself had been obscure and poor I knew. But I reasoned that he had lived in backward times. That my own times were not backward I knew from reading magazines. True, in all of Alton County only my mother and I seemed to know about Vermeer; but in the great cities there must be thousands who knew, all of them rich" (78). Peter's desire to paint like Vermeer is not only a means to escape Olinger, but a way to transcend his fate.

The details of Peter's youth so painstakingly rendered in *The Centaur* are as notable as the mythological allusions. Peter claims of his childhood home, "I can still see everything" (57), and proceeds to transcribe these details to the reader. The thick description of the world of his youth provides the home base from which Peter's artistic vision can depart (his rendering of his father as Chiron the Centaur) and to which it can return. As in most versions of the *Bildungsroman*, the adult Peter points out his younger self's naïveté. At one point he reveals himself to be someone who is as yet unsure of the precise meaning of his world: "I was haunted at that age by the suspicion that a wholly different world, gaudy and momentous, was enacting its myths just around the corners of my eyes" (117). Over the course of the novel, the three arduous days with his father in which he is prevented twice from going home because of car troubles, Peter contracts a fever that leads him out of this naïveté and into a realization that an artistic role awaits him in his future. In the throes of his fever, he writes of the same details that Updike recalls in "The Dogwood Tree," such as telephone wires and trees, and he renders them as Vermeer would:

> The trees took white on their sun side. The two telephone wires diagonally cut the blank blue of the sky. The stone bare wall was a scumble of umber; my father's footsteps thumbs of white in white. I knew what this scene was – a patch of Pennsylvania in 1947 – and yet I did not know, was in my softly fevered state mindlessly soaked in a rectangle of colored light. I burned to paint it, just like that, in its puzzle of glory; it came upon me that I must go to Nature disarmed of perspective and stretch myself like a large transparent canvas upon her in the hope that, my submission being perfect, the imprint of a beautiful and useful truth would be taken. (293)

This is at once an epiphany about the role of the artist and a realization that Peter is being called, with a rapturous (burning) sensation, to fulfill that role. Updike describes this role further in a 1968 interview with Charles Thomas Samuels: "My first thought about art, as a child, was that the artist brings something into the world that didn't exist before, and that he does it without destroying something else. A kind of refutation of the conservation of matter. That still seems to me its central magic, its core of joy."[6]

As a youth, Peter is generally too mired in the mundane rhythm of his world to appreciate its artistic potential. He yearns only to escape this world, which he is able to do on rare occasions when his father encourages him to see a movie and to walk through the streets of Alton, the fictional nearby city resembling Reading, Pennsylvania, which offers him an alternative to the confinement of Olinger:

> At this hour when the workers and shoppers of the city were hurrying by foot, bus, car, and trolley home to their duties, I was for a time released from mine, not merely permitted but positively instructed by my father to go to a movie and spend two hours out of this world. The world, my world with all its oppressive detail of pain and inconsequence, was behind me; I wandered among caskets of jewels which would someday be mine. (138)

This ecstasy of departure does not last long, though; immediately after this description he admits, "Frequently at this moment, my luxurious space of freedom all before me, I thought guiltily of my mother, helpless at her distance to control me or protect me" (138).

Such feelings of guilt at leaving home, even for a short period of time, are common in Updike's early protagonists and produce the central crisis of some, like Joey in *Of the Farm*. Peter is conflicted by his mother's association with her land and his father's restlessness, both of which he seems to have inherited. He yells at his father, "Why can't you stay still?" (164), yet Peter is also repeatedly described as restless. At the end of the book, when his mother suggests that his father become a farmer, Peter realizes, "the thought of my father as farmer frightened me. It would sink me too into the soil" (291). This description not only reveals Peter's abhorrence of the sedentary lives of farmers, but associates such lives with death, his obsession throughout the novel, and aligns him with David from "Pigeon Feathers" who thinks of death as a hole in the ground. Peter is both drawn to a stable, secure home and repelled by it; he notes that his father's habit had dictated the mood of his household: "Haste and improvidence had always marked our domestic details. The reason, it came to me, was that our family's central member, my father, had never rid himself of the idea that he might soon be moving on. This fear, or hope, dominated our home" (273). Peter as a youth was unsure whether he feared or hoped for their moving on, and this uncertainty apparently persists into his adulthood.

Peter Caldwell's ambivalence toward the home of his youth is intensified (and bitterly resolved) in Updike's fourth novel, *Of the Farm*. This book is one of Updike's most contentious and angriest narratives: the pain of return-ing home produces little longing and much suffering in Joey. The story centers on Joey's mother's rejection of his second wife Peggy, a rejection that violently separates the adult Joey from his childhood self. Olinger and the farm near it are an Eden so fallen as to be undesirable. Although Updike does return to this setting later in his career, *Of the Farm* represents his farewell to Olinger as a nostalgic setting that might provide his characters with opportunities for growth and development, if only through an awareness that they must leave. The setting is weary; as Joey's mother says, "Land is like people, it needs a rest. Land is *just* like a person, except that it never dies, it just gets very tired" (*Farm*, 24). Olinger has also become tired as a setting for Updike: Joey's return is full of anxiety and anger, not longing for the lost past. At one point he suggests, "Let's smash . . . all the pictures of me you have sitting around" (119). This desire to destroy the past contrasts with his attempt to take control of the land by mowing the overgrown fields, an act that brings him more physical suffering than emotional satisfaction.

Joey refers frequently to his mother's "mythology" (31), her "saga of the farm" (25), and wants to remove himself from it, to "make [him]self less a myth" (25). He finds it impossible to extricate himself, though, because he is the central character in the myth. The story is a familiar one in Updike's early fiction: Joey's mother sees him as special, as selected to leave this place that, in her opinion, the "know-nothing" residents of Olinger consider "the center of the universe. They don't want to *go* anywhere, they don't want to *know* anything, they don't want to *do* anything except sit and admire each other. I didn't want my only child to be an Olingerite; I wanted him to be a *man*" (29, 30). Complicating this desire for her child's ambition is her rejection of the life he has chosen: his preference for New York over a smaller place as well as his divorce and remarriage to Peggy, the recipient of her vitriol. Joey describes Peggy as "terrain" and "a field" (46, 59), as if to use her to replace the land of his mother's farm. He even imagines her ankles tapering into the earth (88–89), a peaceful harmony of his present and past lives that contrasts sharply with the violence between his mother and his second wife. Yet Peggy's attempts to assimilate into farm life are ridiculous, just as her attempts to win over Joey's mother fail.

Joey must come to terms with the changes the landscape has undergone since his youth. His mother tells him, "It's not the county you grew up in" (34). He begins to feel like his father, a man who claimed repeatedly that the farm gave him "the creeps" (39). When Joey travels to the supermarket with his mother and his stepson Richard, he is keenly aware of the changes that have occurred: "The garish abundance, the ubiquitous music, the surrealist centrality of automobiles made me feel, emerging from my father's dusty car, like a visitor from the dead" (84–85). This is one of the moments when he imagines himself as his father, reincarnated, and his stepson as himself, or as "impersonating" him (85). In an epiphany he listens to his mother telling her story to Peggy and understands that she destroyed his father; she "had brought him to a farm which was in fact her giant lover, and had thus warped the sense of the masculine within me, her son" (134). Her power to destroy continues: "my mother . . . swept forward with a fabulous counter-system of which I was the center, the only child, the obscurely chosen, the poet" (135).

Although he resents it, Joey is clearly affected by this "fabulous counter-system" as it damages his relationship with Peggy, if only temporarily. He is happy to envision himself on the farm alone, without either his mother or his wife, and this fantasy reveals that he remains at the center of his own story, which is the legacy his mother gives him. Still, in the end he rejects the farm, largely because of its association with death. As in many of the stories discussed here, women, the earth, and death are intertwined in the protagonist's mind. The vision of being alone on the farm breaks this cycle, but escape remains a more viable option than solitude: "New York, the city that is always its own photograph, the living memento of my childish dream of escape, called to me, urged me away, into the car, down the road, along the highway, up the Turnpike" (174). As a final gesture of goodwill, he deals with his mother in their old, joking way that "declared nothing and left the past apparently unrevised" (174). The "apparently" in this sentence on the novel's final page bespeaks a change in Joey: he can continue to appear nostalgic for the farm, but in the light of the violent confrontation with the past throughout the book, he has clearly revised his thinking – it is a past to which he no longer desires to return.

Through the emotional intensity of *Of the Farm*, Updike largely put to rest the subjective geography of his home town. Although Olinger is the setting for a handful of later stories and the first part of the recent novel *Villages* (2004), he seems to feel more comfortable with the settings of his adult world in his later fiction, and even in settings well beyond his milieu, such as in *Brazil* and *Gertrude and Claudius* (2000). In his 1984 memoir "A Soft Spring Night in Shillington" (collected in *Self-Consciousness*), he returns to his home town and finds that his relationship to it has changed dramatically:

> I stood there waiting, self-consciously, to feel something, and felt less than I had hoped. The street, the house where I had lived, seemed blunt, modest in scale, simple; this deceptive simplicity composed their precious, mystical secret, the conviction of whose existence I had parlayed into a career, a message to sustain a writer book after book. I had often enough described my old house, its yard, the emotional nuances that hid beneath its details like so many dust mice and cobwebs; its familiar face and I had little to say to one another this evening. (24)

It is as though the stories he has extracted from his youth have taken most of the energy away from the place, and even become more real than the place itself. And yet, a few pages later he writes, "It was exciting for me to be in Shillington, as if my life, like the expanding universe, when projected backwards gained heat and intensity. If there was a meaning to existence, I was closest to it here" (30). He also observes in a preface to a special edition of *Rabbit at Rest* (1990), that on visiting his home after his mother's death in 1989, "I was conscious of how powerfully, inexhaustibly rich real places are, compared with the paper cities we make of them in fiction" (*Odd*, 872). These divergent observations combine to explain how Updike's subjective geography has rendered his home town both the center of the universe and the place he had to flee in order to become the artist he is. New subjective geographies may replace the old as his career evolves, but the artistic principle developed in his early years remains intact.

NOTES

1. Martin Levin, ed., *Five Boyhoods* (New York: Doubleday, 1962), p. 196.
2. Robert M. Luscher, *John Updike: A Study of the Short Fiction* (New York: Twayne, 1993), p. 23.
3. Levin, *Five Boyhoods*, pp. 189–196.
4. Alice and Kenneth Hamilton, *The Elements of John Updike* (Grand Rapids, MI: Eerdmans, 1970), p. 157.
5. James Plath, "Verbal Vermeer: Updike's Middle-Class Portraiture," in *Rabbit Tales: Poetry and Politics in John Updike's Rabbit Novels*, ed. Lawrence R. Broer (Tuscaloosa: University of Alabama Press, 1998), pp. 209–210.
6. James Plath, ed., *Conversations with John Updike* (Jackson: University Press of Mississippi, 1994), p. 45.

GUIDE TO FURTHER READING

Burchard, Rachael C. *John Updike: Yea Sayings*. Carbondale: Southern Illinois University Press, 1971, pp. 53–88, 133–159.

Greiner, Donald J. *The Other John Updike: Poems/Short Stories/Prose/Play*. Athens, OH: Ohio University Press, 1981, pp. 59–197.

Hunt, George W. *John Updike and the Three Great Secret Things: Sex, Religion, and Art*. Grand Rapids, MI: Eerdmans, 1980, pp. 49–101.

Macnaughton, William R., ed. *Critical Essays on John Updike*. Boston: G. K. Hall, 1982.

Schiff, James A. *John Updike Revisited*. New York: Twayne, 1998, pp. 11–27.

2

KRISTIAAN VERSLUYS

"Nakedness" or realism in Updike's early short stories

From the beginning of his career, the kind of realistic writing that Updike practices in his short stories has been devoted to what one of his narrators somewhat ruefully calls "quotidian fluff":[1] an asparagus patch in "Flight" (1959), a listing of supermarket items in "A & P" (1961), the detailed pattern of a bird's plumage in "Pigeon Feathers" (1961). To a certain extent, this preference can be attributed to Updike's apprenticeship at the *New Yorker*, "a loving respect for facticity – for the exactly *what* of matters" comprising the "shared heritage" he found common to all those who worked at the magazine under Harold Ross (*Hugging*, 848). To a larger extent, it reflects the influence of two acknowledged predecessors. One, William Dean Howells, Updike praises for "bringing dullness and mixedness out of the rain of actuality into the house of fiction" (*Odd*, 170). Skirting, on the one hand, the melodramatic plots and morally balanced endings that marked the classic European novel and, on the other hand, the subjects peripheral to ordinary experience (such as whaling ships) that formed the basis of the classic American novel, Howells, with his "fidelity to the mild, middling truth of average American life" (183), provided a model of realism that pointed to "the triumph of American life," the fact, according to Updike, "that so much of it should be middling" (189). Walt Whitman, in contrast, Updike commends for granting the minutiae of that model metaphysical dimensions. Quoting, in a talk on Whitman's "egotheism," the transcendentalist poet's assertion that "the true use for the imaginative faculty of modern times is to give ultimate vivification to facts, to science, and to common lives, endowing them with glows and glories and final illustriousness which belong to every real thing, and to real things only" (*Hugging*, 117), Updike delineates the democratizing ramifications that this credo of such an unlikely prophet of realistic writing augured: real things – an old milk carton as much as a rose, a trolley car as much as a tree – can be "assigned the sacred status that in former times was granted to mysteries" (*Picked-Up*, 518; *Hugging*, 117).

Updike's realism, then, is a curious mix. It foregrounds the tangible and the everyday, but more importantly, it lifts them into the realm of the transcendental by the magic of language. It sticks to the Howellsian "middling" while it hankers after the Whitmanesque sublime. It treats common objects and common emotions with so much loving care that they receive the "vivification" Whitman alludes to and begin to glow with an inner warmth. Nothing much happens in an Updike story except for the slow unraveling of feeling and circumstance. Stories are not pointed to a predestined end. They do not turn on events and they are not pitched to shock or even surprise. Instead, they meander luxuriously and with a looseness and lassitude that provides, not for slackness, but, on the contrary, for probing and infinitely varied contemplation. As the critic William H. Pritchard puts it, Updike's short fiction is characterized by a "meditative, wandering, and associative pattern of writing."[2] Basically, there is only one plot outline: the stories register the infinitesimally small mental adjustments which allow the protagonist to find a vantage point from which the intensely studied shards of his life begin to make sense and reality becomes not only bearable but strangely enchanting.

As he admits in the foreword to the recently collected *The Early Stories, 1953–1975* (2003), Updike, in writing his stories, has freely drawn from an "autobiographical well" (xi).[3] His tales are built around reminiscences of his boyhood in Pennsylvania, his college years at Harvard, his stay at Oxford, the heady twenty months he spent as a young and budding *literatus* in New York, the long and often difficult years of his first marriage, when he and his expanding family lived in Ipswich, a seaside town north of Boston. "[T]hese fragments chipped from experience" have been "rounded by imagination into impersonal artifacts" (*Early*, xii). The ordinary stuff of the author's life has been turned into the extraordinary of his art by means of "careful explication" (x).

Updike takes utmost care to evoke the mood of a time and a place through meticulous descriptions of the minutest material paraphernalia. As the writer-protagonist of one story puts it: "Details. Details are the giant's fingers" (101). In that intriguingly entitled story, "The Blessed Man of Boston, My Grandmother's Thimble, and Fanning Island" (1962), the narrator tries to imagine the life of a complete stranger, the life of his grandmother long since deceased, and the life of the last survivor on an isolated Pacific island. He comes to the conclusion that, on the one hand, exhaustive enumeration of all the circumstances of these lives leads to glut and narrative surfeit, while, on the other hand, a mere outline cannot begin to evoke the feel of daily existence. As a middle course, he settles for selective observation and detailed description: of his grandmother's thimble, the shape of her nostrils, her dwindled body distorted by old age and Parkinson's disease. Thus fully rendered, these vignettes, though dealing with incapacitation and death, emanate a strong sense of contentment – a reveling in the things of this world. For the giant, whose fingers are details, "seizes the stick and strips the bark and shows, burning beneath, the moist white wood of joy" (101). In other stories the quiet elation that follows from careful observation and study is conveyed in the delineation, with pinpoint accuracy, of glass shattering (237), snowplows scraping streaks of asphalt (355), chickadee feet making tiny imprints on fresh snow (356), a blue jay alighting on a twig (510), grape leaves transfused by a "lent radiance" (510). Nothing is deemed unworthy of attention, neither the "several feces like short rotten sticks, strangely burnished" that a man has just excreted (341) nor the physical mechanics of paid sex (682–701). The minutiae of material existence are observed microscopically, because "[t]he pure life of the mind . . . is soon tedious" (285). Or as Updike told one interviewer, "what we need is a greater respect for reality, its secrecy, its music. Too many people are studying maps and not enough are visiting places" (*Picked-Up*, 503). In his memoirs he writes in a similar vein, "Imitation is praise. Description expresses love"; "Truth is . . . the snug opaque quotidian" (*Self-Consciousness*, 231, 234).

Yet Updike's realism cannot be reduced to pure *chosisme* or description for description's sake. On the contrary, in many stories mere accumulation of detail is depressing for the protagonist. Objects piled onto objects make for melancholy or despair ("The Happiest I've Been" [1959], "Packed Dirt, Churchgoing, a Dying Cat, a Traded Car" [1961], "Home" [1960]), while random information leads to madness ("A Madman" [1962]). The Updike protagonist seeks, through memory and imagination, to align objects along a vector so that they become meaningful and accessible. For all that it is anchored in the quotidian and weighed down by the trivia of existence, Updike's realism is floating in a riches of associations. Even house numbers lose their objectivity and become encapsulated in a denser mesh of meaning (284). The Updike protagonists wrestle with the material things of this world mentally. They are not merely observers, but thinkers. And not so much thinkers as ruminators. As one of the narrators puts it, "The world is the host; it must be chewed" (420). Things are there to be contemplated, to be mulled over. Realism is at the same time a subjectivism: it presents the object, but the object as perceived by the active mind of the attentive and ever-curious observer.

In the short story "The Sea's Green Sameness" (1960), the writer stages the confrontation between the mental and the material as a never-ending debate with a tenacious opponent. He posits a bipolar, binary world: "a world of two halves: the ego and the external object" (731). What the writer hopes for is that "once into my carefully spun web of words the thing itself, *das Ding an sich*, will break: make an entry and an account of itself" (733). If in that particular case the verbal struggle with the essence of the "sea's green sameness" ends in defeat, it is because, in describing the monotonous glitter of the Caribbean, the Updike narrator is deprived of memory and metaphor, the two tools which allow him to endow things with "glows and glories and final illustriousness" (Whitman's words). The meeting of mind and material is successful in Updike's stories when objects lose their hard edges and begin to shine with meaning. Such metamorphosis typically takes place when some image can be found that yokes all of far-flung reality together or when things are touched by the comforting warmth of nostalgia.

Not coincidentally, Proust is a pervading presence in the stories. The past humanizes. It acts like a wedge that cracks open a recalcitrant outside world and, if it does not lend direct access to *das Ding an sich*, at least a fall through time relieves the present from its triviality and insignificance. Hindsight turns out to be second sight and the Updike hero is forever dunking his madeleine in a cup of tea, waiting for "the valves of time" to part (92). In "When Everyone Was Pregnant" (1972), the women, big with child, who surrounded the protagonist in the 1950s, are explicitly compared to "Proust and the 'little band' at Balbec" (446). The inexorable sliding onward of time toward death lights up fragments of the past and gives them a special glow and coherence. The same nostalgia pervades "In Football Season" (1962), which relies on the connection between olfactory sensations and memory. It opens with the line "Do you remember a fragrance girls acquire in autumn?" (122), in which the Proustian elements of remembering, smell, and autumn are all combined. As one narrator puts it, "Our lives submit to archaeology" (559), that is to say, they receive meaning through historical perspective. By surging up from the recesses of the past, impressions, suffused by memory, lead to a quiet sort of rapture. Not only does the past shine with a fullness now largely lost. In a story such as "Son" (1973) it becomes obvious that one's very identity comes from being part of a family history. One is what one was.

Acting as the facilitator of coherence – giving the narrator-observer a vantage point from which to deal with the onrush of things on the mind – memory serves a function comparable to that of metaphor. Like memory, metaphor allows the protagonist to find a purchase in life. It provides a perspective from which the far-flung threads of existence can be tied up. The yoking of two things that are dissimilar *in se* constructs meaning. But more than that, it delineates the vector along which Updike's 20/20 realism is at the same time a subjectivism and an idealism. A typical story is "Pigeon Feathers." It deals with death and religious doubts, but ultimately it relies on shimmering linguistic connections and crosscurrents to convey a sense of metaphysical comfort. The story is written from the perspective of a thirteen-year-old boy who is disoriented because of an upsetting move from the town to the country, because of family tensions, because he experiences the threat of mortality for the first time, and because he comes across a passage in H. G. Wells in which the divinity of Christ is questioned. Most of all, though, the boy is pressured by the fullness of things, the ragtag of objects by which one is surrounded and which clamor for interpretation and ordering. It is only when he studies in detail the intricate patterns and color schemes on the wings of the pigeons he has shot that he realizes in an Emersonian moment that everything is interconnected, that the tiniest little artifact finds correspondences in the larger world, that ultimately such concentricity (where everything has a common ground and thus becomes one big metaphor) is itself another name for the divine.

*

Updike's realism – this tight mesh of accurate observation and mental association – is best studied in detail. It is only when paying close attention to the various rhythms of a story and its unique *modus operandi* that one sees how Updike's realism is not only different from the nineteenth-century original, in that it has assimilated the modernist teachings of Proust as well as those of Joyce and Nabokov, but also stands closer to the teachings of poststructuralism than the denominator of realism seems to suggest. Poststructuralism has a history of quarreling with realism. Plot, character, setting, and time – the hallmarks of traditional realism – are taken to have a naturalizing effect, that is, they are assumed to advance an unquestioning acceptance of reality. In the poststructuralist account, realism is associated with undue closure. The reality effect, as it has been decried by the French literary critic Roland Barthes and others, presents outside reality encased in a linguistic armature so that the world comes across as a given that cannot be interrogated or challenged.[4] In spite of its emphasis on minutely rendered concrete phenomena, an Updike story offers no such certainties. If it lingers, it lingers in doubt. It is a search for an all-encompassing metaphor or a moment of stasis. But such closure is always considered to be temporary – a provisional halt in the meaning-making apparatus – and is arrived at only after many narrative loops and dialectical digressions. An Updike story is the reporting of a search more than the announcement of a finding. And though it is not openly self-reflexive – in the often rather laborious and tedious manner of many a postmodernist tale – it nevertheless clearly draws attention to its own linguistic nature and status as fiction.

One story that illustrates how Updike's realism is a heuristic enterprise, in which the protagonist must labor to acquire a slippery linguistic purchase on reality, is "Nakedness," dating from 1974. The story relates a simple incident.

Richard and Joan Maple, a couple we know from previous stories, witness how two naked people leave the nudist beach and enter the "bourgeois, bathing-suited section" (389) – only to be chased away by a policeman.[5]

Against the background of sublime but impassive nature ("the unnoticing commotion and self-absorbed sparkle of the sea" [389]), the story (as part of a section of *The Early Stories* called "Married Life") is one of a series of thumbnail sketches describing subdued marital tensions, in which couples find their bond weakened by the enervating agency of everyday closeness. These tales follow the same recurrent pattern. The friction between the partners usually flares up in bouts of irritation and inexplicable aversion, but it never leads to a clean break. At the end of the squaring-off, there is mostly some sort of uneasy accommodation, some redeeming feature or some reaching back to a happier past, which gives the relationship a new lease on life until the next crisis. In all cases the stories comprise moments when the partners take stock of their situation and unconscious feelings are swept up into consciousness – momentarily. Updike's realism packs a lot that remains unsaid, hidden underneath the surface. It enacts the struggle of meaning to be born. As such, it demonstrates not the firm hold over reality that realism is often associated with (mostly by way of poststructuralist accusation), but rather the flimsy nature of the linguistic wrapping which is used to keep life's vagaries under control.

Significantly, this time around the husband's irritation centers not so much on the physical plumpness of his wife (the fact that over the years she has filled out a little), as on a difference in vocabulary. Since she is decisive and political and he is hesitant and poetic, they deal with the nudists' incident starting from different premises and using antithetical interpretive schemes. A simple confrontation with a strange and unusual phenomenon opens up into a meditative piece, which revolves around the attempts of the mind to deal with the exposed human body and, by extension, all of unmediated external reality. Under the guise of a marital dispute, the story deals with the construction of an adequate "interior mythology" which will account for the facts as they are (389). In particular, it details the impossibility of such an endeavor. Necessarily, naked reality is clothed by the active imagination.

The story follows a strict time scheme and gives us an exact sense of place: the incident at the beach occurs one sunny morning; all afternoon (while mowing the grass under gathering clouds) Richard tries to make sense of it; later that day, around bedtime, he intently watches his wife undressing in their bedroom. Measuring the progress of time (in recognizable increments) and giving a detailed sketch of location are the hallmarks of traditional realism. In tune with the tradition, Updike allows the situation to unfold in the fullness of its circumstances – including even the meteorological ones. The first and the third parts of the story, in particular, give a blow-by-blow account of each and every action taking place. The detailed description includes physical action but it focuses on Joan's and especially Richard's mental activity. In the second part the focus is completely on Richard's attempts to catch nakedness in a reticulated net of memories and meanings. (The reference to Molly Bloom's soliloquy [392] indicates that Updike's realism is indeed indebted to the great avatars of modernism.) The center of gravity is no longer in the relation of the facts, but in their interpretation. The tale takes a linguistic turn. While its ostensible topic is the appearance of the naked beachgoers and while, in general, the incident presents a test for the marital bond, the deeper theme is the relation between language and experience, more in particular the gap that opens up between fact and meaning. As such, the story can be construed as an *ars poetica*, a reflection of realism on its own premises and procedures.

Nakedness is a physical fact, but more than that it is a cultural sign. It occupies a specific place in a culture's repertoire of meanings. This is obvious already when, on first seeing the naked couple, Joan exclaims, "Oh, look . . . We're being invaded!" (389). Within the dominant social code, nakedness is an invasion of foreign significations, an eruption of anarchy and lawlessness within the settled order of things. More to the point, it is semiotically upsetting. What the British sociologist Dick Hebdige wrote about the dress of mobsters and punks also applies to those who choose to go undressed: such flaunting of one's difference amounts to "semiotic guerilla warfare." It constitutes a "mechanism of semantic disorder" meant to offend the "silent majority" and to challenge "the principle of unity and cohesion" which mainstream society is trying to uphold.[6] The confrontation with actual nudity invites a reordering of the linguistic apparatus which society and tradition marshal forth to circumscribe and control the phenomenon.

Of course, such a reordering can be refused. One traditional way of dealing with strangeness is to "other" what is unfamiliar, that is to say, to neutralize what is unusual or destabilizing by forcing it into a network of regulatory, binary oppositions. The result of such stolid categorizing is the production of fixed or essentialized meaning: them versus us, indecent versus decorous, or, in this particular case, undressed versus dressed. The shocked silence among the beachgoers that meets the naked couple at its first appearance marks the moment when the bourgeois semiotic system registers how it is thrown into disarray. But soon the forces of restoration come into action. A woman shouts a disapproving "*Well!*" and an angry old man shakes an uncertain fist at the intruding nudists (389).

The countercultural statement of the naked couple clashes most unambiguously with the repressive bourgeois reaction and "dressed" is most decisively opposed to "undressed" when a policeman descends upon the scene. "His uniform made him, too, representative of a species," the narrator informs us (390). While the sign of rebellion against the Puritan ethos is the exposed (and detumescent) penis (391), the policeman's uniform invests him with the full power of the repressive state. The gun he carries gives him an irrefutable advantage over the nude people and is, therefore, the ultimate arbiter of the conflict. Something soft and "boneless" is opposed to the cold, hard steel of a lethal weapon (390). When the nudists put on their clothes and leave the beach, bourgeois order is restored; that is, the interruption in the mainstream meaning system is summarily dealt with and a reassuring binary ordering of reality is reestablished by main force.

Binary ordering, however, is not the monopoly of the law. It is possible, in opposition to convention and conformity, to develop a reverse discourse that is just as limiting in its semiotic scope and as repressive in its consequences. We know from previous stories about the Maples that Joan is a political activist. Her sympathy immediately goes to the nudists. Her reaction to the incident is frank and unsophisticated but, as it is unable to shed the markings of compartmentalized thinking, it is ultimately unsatisfactory and self-defeating. She, too, imposes upon the incident a prefashioned interpretative scheme, which prevents semiosis from reaching its full blossoming. In calling the young policeman a "pig" (390), she applies the countercultural language of the time. In doing so, she dehumanizes the person and equates his identity with his function. In fact, she takes an interpretative shortcut as drastic as that of the policeman himself. In slapping her shorthand political take on the situation, she does not allow the nudists' unexpected appearance to develop into its full indeterminacy. Within the scheme of the story, she operates as a sort of leftist thought-police. She conquers the nakedness by her political and cultural cocksureness, her linguistic possessiveness, and her "complacent quickness" (390). As a result, she is stumped by the fact that the nudists take no notice of her gestures of sympathy. Her unreflected militancy has made her impervious to mystery and to the far-ranging repercussions – the overdetermined nature – of other people's actions.

Richard – who is given the privileged place of focalizer in the story – reacts with greater circumspection and hesitation. When first seeing the naked couple, his feelings are "hysterically turbulent: a certain political admiration grappled with an immediate sense of social threat" (389). He admires the way the naked couple flout the law. At the same time, he realizes that he is part of the social skein that its interruption threatens to tear apart. He is irritated because Joan has such a ready-made, ideologically prefashioned reaction to this complicated event. While Joan pegs the policeman as "a pig," Richard gropes "for some paradox, some wordless sadness" (390). Richard is aware of the incommensurateness of things and their basic inarticulateness. He realizes that words fall short. His sadness concerns the impossibility of language to deal with reality except by way of unresolvable paradox. In what follows he will undertake an elaborate effort to give nakedness its full personal and cultural resonance. But underneath his frantic search for a summarizing metaphor resides the quiet melancholy thought ("the wordless sadness") that there is no way to arrive at a definitive determination, an absolute coincidence of reality with language. He longs nostalgically for a pristinely pure language that will fix things unambiguously by their names and put an end to the verbal slippage and deferral that marks all human communication. His sadness concerns the fact that no linguistic nakedness is possible, that everything is mediated, that is, unimmediate, shot through with enabling but at the same time falsifying cultural content.

When he sees that the policeman is young, he says softly, "My God . . . He's one of *them*" (390). By situating the police officer within the same generation as the young nudists, he humanizes the policeman. And when he speculates that, in his off-hours, the policeman also may engage in nude sunbathing or skinny-dipping, he complicates the interpretative scheme even further. He opens himself up to unexpected convolutions and drives a wedge between the policeman's identity and his function. His is a nonessentialist stance, in which he delays knee-jerk political designations. The incident is food for an entire afternoon's uneasy thought, in which he tries to give nakedness an existential meaning by projecting it against the background of both his personal history and the whole of Western culture. Poststructuralist theory, in particular the writings of the French philosopher Jacques Derrida, has taught us that semiotic (meaning-giving) processes never come to full closure. The formation of a definitive meaning is blocked by the agency of *différance*, that is, by a process that defers meaning indefinitely. Meaning has to be thought of as a loop that never closes or as a set of receding horizons. By having recourse to a one-dimensional frame of reference, the policeman and Joan are at one in pinpointing the meaning of nakedness unambiguously. Richard, in contrast, ransacks his personal and cultural memory and thus reenacts the circuitousness of the semiotic process itself.

In his far-ranging meditations (while steering the "balky lawn mower through the wiry grass" [391]), Richard goes back to the biblical moment in the third chapter of Genesis when Adam and Eve are driven out of Paradise and for the first (and defining) time in Western thinking nakedness is associated with transgression and shame. More especially, he recalls God's words to Adam: "Who told thee that thou wast naked?" (391). When before the Fall nakedness was a blissful state, it blended into a prediscursive, unnamed naturalness. The curse of nudity coincides with the curse of language. After eating from the Tree of Knowledge of Good and Evil, Adam and Eve become aware of their nakedness and the concept of nudity as a linguistic marker and cultural sign associated with shame and guilt is born. (Adam and Eve hide from God because their nakedness is now something by which to be embarrassed.) Further associations from the Bible (Noah beheld naked by Ham, Susanna and the elders) fill out the moral injunction against nudity and especially against looking at nudity.

The extent to which such biblical teachings have conditioned Richard as a small boy in his outlying West Virginia childhood home is obvious when he remembers an episode in which he and his mother sunbathe on the sun porch (presumably in the buff) and the young boy, even though he avoids looking at his mother's body, is overwhelmed by acute feelings of shame and embarrassment. Later, Richard will indicate how deeply the biblical injunction has conditioned Western thinking as a whole and how the West has imposed its values on the rest of the world (especially those parts in which the Edenic condition was preserved before Western colonization). He recalls from an old sociology text "a nineteenth-century American farmer's boasting that though he had sired eleven children he had never seen his wife's body naked" (393–394). He equally recalls another book in which the writer asserts that a certain port in West Africa "was the last city on the coast where a young woman could walk naked down the main street without attracting attention" (394). In their stark contrast, the anecdotes echo Joan's binary thinking. They oppose non-Western, indigenous prelapsarian innocence to the restricting (polluting) impact of Western morality. And thus they disclose how "nakedness" is a cultural construct and a colonial imposition. Yet in Richard's case, this political signification is by no means the last word on the question. The moral-political reading is enmeshed in a web of further metaphors and associations, further delays in the semiotic process, further probings and investigations.

In particular, the political designation taps into (and competes with) a whole network of aesthetic and personal references, starting with Rodin's remark "that a woman undressing was like the sun piercing through clouds" (392). From an aesthetic point of view, a naked woman is not a political statement, but a liminal experience, a moment of supreme revelation, literally a breakthrough. In calling to mind further examples of famous nudes such as Titian's Venus, Manet's Olympia, and Goya's Maja, Richard implicitly indicates that in exposing the human body with complete "shamelessness" (393), these painters are flouting the biblical injunction, undoing the curse of Adam and Eve, abolishing original sin. These glorious paintings – culminations of a culture while going against the very morality that informs that culture – blur the difference between paint and flesh and therefore confuse the binary divisions between nature and culture. Or as the art historian Lynda Nead puts it, "The female nude is the border, the *parergon* as Derrida also calls it, between art and obscenity."[7] The paintings are artistic but at the same time shot through with a great deal of frank eroticism and thus they also blend the biological and the cultural. All in all, there are nine references to nude paintings. They illustrate how the aestheticization of the human body restores the lost paradisiacal innocence and negates moralistic conditioning. More generally, the cultural discourses that converge on Richard are seen as diverse and contradictory. As much as the accuracy of detail, the interwovenness of these interpretative schemes makes up the thick texture of Updike's realism.

Within this web of cultural references, the realm of the personal that the story carves out is situated within the interlinking semiotic loops that the moralistic and aesthetic registers of the culture offer. More concretely, Richard looks for the personal relevance of nudity in four anecdotes (three of them reminiscences). In the first one – the sunbathing scene with his mother – the moral register unambiguously prevails and the self is purely the product of its environment (that is, of the dominant discourse). In the second (semiotically much denser) personal anecdote, the protagonist looks at his naked body in a mirror. Insight comes in the form of a self-distantiation, an uncoupling of body and mind, whereby the latter takes stock of the former by applying the aesthetic register to the personal. The complications, which indicate the richness of Updike's version of realism, arise from the fact that this self-examination occurs while Richard is lying on top of his mistress in an amorous embrace. The biological imperative – so prevalent in naturalistic tales – is superseded by a far more sophisticated kind of personality-construction, whereby carnal knowledge also is seen as culturally determined.[8] Even when engaged in a sexual activity, Richard fumbles for a defining metaphor. More specifically, in being fascinated by his own body, Richard thinks of himself and his mistress in terms of the many paintings he remembers. In his self-contemplation, he is activating the different places that nudity occupies in the cultural register. Groping through metaphoric designations, he tries to determine what nakedness is, what adultery is. He is restlessly rummaging through the culture to find reference points that will allow him to draw the out-of-bounds within the perimeters of identifiable knowledge.

Richard's relation to (and dependence on) his culture is further exemplified in the third personal anecdote, recounting a true Wordsworthian "spot of time." In describing how Richard felt moved to take off his clothes when visiting a small, secluded pond bathed in "sun-irradiated mist" (393), the narrator strains after metaphysical language to convey the convergence of binary opposites. Richard feels at one with himself and with the universe around him. At first, he yearns to do "something transcendent, something obscene" (393). The stepping out of bounds is denoted as ecstasy (which means just that – stepping outside) or transgression (especially a sexual one). The overcoming of human limitations is at the same time a trespassing of the social law. Yet very soon "sex dropped from him" (393). Released from all biological and social constraints, he feels himself to be "the divinely shaped center of a concentric Creation" (393). This moment of transcendence, when Richard feels lifted out of the ordinary, is followed by the fall into the quotidian, as his momentary elation is interrupted by dozens of ticks clambering up his exposed legs. More significantly, each and every move in this vignette is replete with cultural echoes. The pond is far removed from civilization: "Not a house, not a car looked down from the hills of sand and scrub that enclosed the pond" (393). The remote place is defined as "pure emptiness under the sky" (393). And yet even this emptiness cannot extricate itself from the grip of language, cultural determination, and metaphor. Although the scene at the pond is a reenactment of Eden before the Fall and before the curse of language, the extracultural is always already shaped by the cultural. One cannot slip outside of definitions. Sitting on a warm rock, Richard's pose is compared to that of Rodin's *Thinker* (393). Within a larger context, the anecdote mobilizes a host of literary echoes, including Emerson's "transparent eyeball" passage in his essay *Nature* (1836), Thoreau's *Walden Pond* (1854), and at a further remove Yeats's "Leda and the Swan" (1924), while the bathos introduced by the ticks is reminiscent of the verbal deflation typical of the early poems of T. S. Eliot.

The final personal anecdote and the grand finale of the story takes place when at bedtime Richard (still mulling over the multidirectional meaning of nudity) intently watches his wife undressing. When at a particular moment the nylon of her slip snags, "she halts in the pose of Michelangelo's slave, of Munch's madonna, of Ingres's urn-bearer" (394). Thus, while doing what every woman does at night, Joan is enacting a cultural repertoire, which Richard can master only by, once again, mobilizing metaphor. Reality becomes readable through culture. At first, Joan is irritated by Richard's behavior and she admonishes him (in a last flaring-up of morality and echoing the stern words of God to Adam and Eve in the Garden of Eden): "Don't you have something better to do? Than watch me?" (394). She finally realizes, however, that his attention is a sign of conjugal interest. In reversing the biblical injunction against looking at nudity, Richard aestheticizes his wife. The end result is a collapsing of the perspective of the narrator, of Richard, and of Joan and a conflation of the moral-social, the aesthetic, and the personal registers. Looking at the naked body of his wife, "Richard feels thrilled, invaded" (394). The "invasion" of the nudists on the beach, going through many metaphorical detours and peregrinations, reaches its furthest ramifications in the realm of the absolutely private and personal. Moreover, while cultural reference makes the biological signify, the cultural also loops back into the biological. The last sentence of the story reads, "This nakedness is new to them" (394). In spite of Joan's italicized (and therefore ironical) "*No*" (394), the sudden shift from the third person singular to the third person plural ("them") prefigures the unity of the married couple in intercourse. Such melting into one another signifies the provisional end to the marital tensions. It also connotes the momentary arrival at immediacy, the elision of linguistic detour. Such congealing of meaning is semiotically suspect, as poststructuralist theory posits a self that is constantly in flux, constituted by a network of ever-changing significations. Yet the end of the story suggests that such coming together of all defining discourses in one moment of conjugal bliss is not only epistemologically possible but also humanly refreshing and necessary.

As a story, "Nakedness" typifies Updike's brand of realism in that it consists of a thorough working-through of an incident with no shortcuts allowed. It exposes the multilayeredness of reality. Or to put it more precisely, it shows how "reality," as we perceive it, is the effect of a series of interpretative moves and therefore a social and cultural construct. In his attempts to unveil the ever-shifting network of cross-references that make up the finely articulated and reticulated concept of nudity, Richard, unlike Joan, does the work of the Updike realist. Updike's realism enacts the blossoming of semiosis. The prose is baroque, unsparse, untidy, and full of dangling ends and seemingly unconnected *obiter dicta*. This superabundance of meanings – the refusal of the tale, even a short one of a mere six pages, to lead in a straightforward manner to its predestined end or telos – is a way of demonstrating the fertility of the human mind and of dramatizing meaning-making in action. Without any postmodernist pyrotechnics or tricks – seemingly following the beaten paths of conventional plot development and characterization – Updike presents the mental and textual nature of reality in its full complexity. Richard looks at his own body, at those of strangers, his mother, his mistress, his wife, and mentally at those of the (mostly female) nudes in the paintings he remembers. What results from this constant vacillation and interaction between interpretative schemes and epistemological paradigms is the representation of life experience as a constant repositioning of the self within a discursive field of ever-shifting meanings.

If, in dramatizing this incessant groping for the fitting metaphor, Updike's realism seems to confirm the essential findings of poststructuralism, it differs in one important respect. For all the enacted mobility of meaning, the story yet ends in one all-encompassing moment of stasis. Updike's short fiction, while showing the linguistic nature of existence, skirts the apocalyptic undertones of radical poststructuralism. His stories do not illustrate endless and uncontrollable semiosis. Instead, muted in tone, never brusquely twisted, showing a tender regard for persons and things, they are vivid proof of the fact that, in Updike's own words, "[e]xistence itself does not feel horrible; it feels like an ecstasy, rather, which we only have to be still to experience" (*Self-Consciousness*, 230). Ticks crawl up one's legs to destroy gnostic wisdom and, for sure, before long Joan and Richard Maple will be quarreling again. In the meantime, there has been this one epiphanic moment when everything seems to make sense. Ever so provisionally, the endless deferral of meaning is brought to a standstill. At that still center of the world, when all the metaphors have run their course, Updike reveals the quiet satisfactions of an already vanishing and indefinable now.

NOTES

1. John Updike, *Memories*, p. 313.
2. William H. Pritchard, *Updike: America's Man of Letters* (South Royalton, VT: Steerforth, 2000), p. 63.
3. References to Updike's stories, cited in the text, are to this collection.
4. See Pam Morris, *Realism* (London: Routledge, 2003), pp. 32–34.
5. The stories about the Maples have been collected in *Too Far to Go: The Maples Stories* (New York: Fawcett Crest, 1979).
6. Dick Hebdige, *Subculture: The Meaning of Style* (London: Methuen, 1979), pp. 105, 90, 18, 18.
7. Lynda Nead, *The Female Nude: Art, Obscenity and Sexuality* (London: Routledge, 1992), p. 25.
8. See Nead, *The Female Nude*, p. 16: "the body is always produced through representation."

GUIDE TO FURTHER READING

Luscher, Robert M. *John Updike: A Study of the Short Fiction*. New York: Twayne, 1993.

Pritchard, William H. *Updike: America's Man of Letters*. South Royalton, VT: Steerforth, 2000.

Updike, John. "Howells as Anti-Novelist." 1987. *Odd Jobs: Essays and Criticism*. New York: Knopf, 1991, pp. 168–189.

"Whitman's Egotheism." 1977. *Hugging the Shore: Essays and Criticism*. New York: Knopf, 1983, pp. 106–117.

"Why Write?" 1964. *Picked-Up Pieces*. New York: Knopf, 1975, pp. 29–39.

3

MARSHALL BOSWELL

Updike, religion, and the novel of moral debate

In early 1958, John Updike, flush from the publication of his first poetry collection and the completion of his first novel, *The Poorhouse Fair*, moved his growing family out of New York City and into a seventeenth-century clapboard house in Ipswich, Massachusetts, where, by his own account, he suffered a full-blown existential crisis, one that had actually been brewing for several years. "Amid my new responsibilities," he has explained, "I felt fearful and desolate, foreseeing, young as I was, that I would die, and that the substance of the earth was, therefore, death" (*Odd*, 844). Two books saved him from this abyss: *Fear and Trembling* (1843) by the Danish existentialist writer Søren Kierkegaard (1813–55) and *The Word of God and the Word of Man* (1928) by the twentieth-century German theologian Karl Barth (1886–1968). "[F]or a while," he recently wrote, "I read both theological thinkers greedily, but it was these two titles, I suppose, that gave me a philosophy to live and labor by, and in that way changed my life" (*More*, 843).

What both writers share is a dialectical approach to religious issues in which defining oppositions do not resolve into a satisfying synthesis but rather remain in sustained tension and ambiguity, a philosophical and theological standpoint that Updike quickly seized upon as consistent with his own attempt to treat religious matters in fiction in such a way as to avoid the sort of all-encompassing generalizations that would otherwise destroy the delicate particularizing that literature demands. As such, Kierkegaard and Barth did more than help Updike recover his faith; they also provided him with a model for his own theological and aesthetic vision. One can detect this influence most specifically in Updike's repeated claim that his work seeks to engage his readers in a series of "moral debates" in which the central question is "'What is a good man?' or 'What is goodness?'" [1] I want here to examine this dynamic in a quartet of novels in which such debates take center stage: *The Poorhouse Fair* (1959), *Rabbit, Run* (1960), *A Month of Sundays* (1975), and *Roger's Version* (1986). In all four books Updike uses his battling antagonists as a means by which to affirm his own

Kierkegaardian/Barthian vision even as he complicates and interrogates the moral and metaphysical validity of that same vision.

As an intellectually sophisticated Harvard graduate with a small-town boy's faith in his own uniqueness, Updike took solace from Kierkegaard's elegant argument that faith is a purely subjective experience secure from all rational, objective inquiry. As Updike puts it, Kierkegaard assured him "that subjectivity too has its rightful claims, amid all the desolating objective evidence of our insignificance and futility and final nonexistence; faith is not a deduction but an act of will, a heroism" (*Odd*, 844). This willed act of faith comes about, in Kierkegaard, via a three-stage spiritual movement that Updike has adapted as the structural framework for many of his best fictions. The first stage, the aesthetic, represents an opulent life of desolate self-alienation, in which one avoids "existence," that is, selfhood, "by the most subtle of all deceptions, by thinking." In the second stage, the ethical, the spiritual sojourner recognizes aesthetic avoidance as a form of despair and "chooses" him/herself, through which choice the ethicist "becomes open" both to the world around him and to his/her ethical responsibilities. "Having gone through phantasmal, nebulous images, through the distractions of a luxuriant thought-content . . . , one comes to a very specific human being existing on the basis of the ethical."[2] The third movement, the religious, represents a shift back out of the world of social relations and into the world of faith, of direct encounter with God – that is, "the single individual stand[ing] in an absolute relation to the absolute." This third stage represents an irresolvable contradiction, that between the world's ethical requirements and the requirements of faith, which, as Kierkegaard worries over beautifully and passionately in *Fear and Trembling*, are not necessarily in line with one another, as is vividly illustrated for him by the biblical story of Abraham's near-sacrifice of his son Isaac. Faith, rather, is an irresolvable paradox, one that "makes a murder into a holy and God-pleasing act, . . . which no thought can grasp, because faith begins precisely where thought stops."[3]

To ensure that his most urgent ideas do not turn into mere abstract assertions, Kierkegaard created an elaborate series of pseudonymous "authors" who speak for him – or against him, as the case may be – and who are often, as in the two-volume work *Either/Or* (1843), situated at cross-purposes against one another. Readers must therefore work out for themselves any possible resolutions to these opposing views, a process of readerly self-questioning that Kierkegaard inspires via a strategy he calls "mastered irony," whereby the writer masters his/her material in such a way that the positive meaning emerges as an indirect product of the differential play of those carefully arranged oppositions. Updike connects his own narrative techniques to Kierkegaard's under the rubric of a "'yes-but' quality about [his] writing . . . that evades entirely pleasing anybody." By this Updike means that his work both affirms with reservations and critiques with qualifications. "Everything has at least two sides," he has explained. "My books attempt to show the several sides of something, and leave the reader with the awareness of a difficulty, rather than with the grasping of a slogan or a motto to live by."[4] This tension-filled "awareness of a difficulty" represents Updike's clearest adaptation of Kierkegaard's dialectical strategy.

Karl Barth was also deeply drawn to Kierkegaard's dialectics, so much so that he, too, organizes much of his work around a series of inextricable oppositions. Three central ideas form the triangular coordinate points of Updike's personal Barthian vision: a view of creation as the "something" that reflects God's positive will and which necessarily implies the existence of a corresponding "nothingness" (*das Nichtige*); a vision of evil as that which God did not will; and the argument for a God who is both unprovable but also "Wholly Other" (*totaliter aliter*) from what He has created. The clearest formulation of Updike's own take on Barthian metaphysics can be found in a review he wrote of Frank J. Sheed's *Soundings in Satanism* (1972). Here Updike, citing Barth, argues that evil, properly understood, is really a manifestation of the "nothingness" necessarily posited by God's "something" – that is, God's creation: "A potent 'nothingness' was unavoidably conjured up by God's creating *something*. The existence of something demands the existence of *something else*" (*Picked-Up*, 89). Similarly, Barth argues, in *Dogmatics in Outline* (1947), that "creaturely reality" is always a "*creatio ex nihilo*, a creation out of nothing" for the simple reason that if God "alone is real and essential and free," then heaven and earth, man and the universe "are something else, and this something else is not God, though it exists through God." Evil then gets relegated to "the reality behind God's back," an "excluded and repudiated thing" that nevertheless exists by the necessity of God's will. To quote Barth directly: "[T]his whole realm that we term evil – death, sin, the Devil and hell – is *not* God's creation, but rather what was excluded by God's creation, that to which God said 'No.'"[5] In *Midpoint*, his 1969 poetic statement-of-purpose, Updike treats this final idea as Barth's proof that faith must "flow / From Terror's oscillating Yes and No" (38).

Equally important for Updike, and particularly in the case of *Roger's Version*, as we shall see, is Barth's argument for a "Wholly Other" God. According to Barth, a creation that contained God would be perfect as is and hence in no need of a Savior. Or as Barth insists in a passage from *The Word of God and the Word of Man* that Updike has cited on more than one occasion, "There is no way from us to God – not even a *via negativa* – not even a *via dialectica* nor *paradoxa*. The god who stood at the end of some human way – even of this way – would not be God."[6] This God is, essentially, Updike's God – serene, unprovable, impervious to all scientific evidence that might otherwise diminish the possibility of His existence. This God also gives Updike the "creaturely freedom," not to mention the artistic freedom, he clearly desires as both a sensuous lover of earthly creation and a serious, realistic writer of the post-Christian world.

It is particularly significant that Updike absorbed the work of both writers just as he was forging his own artistic identity, for, after forty years of steady production and as many published books, it is now clear that these two developments reinforced each other in ways that were absolutely formative for the young novelist. The clash between ethics and the inner call to faith staged in Kierkegaard's *Fear and Trembling* – the book that Updike says most changed his life[7] – has remained, perhaps, the central conflict in his work, while Barth's serenely Wholly Other God continues to preside over Updike's work, which, very much like his own description of Shakespeare's universe, dramatizes events that are "purely human, in all the contradictory richness of which human nature is capable – a torrential spillage of self-importance beneath an enigmatic heaven" (*More*, 60). The "contradictory richness" affirmed here becomes not only the fulcrum upon which Updike places his spiritually tuned-in seducers and sinners but also the tension-filled ground from which he can debate with his unsettled readers.

The Poorhouse Fair, which appeared in 1959, pits an aging Christian named Hook against a humanist prefect named Connor. Somewhat awkwardly, Updike set the novel, his first, in a then-future 1977, perhaps to stack the decks a bit against his hero Hook, though the trick does not altogether work. In Updike's "future," Christianity belongs to the poor and aging members of the poorhouse referenced in the title, both of which – Christianity and the old fogeys who still believe in it – seem to be on the edge of annihilation thanks to the pervasive spread of a callow secular humanism, as represented by Connor. Connor is no match for Hook, though, largely because he is little more than an unconvincing spokesman for a view that Updike cannot abide in the first place. This flaw aside, the novel nevertheless provides a fascinating glimpse of Updike's early religious views and his novelistic strategies as they take shape before the reader's eyes.

When, in the novel's opening scene, Hook's irascible pal Gregg lets loose a string of expletives at the realization that Connor has put name tags on the porch rocking chairs, Updike quickly establishes the terms of the book's debate. Gregg resents Connor's do-good meddling, while Hook, the more reflective of the two, captures the real nature of the insult represented by the tags by remarking, ironically, "They put these on the chairs so we won't lose our way" (*Poorhouse*, 10). In Kierkegaardian terms the "tags" partake of what he calls "the universal," that is, the social and human order under which rubric he also lists "the ethical," all of which stand at odds with faithful religious individuality. In this light Connor's well-meaning attempt to order the men's daily habits – they generally sit in the same chairs anyway – becomes a sinister attempt to strip them of their freedom and unique spiritual value. The futuristic setting therefore becomes a way for Updike to dramatize not just the passing of Christianity but, more specifically, the threat posed to his Kierkegaardian sense of spiritual individuality by a creeping, all-encompassing conformity – the "universal" – the latter a burning concern to Updike as he surveyed the sleepy, conservative Eisenhower 1950s.

Updike has pointedly named his man of Kierkegaardian faith. With his outmoded but still vital belief in God, Hook hangs suspended on a saving "hook" above an abyss that his antagonist, Connor, sees only as an indifferent "emptiness." "There is no goodness, without belief," Hook argues. "There is nothing but busy-ness" (116). For Hook, the transcendent lends the gossamer layer of significance to human acts that would otherwise have no meaning beyond themselves. This mustard seed of faith also gives Hook a sexual magnetism that still operates now and again with his elderly female friends, a quality that Updike will later confer on all his larky, adulterous believers. Hook, in effect, becomes the *de facto* leader of the poorhouse residents, many of whom regard him as the avatar of Connor's beloved predecessor, Mendelssohn. In addition to grace and dignity, Hook wistfully recalls, Mendelssohn also possessed "a natural faith," even if "in regards to admini-stration, he would let a few things slip" (28). Given that the work of "administration" falls under the heading of the Kierkegaardian universal, Mendelssohn's disregard for this aspect of his job is hardly a strike against him. In fact, it is a mark of his keen managerial skill. His entire reign, Connor ruefully notes, was a "long era of . . . indifference" during which the old people worked out arrangements for themselves (41), and yet by this same indifference Mendelssohn gave the residents the freedom necessary for them to acquire their own dignity and grace. Hence on the day the novel takes place – that is, the day of the fair – Hook, with his serene faith in God and his belief in the individualized spiritual dignity of his friends, becomes the residents' equally indifferent but loving leader of choice.

Conversely, Connor is all "busy-ness" without, as Updike sees it, dignity or grace. Unlike the God-like Mendelssohn – that is, God according to Barth – Connor strives as prefect "to be accessible" (13), which effort also qualifies him for ethical status in Kierkegaard's terms. Nevertheless, he lacks the third, crucial component: faith. In fact, because he thinks "of no one as God," he has "no gift of conversion" (14), thereby setting him at direct odds with the sexually magnetic Hook. Instead, Connor conceives of heaven as a liberal's earthly paradise, where there "will be no disease" and "no oppression, political or economic, because the administration of power will be in the hands of those who have no hunger for power, but who are, rather, dedicated to the cause of all humanity," and so on (106). Readers must therefore make a choice between Hook's spiritual individuality and Connor's social utopia, for those are the terms of this intricately written but structurally unbalanced apprentice work.

In the unlikely event that readers find Connor's social dreams more congenial and persuasive than Hook's spiritual convictions, Updike strong-arms the debate by having the poorhouse residents stone their hapless prefect. Ironically, for a man so bent on "busy-ness," so preoccupied with building a heaven here on earth, he gets punished precisely for making the world too easy for the old people. "Bore-dom," Hook warns, "is a ter-rible force" (135), so much so that it actually invites the sort of cruelty that rains down upon Connor's head. In the end, Hook's argument is Updike's: the world is fallen, and there is no human way to correct that flaw in creation. In "On Not Being a Dove" (1989), his famous (or infamous, depending on your voting record) essay analyzing his own refusal in the 1960s to protest against the Vietnam War, Updike argues, "In all varieties of Christian faith resides a certain contempt for the world and for attempts to locate salvation and perfection here. The world is fallen, and in a fallen world animals, men, and nations make space for themselves through a willingness to fight" (*Self-Consciousness*, 130). What is more, in Hook's view suffering in a fallen world is advantageous as it "provides the opportunity" for the exercise of virtue (109). So although Connor is compared near the end of the book to a "shepherd," he is clearly an ironic Christ, the prophet for what Updike in *Midpoint* calls "[a]n easy Humanism" that "plagues the land" (38). Updike, like Hook and all his other heroes, will "choose to take an otherworldly stand" (38).

In *Rabbit, Run* Updike essentially revisits the Hook-Connor conflict, with markedly improved results. The novel's hero, Rabbit Angstrom, assumes Hook's role, while the Connor position is taken up by an Episcopalian minister named Eccles. By making his representative Kierkegaardian a selfish, self-absorbed adulterer and his representative humanist a conscientious (if ineffective) minister, Updike successfully tips the scales against his own position and thereby locates the delicate dialectical balance that will characterize his best work for the next four decades. The key to the novel's success lies in the complex, richly textured character of Rabbit himself. In contrast to Hook's avuncular wisdom and decency, Rabbit is intellectually limited, narcissistic, and even cruel – and yet he remains mysteriously irresistible to the end. "Oh all the *world* loves you," sneers his adulterous lover Ruth. "What I wonder is why?" (*Run*, 144). The answer to that question represents the very source of the novel's considerable and lasting power.

Rabbit's last name, Angstrom, is the first and clearest indication of his specific role in the novel's Kierkegaardian scheme. A rough translation of the name might be "stream of *angst*." Kierkegaard endows *angst*, or dread, with tremendous, very specific, and, in his terms, ontological status. It is nothing less than the fear of nothingness, or, better, a recognition of the possibility that a vast nothingness looms beyond us. To feel *angst* is to register one's horrifying, unbounded freedom. Rabbit recognizes this absolute freedom when he quits his job, abruptly leaves his pregnant wife Janice and their young child Nelson, and heads out to Florida. To be sure, Rabbit's reasons for leaving are much less philosophical. A high school basketball star now locked in a desultory marriage with one child on his back and another on the way, Rabbit repeatedly imagines himself caught in a "net," a nice image that invokes his days on the basketball court. And, as he tells his antagonist Reverend Eccles, "[A]fter you're first-rate at something, no matter what, it kind of takes the kick out of being second-rate. And that little thing Janice and I had going, boy, it was really second-rate" (105). Yet even here we see how Updike has managed the difficult trick of transforming this limited, selfish young man into someone readers cannot dismiss so easily. Rabbit's sense of himself as "first-rate" dovetails perfectly with Kierkegaard's argument that truth is inwardness. What Rabbit actually feels is an instinctive, spiritual recoiling against a stifling life of ethical, social engagement. Updike's trick is to transform Rabbit's simple, grasping, but also in its way poetic language into a coded transcription of Kierkegaard's specialized terminology, so that the above can be translated to mean that Rabbit leaves as a result of a "teleological suspension of the ethical," in which the call of inner imperatives takes precedent. "I don't know what [Janice] feels," he tells Eccles. "I never have. All I know is what's inside *me*. That's all I have" (106). Later, in one of the most significant passages in the book, Rabbit explains the content of this inner life in resoundingly mystical terms: "Well I don't know all this about theology, but I'll tell you. I *do* feel, I guess, that somewhere behind all this . . . there's something that wants me to find it" (127).

But Updike, ever the dialectician, no sooner offers this explanation for Rabbit's actions than he instantly presents the other side. Kierkegaard warns, in *The Concept of Anxiety* (1844), that anxiety is not a recognition of freedom *per se* but rather "is defined as freedom's disclosure to itself in possibility."[8] In leaving, then, Rabbit opens up a whole new set of complications that the book is at pains to dramatize, complications that Updike presents as an irresolvable either/or. To reprise Updike's "yes, but" motif, the book says, by his own reckoning, "[y]es . . . to our inner urgent whispers, but – the social fabric collapses murderously."⁹ Rabbit's golf-playing pal, Reverend Eccles, is assigned the job of reminding Rabbit of how obdurately he is imbedded within that social fabric. Whereas Connor promotes a laughably idealized vision of humanistic perfection that reads, at times, like a parody of Dostoevsky's parodies of Nikolai Chernyshevsky or Charles Fourier, Eccles speaks directly out of the domestic ideology of the American 1950s. Quite reasonably, Eccles asks Rabbit, "What do you think it's like for other young couples?" and "Do you think . . . that God wants you to make your wife suffer?" (105, 106). Eccles is also quick to deflate much of Rabbit's mystic self-importance, remarking, "It's the strange thing about you mystics, how often your little ecstasies wear a skirt" (128) – for, of course, Rabbit is trying to recover his sense of grace in the receptive arms of his new lover, Ruth. Tellingly, Rabbit can produce no adequate response to these challenges.

Still, Eccles remains ineffective, and for very specific reasons, all of which flow from Updike's reading of Barth. Rabbit's own conception of the divine as the "something behind all this that wants [him] to find it" clearly signals Updike's Barthian agenda. Conversely, Eccles, as a representative of Kierkegaard's ethical universal, at times "doesn't seem to know his job" (102). Eccles's failure to lure Rabbit back to the universal resides not in his adherence to the ethical creeds of his day, but to his clinging to those creeds at the expense of the spiritual. Eccles is apprised of this error when he confronts his boss, Reverend Kruppenbach, whom Updike has described as "Barth in action."¹⁰ Eccles explains his concerns about Rabbit's behavior. Kruppenbach snaps, "You think now your job is to be an unpaid doctor, to run around and plug up the holes and make everything smooth. I don't think that. I don't think that's your job" (170). Neither does Barth, who declares in "The Word of God and the Task of the Ministry" (1922), "Obviously the people have *no* real need of *our* observations upon morality and culture, or even of our disquisitions upon religion, worship, and the possible existence of other worlds." For Kruppenbach, echoing Barth, Eccles's job is "to make yourself an exemplar of faith . . . so when the call comes you can go out and tell them, 'Yes, he is dead, but you will see him again in Heaven. Yes, you suffer, but you must *love* your pain, because it is *Christ's* pain'" (171). Even though Eccles does not get this, Rabbit apparently does. To Ruth's question quoted earlier as to why everyone loves Rabbit, he replies, "I'm a mystic . . . I give people faith" (144). As with Hook and Mendelssohn, Rabbit conveys an air of spiritual, radiant self-confidence that gives others faith in themselves. And, in a sense, this capacity corresponds to Barth's conception of the ministerial role: "When they come to us for help they do not really want to learn more about *living*: they want to learn more about what is on the farther side of living – *God*. We cut a ridiculous figure as village sages – or city sages. As such we are socially superfluous."[11] And, in the end, Eccles is little more than a "village sage."

This appeal to Barth, however, does not solve the novel's moral debate. After all, Rabbit returns home only to dash out again, whereupon his distraught wife drunkenly drowns their infant daughter in the bathtub. The social fabric *does* collapse murderously, despite – or perhaps *because* of – the irreconcilable demands of the spirit. What is more, Rabbit's acts have earthly, biological repercussions that cannot be assuaged by appeals to the spirit, as Ruth lets him know when she tells him she is pregnant with his child, on receipt of which news Rabbit does the only thing he knows how to do: he runs. The book's final paragraph leaves Rabbit suspended, then, between his spiritual certainties and this new set of complications. As he dashes up Mt. Judge one final time,

> He feels his inside as very real suddenly, a pure blank space in the middle of a dense net . . . It's like when they heard you were great and put two men on you and no matter which way you turned you bumped into one of them and the only thing to do was pass. So you passed and the ball belonged to the others and your hands were empty and the men on you looked foolish because in effect there was nobody there. (306)

Similarly, at the end of the novel, Updike's readers are left holding that ball. The players above might also be understood as two sorts of readers, those who want to nail Rabbit down for fleeing his social responsibilities and those who want to congratulate him for heeding his inner call. The end of the book shakes off both sets of readers, who must then contend with an abrupt empty space instead of a tidy resolution. The debate, in other words, must go on after the book is over – go on, namely, within each reader.

Whereas these two early novels belong principally to Kierkegaard, with traces of Barth superadded to lend a hefty, Germanic theological weight, the remaining two novels treated here, *A Month of Sundays* and *Roger's Version*, part of a trilogy of novels that rewrite Hawthorne's *The Scarlet Letter* (1850), are almost entirely written in Barth's ample margins. In *A Month of Sundays*, for instance, Updike pits one Reverend Tom Marshfield – verily a doubting Thomas, as well as a "marshy field" to contrast with his predecessor Dimmesdale's "dim dale" – against not only his own sexual desires but also his liberal assistant, Ned Bork, this novel's resident Connor/Eccles figure. In the simplest terms Marshfield, like Rabbit, is caught between biology and society, religion and morality, yet whereas Rabbit rushes after solutions based purely on intuition and instinct, Marshfield analyzes his dilemma with the full force of his verbal adeptness, his theological training, and his gift for playful ambiguity. Fittingly, one of the novel's two epigraphs belongs to the twentieth-century existentialist theologian Paul Tillich: "This principle of soul, universally and individually, is the principle of ambiguity." For Marshfield, this ambiguity inheres in the either/or structure of his own theological vision, wherein, quoting Freud, he asserts that "opposites are one. Light holds within it the possibility of dark. God is the Devil, dreadfully enough. I, I am all, I am God enthroned on the only ego that exists for me; and I am dust, and like the taste" (*Month*, 189). Even more importantly, Marshfield early in the novel invites his readers to imagine him as a "circle divided in half, half white and half black" (39). In the white, or Good, half, which belongs to God, Marshfield places a series of items all of which provide order, from the comforting craft of furniture to Karl Barth's prose, from his own "hieratic place within the liturgy" to the "secular sense of order within . . . middle-class life" (40); in the black, or "Depressing," side, Marshfield places Mankind and all the human-willed, as opposed to God-willed, chaos that proceeds therefrom. Marshfield contends that his first mistress, Alicia, reclaimed "a wedge of mankind for the Good and the Beautiful" and thereby "shifted the axis of the divider 10°" (40). The book's primary drama lies less in the tale of adultery he recounts than in the month-long process of writerly therapy that will allow him (hopefully) to realign and rebalance the axis of the divider.

This same process of "realigning the axis" governs Marshfield's account of his battles with Ned Bork, his curate and, he later finds, erotic rival. Bork is a bearded liberal minister who allies his Christian mission to that of the prevailing post-1960s counterculture and, to hear Marshfield tell it, worships a sandaled, bearded Jesus who is less a Kierkegaardian paradox than the godfather of the hippie movement. Marshfield fully shares Updike's avowed "contempt for the world and for attempts to locate salvation and perfection here," and little inspires this contempt more than Lyndon Johnson-era liberalism, which he refers to collectively as "most institutional and political trends since 1965" (40). He dismisses Bork's hippie idealism as a search for "the pacifier of a social cure-all" (60), and later, in a particularly ringing phrase, declares, "Adam did not fall, nor did Christ rise, that the world might be hassle-free" (122).

In his early accounts of the various debates he undertakes with Bork about "the establishment," "the system," and the church's role in improving the world, Marshfield generally reports his own lines and paraphrases Bork's, merely admitting that "there was much to be said on his side" without actually allowing him to say it within the text (71). Be that as it may, Bork gets even better lines than Eccles. For instance, later in the novel, as the debates increase in intensity – and after Marshfield learns that Bork has taken over as Alicia's lover – Marshfield gives Bork a fuller, less patronized speaking role. To Marshfield's argument that Barth would have us "trust the Caesar that is, as against the Caesar that might be," Bork is allowed to reply, "Do you think . . . in Stalin's Russia, say, you would have trusted and served *that* Caesar?," a decisive rebuttal to Marshfield's position that makes Marshfield "grateful to him, for seeing this, and stopping me" (89). Bork also gets to lodge the book's most incisive critique of Barth, who, he says, preaches what essentially amounts to "atheism . . . and then at the last minute whips away the 'a' and says, 'Presto! *Theism!*'" (89–90). This time it is Marshfield who admits that "there were a dozen ledges in his exposition where one could stage an argument" but who holds back, giving Bork, essentially, the last word and leaving the debate unresolved.

As important as Bork is to Marshfield's progress, however, the primary "Other" with which he spars throughout is the feminine writ large. Even his wife, whom he admits he resembles physically, appears to him as "*totaliter aliter*, an Other, a woman" (58), a deliberate invocation of Barth's term for God that signals as clearly as anything else in the novel Updike's playful conflation of sex and religion. The four "sermons" that Marshfield delivers over the course of the text not only mark a gradual progression in his spiritual journey toward harmonic balance but also provide him with an opportunity to play with this blasphemous conflation of the erotic and the theological. In the first sermon he proclaims, "Verily, the sacrament of marriage, as instituted in its adamant impossibility by our Saviour, exists but as a precondition for the sacrament of adultery" (47), which idea Marshfield, at this point in his progress anyway, about two-thirds believes, and Updike possibly about half. By the final sermon, however, Marshfield has given up such games in favor of a more Kierkegaardian reassertion of faith as an "irrational" response to the otherwise unanswerable question, as posed by Pascal, "*Qui m'y a mis?*" (212, 211).

Among the many factors that aid this return to spiritual health is the implied presence throughout of a Ms. Prynne, this novel's Hester and also a figure for the Ideal Reader (228). As the manageress of the "motel" in which Marshfield is staying, she visits his room each day while he is out playing golf, and Marshfield addresses the entire journal, which he hopes she is reading, directly to her. He longs to seduce her, in fact, the journal itself being that seduction. Throughout, God-like, she hovers around him but remains silent, and responds to his text only when he manages to preach that final sermon, which she characterizes as "a sermon that could be preached" (212). Their successful coupling takes place, significantly, three days later. He arrives at the retreat a solitary masturbator – "Masturbation! Thou saving grace-note upon the baffled chord of self!" (4) – and leaves thirty-one days later with his sexuality and spirit back in healthy working order, the male and female principles joined at the apex of the phallic pen/penis in symbolic echo of the text-reader dynamic, the body-spirit dichotomy, and the human-God dialectic. In this way, namely via his appropriation of metafictional self-consciousness, Updike directly thematizes in *A Month of Sundays* his process of debating with the reader, transforming that debate into a seduction the happy end of which is not a resolution of opposites but rather their happy joining in productive dynamic tension.

Roger's Version goes even further in conflating the erotic and the theological. Early in this intellectual whirlwind of a novel, randy, irascible Roger Lambert frankly admits that he draws "comfort and inspiration" from reading both theology and pornography. Whereas theology "caresses and probes every crevice of the unknowable," pornography exalts "our underside, the damp underside of our ordained insomnia"; in both genres "the rock is lifted. And what eventuates from these sighing cesspools of our being, our unconscionable sincere wishes? Cathedrals and children" (*Roger's*, 41). Roger is not merely seeking to provoke. If *A Month of Sundays* uses Barth's "yes/no" oscillation to examine the body-spirit dichotomy, *Roger's Version* explores the larger question of Barth's unprovable Wholly Other God, in which schema theological speculation is treated as a taboo attempt to uncover what should remain unknowable and undisclosed.

Roger's chief antagonist, Dale Kohler – this novel's Dimmesdale – is, in his estimation, the chief spiritual "pornographer," since he believes that he can prove God's existence on a computer. Roger devilishly overemphasizes this point by imagining, in great pornographic detail, a series of afternoon sexual encounters between Dale and Roger's wife, Esther, this cold, calculated novel's resident Ms. Prynne. Although the scenes that Roger imagines between Dale and Esther represent the most explicit visual and tactile descriptions of sexual coupling in Updike's exceptionally lurid *oeuvre*, they are not offered merely to titillate. In his careful reading of the novel, James A. Schiff singles out Updike's emphasis on sight in general, and on Roger's avowed clairvoyant powers of vision. He then argues that Lambert's surname calls to mind the eighteenth-century German mathematician Johann Heinrich Lambert (1728–77), whose first book, *Photometria* (1760), established what is now known as "Lambert's Law of Absorption," namely a formula that measures the exponential decrease of light as it passes through an absorbing beam of uniform transparency.[12] After his first encounter with Dale, for instance, Roger claims to be visited by a "strange unwilled vision" of Dale leaving the office and heading home (28), a motif that will continue throughout the novel as he imagines Dale with Esther, Dale at the computer, Dale at home, and so on. Similarly, the novel is preoccupied with images of "light," both physical and metaphorical, as when Dale, also early in the novel, gets his first hint that Roger might be willing to help him secure a grant to conduct his computer project: "He jumped at the gap, the glimmer of light" (25). Roger's sham claim of clairvoyance in the service of porno-graphic satisfaction, then, adroitly parodies Updike's Barthian insistence that the search for "proof" of God's existence is not only fruitless but also taboo.

Dale, of course, thinks otherwise. He proposes that "[i]f God . . . in fact created the universe, then as a fact it *has* to show, eventually" (21); furthermore, Dale argues that the physical constants and initial conditions now known to have been necessary for creation to have occurred at all *had* to be "fine-tuned" by a purposeful Intelligence, if only because even the slightest alteration in these constants would have made it impossible for the creation of a life-bearing planet like Earth. Dale therefore wants to create a computer model of these initial conditions in the hope that, once the program starts running, the face of God Himself will "show through." Dale's extended use of computer lingo, while frustrating, also functions within the novel as a clever way for Updike to adapt the language of dig-ital technology to Roger's Barthian theology. The computer binary code – that dizzying series of 1s and 0s that constitutes the computer's specialized language – echoes directly Barth's primary dichotomy of the divine Yes and No, whereas Roger sardonically dubs the OR, AND, NOT triad of computer circuitry "[t]he rudiments of the new Gospel" (110–111), a provocative idea inadvertently supported by Dale, who is particularly excited by connections between binary code and Boolean algebra. In Dale's analysis an OR gate renders "one plus one" not "two or zero, . . . but one" (112), thereby pro-ducing a tidy analogue to Kierkegaard's irresolvable either/or, while the AND and NOT gates in Dale's analysis multiply and invert, respectively, providing Updike with a lucky mathematical model for Barth's "something/nothing" dialectic.

For his part, Roger proclaims Dale's argument to be both "aesthetically and ethically repulsive" (24), that last word, used throughout the novel, clearly signaling the "pornographic" nature of Dale's enterprise. "Aesthet-ically," Roger goes on to explain, "because it describes a God Who lets Himself be intellectually trapped, and ethically because it eliminates faith from religion, it takes away our freedom to believe or doubt" (24). Later, Roger quotes in full Barth's statement in *The Word of God and the Word of Man*, also cited earlier here, that "[t]he god who stood at the end of some human way – even of this way – would not be God." Even more importantly, the book suggests that such a search will do more than merely eliminate faith: it will positively kill it. Watching his son poke at a fire during a fractious Thanksgiving dinner, Roger warns, "Don't poke it too much . . . You'll make it go out" (113). Similarly, Dale's quest to reduce creation to the mathematical binary code of computer systems almost succeeds in poking out the dim fire of his spiritual convictions.

For all that, Roger does not merely "win" this argument. In his "Special Message" to the Franklin Library edition of *Roger's Version*, Updike declares, "[T]he debates between Roger and Dale are meant to be real debates, on issues that are, to me, live and interesting" (*Odd*, 857). Hence, in as much as Dale's inquiries are depicted as a brand of theological pornography, Updike has given those inquiries a full hearing in this novel, just as he gives free rein to Roger's pornographic preoccupations. And Updike himself admits, in *Self-Consciousness* (1989), that "[w]riting, in making the world light – in codifying, distorting, prettifying, verbalizing it – approaches blasphemy" (226). So although Dale loses his faith, and Updike's Barthian God remains unproved and therefore securely Other, Dale's argument for an Intelligent Design retains its provocative possibility. Updike ingeniously keeps the debate alive by giving the argument's last word to Roger's neighbor, Kriegman, an atheistic scientist who tells disconsolate, disappointed Dale that he knows "*exactly* how life arose; it's brand-new news, at least to the average layman like yourself. Clay. Clay is the answer" (305). Kriegman goes on to expound on crystal formation in fine clays and so on, but Updike's point is clear: science has inadvertently returned to Genesis, where Adam was formed from the clay of the earth and breathed to life by God. In other words, the debate, as in all of Updike's best work, remains in the end open, dynamic, still restlessly in play.

NOTES

1. James Plath, ed., *Conversations with John Updike* (Jackson: University Press of Mississippi, 1994), p. 50.
2. Søren Kierkegaard, *Concluding Unscientific Postscript to Philosophical Fragments*, ed. and trans. Howard V. Hong and Edna H. Hong, 26 vols. (1846; Princeton, NJ: Princeton University Press, 1992), XII.1, pp. 253, 254.
3. Søren Kierkegaard, *Fear and Trembling/Repetition*, ed. and trans. Howard V. Hong and Edna H. Hong, 26 vols. (1843; Princeton, NJ: Princeton University Press, 1983), VI, pp. 56, 53.
4. Plath, *Conversations*, pp. 16, 75.
5. Karl Barth, *Dogmatics in Outline*, trans. G. T. Thomson (1947; New York: Harper and Row, 1959), pp. 55, 57.

6. Karl Barth, *The Word of God and the Word of Man*, trans. Douglas Horton (1928; New York: Harper and Row, 1957), p. 177. Updike quotes this passage at the beginning of his review of Barth's *Anselm: Fides Quaerens Intellectum* (see *Assorted*, 273) and later in *Roger's Version* (41).
7. See *Odd Jobs*, pp. 843–844, and *More Matter*, pp. 842–843.
8. Søren Kierkegaard, *The Concept of Anxiety*, ed. and trans. Reidar Thomte, with Albert B. Anderson (1844; Princeton, NJ: Princeton University Press, 1980), p. 111.
9. Plath, *Conversations*, p. 33.
10. George W. Hunt, *John Updike and the Three Great Secret Things: Sex, Religion, and Art* (Grand Rapids, MI: Eerdmans, 1980), p. 43.
11. Barth, *The Word of God*, pp. 188, 189.
12. James A. Schiff, *John Updike Revisited* (New York: Twayne, 1998), p. 97.

GUIDE TO FURTHER READING

Campbell, Jeff H. *Updike's Novels: Thorns Spell a Word*. Wichita Falls, TX: Midwestern State University Press, 1987.
Crews, Frederick. "Mr. Updike's Planet." *The Critics Bear It Away: American Fiction and the Academy*. New York: Random House, 1992, pp. 168–186.
Markle, Joyce B. *Fighters and Lovers: Theme in the Novels of John Updike*. New York: New York University Press, 1973, pp. 13–60.
Neary, John. *Something and Nothingness: The Fiction of John Updike and John Fowles*. Carbondale: Southern Illinois University Press, 1992.
Wood, Ralph C. *The Comedy of Redemption: Christian Faith and Comic Vision in Four American Novelists*. Notre Dame, IN: University of Notre Dame Press, 1988, pp. 178–229.
Yerkes, James, ed. *John Updike and Religion: The Sense of the Sacred and the Motions of Grace*. Grand Rapids, MI: Eerdmans, 1999.

II
CONTROVERSY AND DIFFERENCE

4

KATHLEEN VERDUIN

Updike, women, and mythologized sexuality

Near the end of John Updike's novel *The Centaur* (1963), Peter Caldwell contemplates the statue of "a naked green lady" in a pool of water, her lips poised at the scallop shell in her hand (267). Identified a quarter of a century later as a fountain in the Pennsylvania museum the author frequented as a child, this *Drinking Girl* prefigured the "quiescent glade of basically female forms" he later encountered in the Museum of Modern Art (*Looking*, 2–5, 14), and she suggests as well his lifelong attraction to the feminine in its archetypal representations. Updike has several times affirmed the mythic resonance of day-to-day experience – most conspicuously in *The Centaur*, which mythologizes Peter as Prometheus and Updike's own father as the centaur Chiron, but also in the early story "Flight" (1959), where Allen Dow's mother gives "the people closest to her mythic immensity. I was the phoenix" (*Pigeon*, 58). "[T]o a child," Updike told interviewers in the 1960s, "everything is myth-size: people are enormous and ominous and have great backlogs of mysterious information"; his recourse to mythic parallels in *The Centaur* answered, he added, "to my sensation that the people we meet are *guises*, do conceal something mythic, perhaps prototypes or longings in our minds" (*Picked-Up*, 499, 500).

As the mythologist Joseph Campbell writes, "It has always been the prime function of mythology and rite to supply the symbols that carry the human spirit forward."[1] While mythological archetypes magnify, however, stereotypes reduce, and the line between them often blurs. Updike's portrayal of women has accordingly angered some readers as predictably reductive: he "consistently reasserts the worn dichotomy," Mary Allen complains, "that a woman is sexual and stupid (human) or that she is frigid and intelligent (inhuman)."[2] My thesis in this essay is that Updike's women do indeed evoke gender patterns archaically entrenched in Western culture – primarily, it seems to me, the archetypes of earth mother, seductress, and witch. But if the author projects a mythology of women, that mythology turns first on a myth of self, and both run like a double helix through his work.

Self-consciousness: hero

"The mystery that . . . puzzled me as a child," Updike recalled in his early memoir "The Dogwood Tree: A Boyhood" (1962), "was the incarnation of my ego – that omnivorous and somehow preëxistent 'I' – in a speck so specifically situated among the billions of history. Why was I I? The arbitrariness of it astounded me; in comparison, nothing was too marvellous" (*Assorted*, 182). Updike's near-obsessive reiteration of this enigma confirms its personal significance: he raises the same question in his 1969 autobiographical poem, *Midpoint* (4), and again in his 1989 memoir, significantly titled *Self-Consciousness* (6). In *Rabbit, Run* (1960) the title character surveys familiar surroundings in sudden terror: "Why was he set down here, why is this town, a dull suburb of a third-rate city, for him the center and index of a universe that contains immense prairies, mountains, deserts, forests, coastlines, cities, seas? This childish mystery – the mystery of 'any place,' prelude to the ultimate, 'Why am I me?' – starts panic in his heart" (282–283).

For Updike, by his own admission, this shock of cosmic precariousness and a resultant fear of dying – the sensation of *angst* described by existentialist philosophers – impelled the religious conversion of his twenties, when he read the Christian existentialist Søren Kierkegaard (1813–55) and the neo-orthodox theologian Karl Barth (1886–1968). As Updike recognizes, Christianity uniquely promises continuation of a unitary subjectivity, "that core 'I' which we imagine to be so crystalline and absolute," into eternity (*Self-Consciousness*, 218); as his character the Reverend Thomas Marshfield remonstrates in *A Month of Sundays* (1975), "all those who offer instead some gaseous survival of a personal essence, or one's perpetuation through children or good deeds or masterworks of art, . . . are tempters and betrayers of the Lord" (209). But Updike's experience also provides a textbook example of the "identity crisis" theorized by the psychologist Erik Erikson, "when each youth must forge for himself some central perspective and direction, some working unity" – a crisis sometimes precipitated by an "ego-chill, a shudder which comes from the sudden awareness that our nonexistence . . . is entirely possible." In Erikson's analysis, moreover, such psychic panic drives "our myth-making, our metaphysical speculation, and our artificial creation of 'ideal' realities in which we become and remain the central reality."[3]

Updike's protagonists thus typically replay the definitional crisis recounted by the author: arrested by a fear of death, they assert Christian orthodoxy, usually to a religiously indifferent audience. The early story "Pigeon Feathers" (1961) forms a blueprint: the boy David Kern, confronted by his own mortality, batters his mother with questions about the afterlife and sneers when his minister compares heaven to "the way the goodness Abraham

Lincoln did lives after him" (*Pigeon*, 133). David's inner conflict resolves spontaneously, however, when he shoots pigeons in the darkened cavern of his family's barn. The paradox of overcoming death by dealing death is illuminated in Ernest Hemingway's meditation on the bullfight, *Death in the Afternoon* (1932): "Once you accept the rule of death thou shalt not kill is an easily and naturally obeyed commandment. But when a man is still in rebellion against death he takes pleasure in taking to himself one of the Godlike attributes – that of giving it."[4] "The love of killing (*vide* Hemingway)," writes Updike in a presumable gloss on this insight, "springs from the fear of being killed: a counterblow, as it were, delivered against the encircling dark" (*Odd*, 67). The image of counterblow explains in turn David's strange euphoria: "He felt like a beautiful avenger" (*Pigeon*, 146).

In the words of Mircea Eliade, "Many heroic mythologies are solar in structure. The hero is assimilated to the sun; like the sun, he fights darkness, descends into the realm of death and emerges victorious."[5] As David aims his shotgun at the "small round holes" below the barn's eaves (145), however, his vengeance imitates the sexual act and skids into a mythological binary of gender. Updike's image of cosmic avenger revives the ancient cultural moment when human consciousness repudiated definition as mere natural organism – exemplified when the Sumerian hero Gilgamesh rejects the fertility goddess Ishtar or the Babylonian Marduk destroys the female sea monster Tiamat. From the hero's standpoint, primordial Nature is deflected mercilessly upon the feminine. In Northrop Frye's assessment, "It seems almost a symbolic necessity in mythology to think of nature, more particularly vegetable nature, as female, a mother whose fertility brings all life into being"; but as simultaneously "the tomb of all forms of life, she has a menacing and sinister aspect."[6] Updike appears to participate in this prejudicial mythology, and again the paradigm is raised in "Pigeon Feathers": absorbed in her farm, David's mother insults her son's anxiety by inviting him to "[l]ook out the window at the sun; at the fields." She is, David grumbles in imitation of his anxious, churchgoing father, "so simple, so illogical; such a femme" (137).

Nature: Mother Earth

The myth of Mother Earth dominates the whole of Updike's fiction, rendering archetypal, in *Of the Farm* (1965), the bond between the land and Joey Robinson's mother, who resembles at once David's mother in "Pigeon Feathers," Cassie Caldwell in *The Centaur*, and much of what Updike has recalled about his own mother: like Allen Dow's mother in "His Mother Inside Him" (1992), evidently, Linda Grace Hoyer Updike "planted in him the idea that land was sacred, a piece of Mother Earth" (*Afterlife*, 237). In an earlier essay Updike had noted that his mother's "old hobbies, which I thought eccentric – organic gardening, natural foods, conservation – now seem to me simple good sense. More deeply than any patriarchal religion, I believe what she instilled: the notion that we should live as close to nature as we can, and that in matters of diet and behavior alike we should look to the animals for guidance" (*Odd*, 69). But this graciously filial equation between earth-loving mother and Mother Earth also perpetuates the deep polarities legitimated by myth. As Gaea, the Earth, woman necessarily complements Father Sky (cf. *Centaur*, 297; *Month*, 220), but she remains his opposite and presumed inferior. Source of unabashed fertility – "Our lovely green-clad mother spreads her legs – / Corrosive, hairy, rank" (*Midpoint*, 40) – Earth allies most nearly to the sex goddess Venus, like her avatar Vera Hummel in *The Centaur* "[a] woman . . . of over-arching fame," yet ominously stretching back to a time when consciousness, for Updike the ultimate marker of humanity, "was mere pollen drifting in darkness" (276, 22). To penetrate such a being, Updike fantasizes, is to descend into a hellish inversion, "the murky region, where up is down and death is life, of mythology" (*Odd*, 71). As the novelist Joyce Carol Oates has observed, Venus in Updike's imagination "is life itself; the very force of life, playful, promiscuous as Nature, ultimately uncaring as the ancient Magna Mater was so viciously uncaring of the beautiful adolescent youths she loved and devoured."[7] "The fullness ends," Rabbit Angstrom agrees, "when we give Nature her ransom, when we make children for her. Then she is through with us, and we become, first inside, and then outside, junk" (*Run*, 225).

The cycle of generation is thus revealed as a biological trap, and women join the earth goddess in her darker phase as death-bringer. Updike's fictional author Henry Bech, reluctantly visiting a Southern women's college, finds himself literally suffocated by surrounding fecundity: "Their massed fertility was overwhelming; their bodies were being broadened and readied to generate from their own cells a new body to be pushed from the old, and in time to push bodies from itself, and so on into eternity, an ocean of doubling and redoubling cells within which his own conscious moment was soon to wink out" (*Bech*, 112). As though further to emphasize the regnant paradigm, Updike's males experience their shock of *angst* in the presence of an unsympathetic woman, seemingly the hero's necessary foil: wakened to hear her husband Jerry "protest that some day he would die," Ruth Conant in *Marry Me* (1976) "had said, 'Dust to dust,' and rolled over and gone back to sleep. Jerry never forgave this" (78). Their indifference to mortality a tacit negation of Christian supernaturalism, the women in Updike's fiction betray an equally untroubled acceptance of Nature's second "organic imperative," sex (*Assorted*, 231). Marshfield is bemused to find, in the course of his adulteries, that "women really don't see much wrong with it" (*Month*, 174), and Foxy's admonition to Piet Hanema in *Couples* (1968), "*Have me without remorse*" (264), modulates with the decline of decorum to Verna's "Nunc, it's no big deal" (279) in *Roger's Version* (1986) or the businesslike consensual expletive ("*Shit*") that prefaces Pru's what-the-hell seduction of her father-in-law (346) in *Rabbit at Rest* (1990). Even as late as *Gertrude and Claudius* (2000), Hamlet's adulterous mother exalts Nature as "God's older and purer handiwork" (90).

Cast as ancillary to a devouring earth goddess, women in Updike's work transmogrify into adversaries of a patriarchal religion that presumably demeans their natural prerogatives: "Did you *see*," Peggy Fosnacht demands on the occasion of the Pope's visit in *Rabbit Is Rich* (1981), "what he said in Chicago yesterday about *sex!*" (286). In "Augustine's Concubine" (1975), Updike traces a twin aversion to Nature and the feminine back to the *Confessions* of St. Augustine (CE396–430), historically the great exemplar of self-consciousness: "*Concupiscentia*. Its innocence disturbed him, the simplicity of her invitation to descend with her into her nature, into Nature, and to be immersed"(*Problems*, 137). Little wonder, perhaps, that in *Couples* Piet can lament that "[t]he voracious despair of women had swallowed God" (258), or that Glenn Morrissey, in a much later story, is still discerning in women's faces an ancestral Tiamat, "that female openness and depth of interrogation which remind men of the dark, of the ocean, of the night sky, of everything swallowing and terminating" (*Afterlife*, 250–251).

Adultery: Iseult

Updike married in 1953; the first of his four children was born in 1955. In one of several accounts of his religious conversion, he frankly attributes the existential crisis he suffered to domestic confinement: he read Kierkegaard's *Fear and Trembling* (1843), he acknowledges, "in 1955 or early 1956, as a nervous newcomer to New York City, husbandhood, and paternity. Amid my new responsibilities I felt fearful and desolate, foreseeing, young as I was, that I would die, and that the substance of the earth was, therefore, death" (*Odd*, 844). "I had taken pride, at first, in Perdita's pregnancies," Ben Turnbull remembers of his first marriage in *Toward the End of Time* (1997), "but by now the process felt stale, a stunt stained with Nature's fatality" (82). In *Of the Farm* Joey Robinson hears a sermon on the creation of Eve that ostensibly desexualizes Christian marriage into sustained companionship, man and woman alike intended "to *work* together" (150); yet the young minister (about whom, Joey's mother mutters darkly, "[t]here's been talk" [154]) provocatively pairs the "visceral and nostalgic warmth" of women with Christian supernaturalism as competing alternatives of comfort to death-foreseeing males (152). As the drunken Freddy Thorne puts it in *Couples*, "In the western world there are only two comical things: the Christian church and naked women. We don't have Lenin so that's it. Everything else tells us we're dead" (146). In what seems a transparently self-serving paradox, then, Updike's Christian protagonists repeatedly flee "Nature's fatality" by gratification of natural instinct; religious orthodoxy and the temptation to adultery writhe in symbiotic tension.

The acknowledged primer for Updike's construction of adultery is his 1963 essay on Denis de Rougemont's *Love in the Western World* (1939; English translation 1956), an investigation of Europe's long romance with love outside marriage. De Rougemont proposes that the medieval myth of Tristan and Iseult exalts the unattainable and illusory; it is not each other the lovers love, in this modality, but themselves, and the heightened self-consciousness that their frustrated passion incites. De Rougemont personifies this "love-myth," Updike notes in a telling conflation, as "a Venus born of the foam of Eastern religions and imported into Europe . . . Her essence is *passion itself*; her concern is not with the possession, through love, of another person but with the prolongation of the lover's state of mind" (*Assorted*, 285). Iseult thus functions as "the mythical prototype of the Unattainable Lady to whom the love-myth directs our adoration, diverting it from the attainable lady (in legal terms, our 'wife'; in Christian terms, our 'neighbor') who is at our side" (285). Yet Updike also asserts the love-myth's consolations:

> Might it not simply be that sex has become involved in the Promethean protest forced upon Man by his paradoxical position in the Universe as a self-conscious animal? Our fundamental anxiety is that we do not exist – or will cease to exist. Only in being loved do we find external corroboration of the extremely high valuation each ego secretly assigns itself. This exalted arena, then, is above all others the one where men and women will insist on their freedom to choose – to choose that other being in whose existence their own existence is confirmed and amplified. (299)

These statements suggest the author covertly in dialogue with himself, and the Tristan myth looms large in Updike's fiction: "I fell into the local version of the sexual revolution," Updike comments, "and out came a bundle of variations on the story of Tristan and Iseult" (*More*, 764). The medieval lovers appear by name in "Four Sides of One Story" (1965; *Music*, 87–100); "Tristan's Law" ("appealingness is inversely proportional to attainability" [*Problems*, 152]) is cited in "Problems" (1975); *Brazil* (1994) features a couple named Isabel and Tristão; "The Two Iseults" appears as a contents subheading in *The Early Stories, 1953–1975* (2003); *Gertrude and Claudius* draws on troubadour poetry highlighted in its dedication; and "Tristan and Iseult"(1990) recasts the Unattainable Lady amusingly as a large-bosomed dental hygienist (*Afterlife*, 148–153). To possess Iseult, however, is, *ipso facto*, to kill the romance. "You sleep with somebody in a moment of truth," the narrator complains in *Roger's Version*, "and the obligations begin to pile up nightmarishly" (286).

Updike exposes this "love-myth," then, as doomed to disappoint; yet the proliferous adulteries of his fiction testify also to the incontrovertible excitement of the illicit encounter. Disgraced by serial infidelities and rusticated to a rehabilitation center in Colorado, Updike's fallen minister Marshfield reshapes his daily therapeutic journal into an exercised apologia: "Wherein does the modern American man recover his sense of worth, not as dogged breadwinner and economic integer, but as romantic minister and phallic knight, as personage, embodiment, and hero? In adultery" (*Month*, 46). Mounted in opposition to faith, sex here seems nihilistically to triumph as "the emergent religion, as the only thing left" (*Picked-Up*, 505).

For Updike's Christian protagonists, however, the demands of self-consciousness take precedence over Nature's self-forgetfulness, and guilt thus forms an indispensable component, "sex as a 'knowing'" harking back to Eden's Tree of Knowledge (*Midpoint*, 28). In a telltale comment, Updike savors a society where "erotic adventure is still enough freighted with guilt and pain to seem a mode of inner pilgrimage" (*Hugging*, 388). But this inner pilgrimage, one notices, remains largely the preserve of men. While the women in Updike's novels consistently deny culpability ("Never their fault. The serpent beguiled me" [*Couples*, 236]) or subsume their indiscretions into renewed complacency, Updike's male adulterers are given to protestations like Jerry Conant's: "to abandon my family is a sin; to do it I'd have to deny God, and by denying God I'd give up all claim on immortality" (*Marry*, 55). Indeed, several of Updike's men employ their sexuality to reenact the fantasy of cosmic vengeance first seen in "Pigeon Feathers": Piet is denounced by an irate husband as "[t]he Red-haired Avenger" (*Couples*, 402, 412), and Jerry gloats that "he had given his enemy the darkness an eternal wound. With the sword of his flesh he had put the mockers to rout. Christ was revenged" (*Marry*, 287). Perhaps most explicit is the way Marshfield rationalizes the seduction of his divinity professor's daughter: "His course epitomized everything I hated about academic religion" and "I was slaying him that the Lord might live" (*Month*, 50, 54). The act of "fucking" – increasingly the verb of choice as Updike's men pursue their "sexual pilgrimage" through the bodies of women (*More*, 821), and related etymologically to the Latin *pugnus*, a fist – metamorphoses improbably into an act of righteous punishment, enlarged to grandiose proportions as Henry Bech among his Southern hostesses remembers how the North "had once fucked the South so hard it was still trembling" (*Bech*, 110) or Rabbit Angstrom muses in *Rabbit Redux* (1971), "Us and Vietnam, fucking and being fucked, blood is wisdom" (310).

Feminism: witch

The Witches of Eastwick (1984) represents Updike's most concentrated attention to the feminist movement. But this work, too, casts shadows by its mythological frame: he would "not have begun this novel," Updike comments, "if I had not known, in my life, witchy women, and in my experience felt something of the sinister old myths to resonate with the modern female experiences of liberation and raised consciousness" (*Odd*, 855). In *Witches* Alexandra Spofford, Jane Smart, and Sukie Rougemont (her surname, of course, immediately suggestive), three middle-aged women of a small Rhode Island community, take to practicing witchcraft: they have transformed their unsatisfactory husbands respectively into a jar of dust, a dry sheaf of herbs, and a plastic placemat. While Darryl Van Horne, the novel's comical Satan figure, denounces Nature in a nauseous outburst worthy of Bech – "all that budding and pushing, the sap up the tree trunks, the weeds and the insects getting set to fight it out once again, . . . Christ, it's cruel" (*Witches*, 82) – the three witches fall in line with Updike's earlier females by endorsement of Nature's processes: "There must always be sacrifice. It was one of nature's rules," Alexandra pronounces as she crushes crabs on the beach (16). The crabs, however, are the first instance of the "bad-luck word, the Latin for 'crab'" (236). Fear of cancer – itself merely the "D'naughty DNA" (268), the life force run amok – metastasizes through the novel and concentrates finally in the witches' victim, Jenny Gabriel. Apprehensive as Jenny declines, the three attempt to retrieve the poppet made in her image from the swamp where Alexandra has flung it, "to be gone, swallowed up, dissolved, forgiven by nature's seethe" (261), only to find it entirely eaten: "Nature is a hungry old thing," Alexandra shrugs (286).

Updike was aware, of course, that feminists were claiming both witch and Mother Earth as totems (*Hugging*, 303–307, 341–345; *Odd*, 425–432), but *Witches* exposes his trio's feminism – "our divorces and finding ourselves and so on" (65) – as by turns shallow and insidious: the author appears to have mustered his characters to challenge equally dubious myths essentializing women as peaceable and benign. "It was a convention of feminist thought, at least in the sixties and seventies," Updike explained in an interview, "that men were murderous in their use of power, and that women, were they

allowed power, would of course *not* be – even though Indira Gandhi and
Golda Meir and other female leaders throughout history had not proven to
be conspicuously more clever at avoiding war than men had. So I was trying
to explore, on the realistic level, the whole question of power in women."[8]

This ambivalence toward power in women emerges again in *S.* (1988),
the third in Updike's trilogy inspired by Hawthorne's *The Scarlet Letter*
(1850); Hawthorne's novel is likewise "a myth by now," Updike avers, "and
it was an updating of the myth . . . that interested me."[9] Updike's latter-
day Hester Prynne is the resilient Sarah Price Worth, reinventing herself in
a putatively Buddhist ashram in Arizona. Ashram, Arizona, the "Arhat"
who leads the motley commune, the A-frame lodgings, and a prevalence
of Vitamin A permit scope for Updike's irrepressible cartoonist's instinct;
the letter's referent, as in Hawthorne, remains of course Adultery, as Sarah
leaves her husband and conducts various sexual experiments (including an
interval with another woman, Alinga). As the novel progresses, however,
Sarah is better defined by Avarice: she disingenuously bilks contributors,
embezzles funds, and builds herself a prodigious bank account in Switzer-
land. Where Hester famously remains silent, moreover, Sarah carries on an
irritating, self-congratulatory prattle: the novel's text consists entirely of her
letters and the compromising audiotapes she surreptitiously prepares. Philo-
sophically illiterate ("all I remember now is essence precedes existence, or
is it the other way around?" [*S.*, 5]), impervious to guilt ("and then like
Eve and Adam digesting the apple we must feel so *guilty*. I didn't, I don't
think" [9–10]), Sarah predictably dismisses the question of God's existence
as "rather boring" and echoes the Nature-worshiping bromides mouthed
by Updike's other women: "[I]t seems so obvious that *some*thing exists,
something incredibly and tirelessly good, an outpouring of which the rocks
and I and the perfect blue sky with its little dry horsetails are a kind of
foam . . ." (42).

Debased from the austerities of Eastern mysticism, the ashram's pseudo-
esoteric discourse is similarly ludicrous: "Repeat, please. 'Buddhatvam
yoshidyonisamsritam.' . . . It means, 'Buddhahood is in the female organ.'
The yoni. The cunt. Buddhahood is in the cunt. OM mani padme HUM"
(106). But however puckishly presented, this image encodes a substratum
of startling misogyny. Suggested already in the "saucy pink cloth" of the
novel's cover (*More*, 761), the "cunt," the "symbol of Lakshmi, . . . the
Mother Goddess," comprises also a "nothingness" (*S.*, 108, 109) reminiscent of Karl Barth's *das Nichtige*, Satanic nonbeing (*Picked-Up*, xix,
88–89; *Centaur*, 246): Buddhist nirvana joins vaginal vacuum as "what we're
afraid we're going to get anyway . . . utter death, utter extinction" (*S.*, 228),
the terror at the core of Updike's psychic plot. And considered as myth,

Sarah radiates an equally ominous aura, for she adopts as her new name "Kundalini," defined by the charlatan Arhat as "the female energy" in "all things. She sleeps coiled at the base of the spine, in the root chakra" (75). Updike teases us that Sarah is indeed reptilian – "*What's the point of living if you can't shuck skins?*" (222) – and the image recapitulates the archetypal collusion between woman and snake in Eden (cf. *Looking*, 29). Moved to pride of place as the novel's title, the single initial with which Sarah signs her correspondence forms an outline curvaceous but unmistakably serpentine.

Domesticity: demythologizing

"The real God, the God men do not invent," Updike long ago insisted, "is *totaliter aliter* – Wholly Other" (*Assorted*, 273); his will to mythologize women arises, one speculates, from an arguably perverse insistence on their similarly numinous otherness, an alterity that feminism placed at risk. In his poem "Pussy" (1977), both forms of otherness merge – "Your pussy, it is my pet, it is my altar, *totaliter / aliter*" (*Tossing*, 81) – and "Cunts" (1973), from the same volume, bluntly frames the issue: "It is true, something vital ebbs from the process / once the female is considered not a monstrous emissary / from the natural darkness but as possessing personhood / with its atten-dant rights, and wit" (78). Anticipating Ben Turnbull's ambivalence toward "that sacred several-lipped gateway to the terrifying procreative darkness" (*Toward*, 54), "monstrous emissary / from the natural darkness" calls up again the privileged myth of hero embattled against Nature and death. Yet the phrase must surely indicate, in a writer of so much subtlety, not one but two authorial voices, an intentionally ironic self-critique: the archetypal identities collapse of their own absurdity. Read on a level of social realism and relieved from the affected vanities of cosmic myth, Updike's fiction also documents a sorry record of women's frustration since the Eisenhower era.

The most substantial exemplum remains the tetralogy of Rabbit novels, produced by Updike at roughly ten-year intervals, and their novella-length coda, *Rabbit Remembered* (2000). "You're supposed to look tired. You're a housewife," Rabbit tells his wife Janice in *Rabbit, Run*, and Janice and her mother commiserate with others like themselves through the maudlin wish-fulfillment of late-1950s television's *Queen for a Day* (12, 216). Even the sordid underlayer of female experience – the prostitute Rabbit recalls from his Army days, her "backside . . . bitten so often it looked like a piece of old cardboard" – pokes through a bourgeois conspiracy of silence as Ruth Leonard, a semiprofessional in her own right, points out that "a lot of married women have had to take it more often than I have" (*Run*, 180, 185). Although Ruth predictably taunts his faith with "I could throw up every Sunday morning" (89), Rabbit, undressing her for the first time, mythologizes her geologically as "an incredible continent, the pushed-up slip a north of snow" (80), and he is bothered when her prophylactic precautions reassert the mundane: "There's that in women repels him; handle themselves like an old envelope" (86). Yet Rabbit subsequently treats both mistress and wife with similar indifference, forcing Ruth to perform an expiatory fellatio and exploiting Janice's postpartum, bleeding body in ways she resents as "cheap" (186–187, 248): the fraudulence of Rabbit's supposed idealism is unequivocally displayed. And Ruth's habitually sardonic tone – "You all think you're such lovers" (76) – adumbrates Alicia's "shaky hardness that thirty years of being a female in America had produced" in *A Month of Sundays* (82).

The pathetic adolescent Jill Pendleton, in *Rabbit Redux*, deepens Updike's case against male exploitation – "she's full of holes," her companion invites as Rabbit watches numbly (298) – but Janice, originally dismissed by Rabbit as "dumb" (*Run*, 22 *et passim*), follows a personal trajectory of increasing independence as the Rabbit novels track cultural change. Her own experience with adultery, affably facilitated by one of her father's employees, clearly builds her self-esteem: with her adult son Nelson's lapse into substance abuse, she takes over the family Toyota franchise, and by *Rabbit at Rest* she is earning a realtor's license. "It's wonderful to work," says Janice, "[w]omen of our generation came late to it" (*Licks*, 193); and in the cultural mirror of the television screen, *Queen for a Day* gives way to broadcaster Diane Sawyer (*Rest*, 299). Meanwhile, the pragmatic Ruth has made the best of things by marrying a farmer, and Updike subverts Rabbit's romanticism even posthumously when Annabelle, the previously secret fruit of their affair, confesses to molestation by her stepfather (*Licks*, 346–347).

By these sympathetic depictions, and perhaps more by regularly undraping the callous egotism of his males, the author may well deserve Mary O'Connell's complimentary placement "among the precursors of the contemporary movement among men to reexamine their cultural inheritance as males."[10] In fact, Updike insightfully locates the origins of feminist protest not in political polemic but in the kind of stultifying boredom prompting Rabbit's attempted seduction by the wife of his solicitous minister (*Run*, 241–242). As little as Updike's wifely characters care for their husbands' theology, they may also claim their freedom through adultery: as Marshfield demands, "And wherein does the modern American woman, coded into mindlessness by household slavery and the stupefying companionship of greedy infants, recover her powers of decision, of daring, of discrimination – her dignity, in short? In adultery" (*Month*, 46). In the early story

"Lifeguard" (1961), written shortly after Updike had moved his family to the Atlantic community of Ipswich, the title character looks down with manifest arrogance on indolent young matrons with their brood of toddlers: "Many of these women are pregnant again, and sluggishly lie in their loose suits like cows tranced in a meadow"(*Pigeon*, 215). In hindsight, however, the author recognizes in this bovine company an incipient army:

> The sexual revolution created by women – men allegedly have always been sexual anarchists – was on the way, and, in its wake, its sobering hangover of feminism . . .
> The flight from the spotless kitchen had begun. If the first acts of rebellion took the form of adultery, with the relatively conservative yen to be married to a (slightly) different man, the dreams of the sunbathers could and did evolve beyond heterosexual attachment entirely, toward an Amazonian paradise of self-sufficient women. Perhaps that society already existed on the beach, and I, a puppyish wrong-sex tagalong, did not realize what I was witnessing. Out of suburbia, matriarchy. These women were donning bronze armor.
>
> (*More*, 40)

Updike's most compelling reconsiderations of gender roles, whether mythological or socially coerced, emerge poignantly in his chastened pictures, recurrent in recent years, of the women closest to him. The wife who moves through much of his fiction before the 1980s – artistic, philanthropic, often endearingly barefoot – noticeably resembles his first wife, the daughter of a Unitarian minister; she endures repeated casting as inimical Other, her primary function to localize a standard oppositional role. Marshfield's wife Jane is pointedly Unitarian, and in *Marry Me* Ruth Conant laments helplessly that her husband "sees death everywhere . . . When I say *I'm* not afraid of death, he tells me I'm a spiritual cripple" (88); she is a Unitarian, the narrative voiceover intones, "and what did this mean, except that her soul was one unit removed from not being there at all?" (96). This mean-spirited jab recalls the belligerent challenges to Unitarianism elsewhere in Updike's work (*Assorted*, 280; *Witches*, 125); his own stubborn church affiliation, Updike admitted in *Self-Consciousness*, may have constituted an effort "to preserve a distance from . . . my Unitarian wife" (143). In a motion incurring the critic Frederick Crews's mordant judgment that Updike had "radically divorced his notion of Christian theology from that of Christian ethics,"[11] the author acknowledges a moral negotiation worthy of his own protagonists: "I read Karl Barth and fell in love with other men's wives" (98).

But Updike's fiction is also justly honored for its grief-stricken evocations of the pain of broken families, in stories such as "Leaves" (1964; *Music*,

52–56) or the profoundly sorrowful "Separating" (1975; *Problems*, 116–131). These narratives gain a rich humanity from their autobiographical occasions, just as the unfulfilled prophecy of "a marriage composed of spats, mutual disappointments, and, toward the end, a mellowing hoard of shared memories" (*Assorted*, 128), from Updike's early homage to baseball's Ted Williams ("Hub Fans Bid Kid Adieu" [1960]), radiates subtextual tenderness when we learn that it was written after an aborted extramarital tryst.[12] Perhaps the most moving expression occurs in "Gesturing" (1979), one of the Maples stories collected in *Too Far to Go* (1979): "He saw through her words to what she was saying – that these lovers, however we love them, are not us, are not sacred as reality is sacred. We are reality" (231). The sacred moves intentionally here from exceptional to ordinary, a sacralization of domesticity with its comforting responsibilities, shared jokes, and complicated layers of intimacy. "Perhaps I could have made a go of the literary business without my first wife's faith, forbearance, sensitivity, and good sense," Updike confesses in his foreword to *The Early Stories*, "but I cannot imagine how" (x).

A similar dialectic between myth and reality informs Updike's mature reflections on his mother. In a piece for the women's magazine *Vogue*, Updike admitted, "The largeness of our mother-myth has a paradoxically dwindling effect upon the women concerned: they must be in all things motherly and become therefore natural processes rather than people" (*Odd*, 67–68). "[M]uffled" in her son's youth "behind the giant mask of motherhood" (69), Linda Updike is revealed in this essay as a woman of determined literary ambition, "sitting in the front bedroom, with its view of horse-chestnut trees and telephone wires, and tapping out pages to send to New York magazines in brown envelopes. The brown envelopes always came back" (68). In one of the fictionalized tributes following Updike's mother's death in 1989, Allen Dow understands his deceased mother's alliance with nature in terms of desperate refuge: "Being a woman had no doubt frustrated her, keeping her at home, tying her to the fortunes of men less intelligent than herself, denying her a career . . . Finding human relations difficult, she had turned to nature for comfort" (*Afterlife*, 238–239). The prizewinning "A Sandstone Farmhouse" (1990) attempts a culminating *Trauerarbeit* as Joey Robinson weeps before his mother's casket:

> She was in there, and in his mind there appeared a mother conceived out of his earliest memories of her, a young slim woman . . . hurrying to catch the trolley car . . . a torrent of empathy and pity for that lost young woman running past the Pennsylvania row houses, under the buttonwood trees, running to catch

the trolley . . . This was the mother, apparently, that he had loved, the young woman living with him and others in a brick semi-detached house, a woman of the world, youthfully finding her way . . . She had tried to be a person, she had lived. There was something amazing, something immortal to him in the image of her running. (*Afterlife*, 126–127)

If the mother figure submits to mythological enlargement in these passages, it is no longer as earth mother, walking her fields in otiose detachment, but the appalling feminist archetype of thwarted woman fighting madness in her attic.

As the literary scholar Stephen Greenblatt insightfully states, "self-fashioning" may be "achieved in relation to something perceived as alien, strange, or hostile. This threatening Other – heretic, savage, witch, adulteress, traitor, Antichrist – must be discovered or invented in order to be attacked."[13] Drawn from deep cultural veins of mythology, romance, and folklore, and circling always back to primal Eve, Updike's major feminine archetypes help justify a self-defining myth, patented and recited through his fiction, that the author universalized in 1997 as "[m]an in a state of fear and trembling, separated from God, haunted by dread, twisted by the conflicting demands of his animal biology and human intelligence, of the social contract and the inner imperatives" (*More*, 852). Like the ceremonies commended in the story that concludes *Pigeon Feathers* (279), myths stave off what Eliade calls "the terror of history," desacralized time as "a precarious and evanescent duration, leading irremediably to death":[14] but as such, Updike's unsparing scrutiny reveals, they may be commandeered as well to demean and dehumanize. *Seek My Face* (2002), in a sense a portrait of the artist as an old woman, presents his most complicated female character to date – perhaps because so many of Hope Ouderkirk's aspirations suggest the author's own. The autobiographical currents in Updike's fiction – painfully obtrusive, reviewers agree, in the retrospective, valedictory *Villages* (2004), with its thematic "Why do women fuck?" (19, 204, 234, 319) – threaten indeed to cross boundaries of taste and privacy: Promethean ambition, to sustain the mythic metaphor, pooling into a looking-glass for Narcissus. But in laboring to make sense of his own life and of the women, both real and imagined, who passed through it, Updike has also kept faith with the "strenuous confessional exercises" he long ago admired in the American literary tradition (*Assorted*, 306); and his literary endeavor, in what is now his eighth decade, continues to interrogate those myths of flesh and spirit, death and life, female and male, that immemorially divide the Western mind.

NOTES

1. Joseph Campbell, *The Hero with a Thousand Faces* (1949; Princeton, NJ: Princeton University Press, 1972), p. 11.
2. Mary Allen, "John Updike's Love of 'Dull Bovine Beauty'" (1976), in *John Updike*, ed. Harold Bloom (New York: Chelsea House, 1987), p. 95.
3. Erik H. Erikson, *Young Man Luther: A Study in Psychoanalysis and History* (New York: Norton, 1958), pp. 14, 111.
4. Ernest Hemingway, *Death in the Afternoon* (London: Jonathan Cape, 1932), pp. 220–221.
5. Mircea Eliade, *The Sacred and the Profane: The Nature of Religion*, trans. Willard R. Trask (1959; New York: Harper and Row, 1961), pp. 157–158; see also p. 79.
6. Northrop Frye, *The Great Code: The Bible and Literature* (New York: Harcourt Brace, 1982), pp. 152, 68.
7. Joyce Carol Oates, "Updike's American Comedies" (1975), in *John Updike*, ed. Harold Bloom (New York: Chelsea House, 1987), p. 60.
8. James Plath, ed., *Conversations with John Updike* (Jackson: University Press of Mississippi, 1994), p. 264.
9. John Updike, quoted in James A. Schiff, *Updike's Version: Rewriting The Scarlet Letter* (Columbia: University of Missouri Press, 1992), p. 8.
10. Mary O'Connell, *Updike and the Patriarchal Dilemma: Masculinity in the Rabbit Novels* (Carbondale: Southern Illinois University Press, 1996), p. 237.
11. Frederick Crews, *The Critics Bear It Away: American Fiction and the Academy* (New York: Random House, 1992), p. 171.
12. Paul Gray, "Perennial Promises Kept," *Time*, 18 October 1982, p. 80.
13. Stephen Greenblatt, *Renaissance Self-Fashioning: From More to Shakespeare* (Chicago: University of Chicago Press, 1980), p. 9.
14. Mircea Eliade, *Cosmos and History: The Myth of the Eternal Return*, trans. Willard R. Trask (1954; New York: Harper and Row, 1959), p. 150; Eliade, *The Sacred and the Profane*, p. 113.

GUIDE TO FURTHER READING

Hunt, George W. *John Updike and the Three Great Secret Things: Sex, Religion, and Art*. Grand Rapids, MI: Eerdmans, 1980.
Malone, David. "Updike 2020: Fantasy, Mythology, and Faith in *Toward the End of Time*." *John Updike and Religion: The Sense of the Sacred and the Motions of Grace*. Ed. James Yerkes. Grand Rapids, MI: Eerdmans, 1999, pp. 80–98.
Olster, Stacey. "'Unadorned Woman, Beauty's Home Image': Updike's *Rabbit, Run*." *New Essays on Rabbit, Run*. Ed. Stanley Trachtenberg. Cambridge: Cambridge University Press, 1993, pp. 95–117.
Ra'ad, Basem L. "Updike's New Versions of Myth in America." *Modern Fiction Studies* 37 (1991), pp. 25–33.

5

JAY PROSSER

Updike, race, and the postcolonial project

In his *oeuvre* fundamentally about middle America, what Updike has to say about race concerns white America and its constructions particularly of African Americans. As Brian Niro has pointed out, race is an "American fixation," and "slavery has forged the concept of race in the United States into an almost exclusively black and white dynamic." Since then, "America has consistently worked to polarize racial discourse."[1] Slaves are a founding presence of the nation. In order to free itself of the British Empire, to become a postcolony, America needed to have a sense of the opposite of freedom. Carrying the concept across from history, Toni Morrison has argued that American literature has been established through mirror-image binaries. Blackness has served as a "persona [performing] duties of exorcism and reification and mirroring."[2] This manicheanism – an opposition between light and dark of almost divine dimension – has been not only conscious but unconscious. From the short stories – "A Gift from the City" (1958; *Same*, 163–192) and "The Doctor's Wife" (1961; *Pigeon*, 197–210) – to the novel *Rabbit Redux*, in Updike blackness stands as other, love or hatred, guilt or fear, a measure of white American consciousness. Updike shows the myths and ideology that nevertheless make a nation's reality. Even when outside of the United States and dealing with postcolonial countries, as in *The Coup* and *Brazil*, the mirror relation obtains, this time held up to America as nation. These novels are illuminating less of Africa and Brazil than of America's ideals and failures. Inside a racial unconscious Updike has replicated otherness but also fictionalized solidarity. His works show the divide but also create surprising, generative encounters. His interest in race spans American history to a future vision, especially of America's place in the globe. It continues to his latest fiction and, in his memoir *Self-Consciousness*, to his intimate self.

Updike's first and most substantial novel about race, and the one most set in America, is *Rabbit Redux* (1971). There has been much debate about the subject, with some critics finding the black character the most credible in white American literature, and others finding Rabbit and the novel racist. The uncertainty stems from the fact that the novel is told through Rabbit's consciousness, with Rabbit himself an analogy for America. Particularly in the Rabbit tetralogy, Updike is master of free indirect discourse, and his use of the present tense adds to the immediacy, so that Rabbit's consciousness seems very unmediated. The beginning of the second novel offers an example of how this problematically affects race. To Rabbit, blacks are definitely other, almost a different species. Unable to bring himself to say black, using the older, more racialized "Negro," Rabbit thinks, "The bus has too many Negroes" (*Redux*, 12); "it stinks of *Negroes*" (35). Rabbit fears blacks as alien beings – "as if their thoughts are a different shape and come out twisted even when they mean no menace" (13). Although he works with two, Farnsworth and Buchanan, he does not feel at ease talking to blacks. Blacks are impinging on his world. They are the "seeds of some tropical plant . . . taking over the garden" (13) – his rabbit patch.

The novel is set in 1969 and depicts the militant wave of Civil Rights, Black Nationalism, that followed the assassination of Malcolm X, during a year of race riots. Working at the printing press and setting to type the local newspaper, *The Brewer Vat*, Harry is in prime place to witness events, for example the race riots that really took place in 1969 in York, Pennsylvania, near to the novel's fictional Brewer. He observes crime and increasing sensitivity to racial representation. "LOCAL HOODS ASSAULT ELDERLY," the *Vat* reports, where "LOCAL" has replaced "BLACK" (135). The radical black paper offers another side to crime stories: "PIG ATROCITIES STIR CAMDEN" (199).

The novel is about how Rabbit comes down from the bus and his life fuses with the events of newspapers. The plot turns when he goes to a black bar, Jimbo's Friendly Lounge. The only white man, Rabbit fears that he is "among panthers" (117), that blacks pose a threat to his middle American (white) future. Yet he also feels desire and nostalgia, and through singer Babe's music blacks represent a rural lost America. He meets Skeeter, who may be related to his workmate Farnsworth. Skeeter is a Black Nationalist, a rhetorician, imagines himself to be a black messiah, does drugs, and may be suffering delusions. He is a brilliant trickster-type figure, evocative of Huey Newton, founder of the Black Panthers, and Stokely Carmichael, another Black Nationalist leader. In 1969 Bobby Seale, fellow founder of the Panthers, was being tried for conspiracy to incite riots at the 1968 Chicago Democratic National Convention; the fact that at the trial Seale had to be bound and gagged to silence his courtroom outbursts is mentioned on Rabbit's television. Unmoored, left by wife Janice, Rabbit takes first of all as his lover a white girl, Jill, whom he also meets in the bar, and then Skeeter, to live with him and son Nelson. Although it is Skeeter who should feel fear, with a warrant out for his arrest and the police looking for him, Rabbit is scared but also fascinated by this threat to technocratic order. As Skeeter says, "We fascinate you, white man. We are in your dreams. We are technology's nightmare" (234). In Rabbit's relation to Skeeter we move inside a white racial unconscious. The chapter "Skeeter" offers the mirror in concentrated form. At one point they switch on the television to find (black) Sammy Davis Jr. opposite (white comedian) Arte Johnson: "They are like one man looking into a crazy mirror" (247).

Skeeter is an agent for potential change in Rabbit's mind. He brings with him books on the history of slavery in America; on the awakening of black consciousness by the first black intellectual and founder of the National Association for Advancement of Colored People, *The Selected Writings of W. E. B. Du Bois* (1970); by Martinique psychiatrist and key theorist of postcolonial studies Frantz Fanon, who certainly dealt with racism in the unconscious, *The Wretched of the Earth* (1961); and Black Nationalist classics such as Eldridge Cleaver's *Soul on Ice* (1968). The characters read aloud, and Updike quotes liberally from these texts. Rabbit is also educated by Skeeter's experience. In what feels like a direct corrective to Rabbit's consciousness, Skeeter tells how whites move away from blacks on buses as if they were covered in scabs. Racism and the process of reeducation are portrayed very bodily. Rabbit is attracted to Skeeter as if to an organism that is intimate but waste – "out of the same curiosity that made him put his finger into his belly-button and then sniff it, the metal waffle-patterned lid on the backyard cesspool" (208).

Racial difference is exaggerated through sexual difference. Thinking of sex even when he sees blacks on a television game show, Rabbit fantasizes that the women have "[b]ig lips, suck you right off, the men are slow as Jesus, long as whips, takes everything to get them up" (18). "Cocks like eels. Night feeders" (134). From the beginning, Skeeter's penis is a source of wonder. Even Skeeter's upper lip reminds Rabbit "of the stitch of flesh that holds the head of your cock to the shaft" (337), which white men do not have on their lip. There are memorable scenes of masturbation and triangulation between Skeeter, Jill, and Rabbit, as Skeeter has Rabbit read, particularly from *Life and Times of Frederick Douglass* (1892). In a race reversal of black and white, Rabbit is designated slave, Skeeter master, and Jill slave girl – a rape scene Rabbit enjoys watching. A homoeroticism comes from racial difference. Rabbit wipes Skeeter's sperm up with his handkerchief, pressing his nose right to Skeeter's seed. A later point in the novel, when Rabbit masturbates to the fantasy of a "Negress" in a barn hung with gallows

(378), recalls the passage from Douglass's narrative. Douglass has penetrated Rabbit's consciousness.

The novel shows Rabbit's partial transformation. In the beginning we see his misconceptions. Two African Americans return a pocketbook to Jill, not the knife Rabbit expects. He lends twenty dollars to Buchanan and is surprised to get it back. The turning point is the fire that burns down his house, with which Rabbit enters the news and which he himself sets to type. Taking Skeeter in, Rabbit is, as his father Earl Angstrom says, "playing with fire" (237), a symbolism literalized by plot. James Baldwin's *The Fire Next Time* (1963), a text for Black Nationalism which sees America as "a burning house" and envisions social conflagration, may be an intertext.[3] Other whites' racism becomes a foil for Rabbit's changing consciousness. Earl calls "American Negroes" "the garbage of the world" and is all for shipping them back to Africa (166). The taxi driver who terms blacks "Jigaboos" similarly embarrasses Rabbit (271). He is threatened by Showalter and Brumbach, his neighbors more unambivalently invested in the white middle class. Although Jill is killed and Skeeter escapes with both her money and his own suitcase, Rabbit looks at Skeeter's abandoned books and the racist graffiti on the remains of his wall and believes, with Skeeter, that the fire is "honky action" (333). He decides that the problem with Skeeter is "other people" (358).

Updike in his introduction to the tetralogy argues that the Skeeter chapter is a 1960s "'teach-in.' Rabbit tries to learn. Reading aloud the words of Frederick Douglass, he becomes black, and in a fashion seeks solidarity with Skeeter" (*Tetralogy*, xvi). The novel's solidarity, occurring when we enter into Skeeter's consciousness and he thinks that he cannot make these "ofays" understand (258), is minimal. But perhaps this indicates the limits of Rabbit's and whites' understanding.

It is clear that blacks stand for some consciousness in the American nation. "Their whole beings seem lubricated [in] pain" (103) – they embody in the history of slavery imperialism at home. But the novel also addresses imperialism that is abroad and current. The race riots of 1969 are intercut on the news with the Vietnam War, and Rabbit struggles to piece these together. Black Nationalism is bringing home US imperialism. Pan-African and coinciding with the anticolonial struggles, particularly in African and African-diasporic countries, in which Fanon was key, Black Nationalism places loyalty beyond the US, breaking the tautology of geography as nation. A Vietnam vet, Skeeter tells Rabbit (who is too old for Vietnam and was too young for Korea) of the exploitative suspension of racism in Vietnam, the only place where the US does not discriminate against blacks.

The subplot – and what allows Rabbit to bring Skeeter and Jill into his home – widens racial difference beyond African Americans. Janice is having an affair with Charlie Stavros, a Greek American whom Rabbit compares to blacks and whom we first encounter in a Greek restaurant in the black district. Rabbit finds him greasy and hairy. Domestic plot echoes national, as we learn that Jackie Kennedy has just married Aristotle Onassis, a foreigner and definitely not of America's blueblood family. Jokes about Tonto and the Lone Ranger extend the trope, in another television skit the white man going off with Tonto instead of his wife – Tonto, whom Rabbit never understood, an American Indian. Rabbit calls Stavros "Tonto" and Janice an Indian "squaw" (49, 50). Rabbit to Janice is lardy white and to Charlie "[p]aleface" (49). The US is itself playing Lone Ranger all over Asia. Charlie and Janice, Skeeter and Jill, Rabbit's sister Mim and even his twelve-year-old son Nelson are against the Vietnam War. Rabbit supports Vietnam, naïvely believing in the beneficent, democratic US of Cold War politics. As Stavros says of Rabbit, "He's a normal product . . . He's a typical good-hearted imperialist racist" (47). But Rabbit's is also an America that is over. As Stavros continues, what Rabbit thinks, "We-them, America first. It's dead" (53). Even Rabbit recognizes, when at a ball game racist abuse is hurled at players, "something has gone wrong" with America (83). The US flag decal on the back window of his Falcon (US) car is still there at the end of the novel but fast fading.

The novel sees very early the price of America's imperialist project. In 1969 America landed on the moon, its empire expanding beyond Vietnam, Korea, earth itself, into space. This provides the organizing frame of the book, but the triumphant moment is presented by the television and experienced by characters as puzzling, with intercut quotations fragmented and hanging, its significance confused. For Rabbit and the others the significance may be that they have come ungrounded, that America in the 1960s is falling into space. But expansion is irreversible. The next in the tetralogy, *Rabbit Is Rich* (1981), is set in 1979. Although the reader learns of Skeeter's death in what newspapers call a "shoot-out" with police, when officers "had no choice but to return fire" (31), America has gone global. The Toyota franchise of Springer lots has expanded, and Rabbit himself now heads it and drives a Toyota. America is running out of gas and will have to turn to external sources for its oil dependency and create a new empire. With the final book in the tetralogy, *Rabbit at Rest* (1990), it is significantly a black but mixed-race kid that spurs Rabbit's death. Shooting hoops with this kid wearing a tiger tanktop, Rabbit has a heart attack. Not wanting to get involved, the boy runs away – running after basketball, like Rabbit in the first novel. The tiger has replaced the rabbit in America's future.

There is a mixed-race child in the other Updike novel set in America that deals, but much less substantially than *Redux*, with race. In *Roger's Version*

(1986), Roger Lambert, a professor at divinity school, gets sexually involved with niece Verna, who has a mixed-race child. Paula, a transformation of Hawthorne's Pearl, comes to live with Roger at one point, after Verna becomes abusive. In the midst of Reaganite family values and individualism, Roger crosses to the other side of the river to see the single mother living in the projects. We see scenes from the ghetto: boarded-up stores, weeds, trash, dilapidated homes, smashed locks, graffiti. The ghetto is black but turning Hispanic and Vietnamese. "We had dabbled overseas and in extracting ourselves had pulled up these immigrants like paint on a stirring stick" (*Roger's*, 53).

When Updike travels outside of the US he explores the postcolonial relation between the US and its others. This is especially so in *The Coup* (1978). Set in an imaginary African country, Kush, the novel has been charged by some critics with being a fictionalization of Africa. Both *The Coup* and *Brazil* derive much of their information from books, as Updike's acknowledgments indicate. Updike at least wrote *The Coup* after a visit to Ethiopia in 1973 – unlike his contemporary American Saul Bellow, who wrote his African novel despite never having been to Africa. *The Coup* does not have so much in common with as it reverses Bellow's *Henderson the Rain King* (1959). In *Henderson*, a rich white American ventures across Africa, is imprisoned, is forced into dialogue with Dahfu, an African king, and is hailed as rainmaker. In *The Coup*, Updike's Colonel Hakim Félix Ellelloû, the ruler of a country under a curse of drought, talks with the old king Edumu, and then beheads him in the belief that the king, whom he deposed some twenty years earlier in a coup, is cause of the curse and that his death will bring rain. In the Oedipal frame of the novel, the king is closest to the father. Ellelloû undertakes a pilgrimage across the country, to find that the king's head has become the sphinx of oracles. Once Ellelloû is arrested and imprisoned and the country overtaken in another coup, the rains come.

In a move more daring than that of any other American or British novelist on Africa, Updike writes through an African consciousness. The novel is in the first person (it is possibly the memoirs Ellelloû is rumored to be working on at the end), but shifts into the third person. Ellelloû suggests as reason the African denial of ego, but the narrative shift also implies that he views himself as construction, an idea of statesman. He does not speak in an African voice. He learned English – with an American accent – in the US, where he attends college during his years of exile under the colonial government. The comments on black skin color cannot derive from an African or even a black consciousness, as evidenced, for example, when a waitress's legs are admired for being "the color of good healthy shit" (*Coup*, 241). As with Skeeter, blackness is eroticized, and with the women it is their race that is their sex. This is what bell hooks calls "eating the Other," "[w]hen race and ethnicity become commodified as resources for pleasure."[4] Arabic qualities are stereotyped: valor, thievishness, hospitality.

Edward Said identified orientalism as a construction, where the West constructs itself through a construction of the East.[5] Formerly Noire under the French (French for "blackness"), Kush is a fabricated country – "an idea of Kush" (11). "Kush" is the name of an ancient African kingdom below the Nile, now in northern Sudan. It borders on "Zanj" – a fictional place ruled by Ian Smith: confusingly the real former white prime minister of Rhodesia (now Zimbabwe). The true histories of sub-Saharan nations, Mali, Egypt, and Libya, intermingle with the fictional Kush's. As previous writers on Africa, namely Joseph Conrad, have shown, Africa to the imperialist mind is "an idea," a blank or dark space on the map, a story told by a white man on the deck of a boat in the metropolis.[6] But construction is used to rule. As a discourse, orientalism is imaginary but part of imperialist mechanics. Created by imperialism amidst warring and nomadic tribes for whom national borders are meaningless, Kush – like the similarly fabricated Iraq – is nonetheless real. Updike is aware of the mediation of Africa by the Western mind. At one point the slideshow alongside the king's talking head projects jumbled iconic images of Africa for tourists – "Kodachrome fixations of dunes, of peanut pyramids, of the hydroelectric dam . . . , of feathery tribal dances . . . , of a camel ruminating" (215).

The dynamic is that of the mirror again, with Rabbit and Skeeter writ large and postcolonial. The novel is set during the Cold War, and the US and the Soviets, the "superparanoids" (57), are extending their empires to satellite states. Their manicheanism is of good versus evil empires, oppositions between capitalism and Marxism, liberty and equality, Christianity and Islam. A form of Islamic Marxism that structures the politics of Kush under Ellelloû takes a more fundamentalist turn. The girls in the Kush capital attend the "Anti-Christian High School" (11), "dedicated to the extirpation of the influences of Christian mission education" (5). Ellelloû attends McCarthy College during 1950s McCarthyism, the start of the Cold War, in fictional "Franchise," Wisconsin. Here, through Oscar X, an American Black Nationalist more typecast than Skeeter, Ellelloû discovers Islam. Kush is an idea of Black Nationalism – or "residue," as Ellelloû remarks (162). Early black politics in the US are paralleled with anticolonial struggles among blacks in the African diaspora. Shifting in and out of Ellelloû's consciousness, the narration satirizes America as other. With its consumerism and waste, peanut butter, crash diets and jogging, America is a "fountainhead of obscenity and glut" (3), an "insidious empire" (43). Of his four wives, it is the white American – whom Ellelloû meets in the drugstore in Franchise on "Commerce

Street" (132) – who has taken the *hijab*, the veil. The coup against Ellelloû is supported by US aid, and he is replaced by his finance minister who is all for UNESCO, economic development, and foreign investment. And "to the American press . . . [Ellelloû] was never presented save snidely and . . . his fall was celebrated with a veritable minstrelsy of anti-Negro, anti-Arab cartoons" (7).

Postcolonialism is proving to be a phenomenon not after colonialism but "intensified colonialism – or . . . imperialism," as Peter Childs and Patrick Williams argue.[7] The king was a puppet under French (old) colonialism. With European colonialism deposed, a new imperialism emerges, particularly American, disguised as economic and political liberalism. The novel stages the clash between Islamic fundamentalism and neoliberalism. In manicheanism the polarities are more akin than they seem and are really mutually perpetuating, the divides interdependent. Old imperialism has left the infrastructure decrepit and robbed, and a new economic imperialism – globalization *avant la lettre* – exploits its wake. The golden parabolas glimpsed by Ellelloû as a mirage, and appearing in other places in Updike (for example, *Redux*), turn out to be McDonald's. Even under Islamic Marxism foreign aid comes in the wrong form and with capitalist costs. At the same time as providing food relief, the multinationals create oil wells that interrupt nomadic grazing patterns, in turn producing more drought. In an early episode Ellelloû burns up aid cereals – the "Kix Trix Chex Pops," the "fetchingly packaged pap" (36) – the starving cannot eat, because not only does Kush not have milk, it does not have water for the milk powder the US has supplied. In another Updike conflagration a USAID worker, a "toubab" or foreigner (37), is immolated on a pyre. As Ellelloû says of his successor, "Where their libraries come, Coca-Cola follows; as our thirst for Coca-Cola grows, our well of debt deepens" (284). In the middle of the desert town bearing his name, a mirror image to American commercialism and corporatization (Franchise in fact), there is nothing behind the main drag. Lawn sprinklers operate in the drought outside head offices. Because of the complexity of voice and imagery – the shifts between first and third person, the mirroring between West and East – the satire is funnier and more incisive than that of, say, Eastern mysticism in *S.* (1988). For who is parodying whom?

But *The Coup*'s absurdism is also prescient. Among Kush's "natural resources" (6) are listed diseases that, alongside famine, are still devastating Africa. And the life expectancy of thirty-seven, now with AIDS, looks optimistic in some sub-Saharan countries.[8] Anti-Arabism is thriving. And we have seen an expansion of American empire and interventionism. *The Coup* foresees America's binds to its postcolonial world.

A novel of romance, *Brazil* (1994) is a more direct translation of its sources. The main source provides the conceit, the story of Tristan and Iseult. Based in Updike on Joseph Bédier's 1900 version, *The Romance of Tristan and Iseult*, the story goes back to a millennium-old European romance of courtly love, which Richard Wagner, mythographer in music of heroes and nation, turned into opera. The frame romanticizes love and nation – all through a text not indigenous to Brazil.

But another source is indigenous, Brazilian sociologist Gilberto Freyre's *The Masters and the Slaves* (1933), which sets mixed-raceness as the founding myth of Brazil. The novel contains sentiments straight from the racial typology of Freyre, noting the "well-known melancholy of the Portuguese race; no less an authority than Gilberto Freyre assures us that, had not the early colonizers imported Africans to cheer up their settlements, the whole Brazilian enterprise might have withered of sheer gloom" (*Brazil*, 229). As such, the particular romance that underlies Updike's book is with Brazil's mixed-race identity, or *mestiço*. Black Tristão and white Isabel's love stages an encounter in the mirror. The novel begins with the point where skins join: "Black is a shade of brown. So is white, if you look. On Copacabana, the most democratic, crowded, and dangerous of Rio de Janeiro's beaches, all colors merge into one joyous, sun-stunned flesh-color, coating the sand with a second, living skin" (3). As Isabel's uncle draws the contrasts to "apartheid" nations, Brazil is "not South Africa, thank God, or the United States" (23).

The plot unpacks this myth of color-blindness and shows its limits, how there is a divide in spite of what Brazil may think of itself. The couple are hounded by racial prejudice, first by Isabel's uncle in Rio and father in Brasilia; by radicalized students of the 1960s and 1970s, in café scenes of students talking revolution (recalling those of *The Coup* and set during some of the same moments) in the wake of Martin Luther King's assassination when, as a Marxist character puts it, "The end is near for the lily-white imperialists of the North" (99); then by eighteenth-century *bandeirantes* (converted Jews fleeing the Inquisition), one of whom Isabel is forced to marry and who make Tristão, because he is black, a slave. When in a fantastic race-change he becomes white and she black, the tables threaten to be reversed. From the factories he manages in São Paulo as a white man, Tristão makes his way back to the beach where, in a final irony, he is killed by a black boy in a T-shirt inscribed "BLACK HOLE" (254), the name of a nightclub. Freyre is disparaged by one character as "that master of self-congratulation" (101).

Addressing stereotypes in a magical realism modeled on what Updike deems "truly Brazilian fiction" (Afterword, no page), *Brazil* nevertheless makes a fairytale out of national-racial myths. The race-change is brought about by a shaman who blows smoke over Isabel and paints her with dyes.

Black Isabel becomes associated with spice, an exoticization like that of Skeeter, white Tristão with thin-lipped authority and reason: "It was as if his brain, now that he had white skin, had become a box squared off with linear possibilities – a grid of choices, alternatives, projections" (201). Racial difference is burdened with physiognomy, blackness with "thingness" (206). Above all, sexual difference supports the stereotypes of race. When Tristão is white, his penis, though still a "yam," is smaller (203). And black Isabel's "clitoris felt longer and firmer than before" (209), in dangerous proximity to the Hottentot myth of black women having large genitals. The biological racism from the beginning of *Rabbit Redux* is carried to observations about other bodies: the New Christian *bandeirantes* with their oversized noses; even jokes about achondroplasia, or what Updike calls dwarfs. Indians, too, are bifurcated into either marauding savages or infantilized servants. History is rendered sometimes offensively, as occurs with that of the Indians: because of diseases "with much obnoxious farting and coughing, they would die" (174) – in effect a genocide of colonialism.

Jokes express the unconscious in part, and Updike does get at some taboos around race. After the race-change he explores the difference in Isabel's and Tristão's sexual coupling. "Being a white woman fucked by a black man is more delicious, she had sadly to conclude, than a black woman being fucked by a white man. The former, to a descendant of the masters of colonial Brazil, had the exaltation of blasphemy, the excitement of a political defiance; the latter transaction savored of mundane business" (204). Like Fanon in two chapters in *Black Skin, White Masks* (1952), "The Woman of Color and the White Man" and "The Man of Color and the White Woman," Updike recognizes the repercussion on interracial sexual relationships of slavery as an interwovenly sexual and commercial mode of reproduction.[9] He also hints at the fetishization of blood characterizing laws to clarify racial difference and particularly to prevent miscegenation. It is easy to miss, but there is a hint that Isabel and Tristão have the same father and so literally share some of the same skin. The taboo on incest, an extreme form of endogamy, "even combines in some countries with its direct opposite, inter-racial sexual relations, an extreme form of exogamy"[10] – particularly countries such as those in the Americas where family was used to propagate "property" over generations.

Miscegenation is an American coinage, and the United States was the only nation to carry the prohibition against interracial sexual reproduction into the postcolonial period, so the taboo can seem definitive of Americanness.[11] Brazilian critic Dilvo I. Ristoff sees the novel as Updike "Brazilianizing" his "distinctly American" "dilemma." Ristoff quotes Updike's "Special Message" to the Franklin Library edition: "A country's sense of itself is an activating part of its reality, and this sense derives in part from outsiders. Because others have romanticized and sexualized Brazil, Brazil is saturated in romanticism and sexuality." Updike envisions his Brazil as "an image of the world that is coming, one world of many mixed colors."[12] When America becomes visible in the novel, there are sharper touches: affiliation between nations in the Whitman epigraph, the betrothal ring engraved with DAR, Daughters of the American Revolution, stolen from an American tourist and eventually passed on to the Indian shaman for the race-change. The problem is that there is no mediating consciousness. The narrative remains mostly omniscient and distant, so the romancing feels like Updike's. The other side of the mirror is missing. After all, America, too, has a history of mixed race, and transporting it off American soil can seem like evasion. It has been worked by other writers, most masterfully by William Faulkner in *Go Down, Moses* (1942).

Overwhelmingly, Updike's other discursive sources are outsiders' avowed projections of Brazil. From Claude Lévi-Strauss's *Tristes Tropiques* (*Sad Tropics*) (1955), he takes material on the Indians and the idea of traveling though space as time travel. *Brazil*'s chapter titles, given mostly by setting, have a palindromic structure, the novel itself mirroring Brazilian history. Starting during the time of military rule of 1964–1985, the travails of Tristão and Isabel go back in history to the colonial era: "Moving inland, they seemed to move backwards in time" (112). As Lévi-Strauss has been charged with "imperialist nostalgia," a way to make "racial domination appear innocent and pure,"[13] this inversion can seem an imposition by the outsider – South America as backward to the progressive northern hemisphere. Another source is Elizabeth Bishop and the editors of *Life*'s *Brazil* (1962), a book Bishop would be so unhappy with that she almost disowned it.[14] Her *Brazil* has a *National Geographic* feel, where "National" is an American nationalist perspective. As in *The Coup* – in which Updike acknowledges *National Geographic* as a reference text – the protagonists' pilgrimage across the country offers an excuse for packing in history and geography, and it does feel as though Updike is getting these straight from the pages of *National Geographic*. Brazil for tourists is shown: Brasilia, Ouro Prêto, the Manaus opera house, the Mato Grosso or large scrubland in the country's middle; in Rio, the Copacabana apartment and the shanty on the Hill of Babylon no bigger than the apartment's bathroom. All the expected references are made (Updike thanks the *Real Guide* and the *Lonely Planet*): to cachaça, the drink of Brazil, samba, the music, inflation – as if Updike had a box of toys labeled "Brazil" and was determined to use them all. Although Updike went to Brazil before writing the novel, *Brazil* feels, as Ristoff points out, hurried. Above all, the elucidation of America, the self-consciousness, is lacking.

Thus it is apt and best in his memoir, *Self-Consciousness* (1989), when Updike brings the subject home. Two chapters, "At War with My Skin" and "A Letter to My Grandsons," concern race and work in conjunction with each other. In the first, Updike writes of his psoriasis and the effect of mottling on his body as "naked, naked shame" (*Self-Consciousness*, 43). He experiences a kind of stigmatization, where stigmatization begins as marks on the skin and is internalized as social difference, analogous to being black. Psoriasis makes for skin consciousness that is self-conscious but also unconscious. "Psoriasis keeps you thinking. Strategies of concealment ramify, and self-examination is endless. You are forced to the mirror, again and again; psoriasis compels narcissism, if we can suppose a Narcissus who did not like what he saw" (45). Updike's fiction all along has been interested in surfaces, even of inorganic objects, and in actual skin – pimples, sweat, thinness, pallor, dappling, marks, blotches, scars, defects as well as color. His very writing is connected to skin: "Only psoriasis could have taken a very average little boy, and furthermore a boy who loved the average, the daily, the safely hidden, and made him into a prolific, adaptable, ruthless-enough writer" (75). His engendering of art from flawed skin is echoed in "From the Journal of a Leper" (1976), where a psoriatic potter makes perfect pots, which, when his skin is cured, become flawed (*Problems*, 181–196).

Updike tells of a life lived because of his skin, especially – since the sun temporarily cures psoriasis – his struggles to acquire a tan. Once the sun has faded from the beaches of New England, he goes to the Caribbean, "where an old-fashioned Shillington boy would never have thought to go" (61). Here he has his first encounter with blacks, because, as he admits, blacks at home are mostly "ghettoized" (65). It changes his perception of skin. His whiteness standing out in the black vestiges of the British Empire, he feels he is seen for his whiteness rather than for his psoriasis – and not stigmatized. But he is also self-conscious about how his encounter with blacks changes him more profoundly. Quoting another memoir, by a Danish author about white settlers in Kenya, he writes, "So, as Isak Dinesen grandly puts it in *Out of Africa*, 'The discovery of the dark races was to me a magnificent enlargement of all my world'" (66).

This consciousness of alterity is not worked through in Updike's writing, particularly, as you might guess, in relation to sex. "For of course my concern with my skin was ultimately sexual, the skin being a sexual organ and the moment of undressing the supreme personal revelation and confiding" (72). He recalls his desire for black Caribbean girls, particularly for a mixed-race girl who "had a mischievous Caucasian touch to her features" and whom he ponders under his mosquito netting (64). In these encounters, is the skin divide replicated, or the mirror crossed and manicheanism broken down? With his own skin tanned and healed, his self-consciousness, about psoriasis can be abandoned, and with it racial affiliation – the divide put back up. Yet Updike's psoriasis and self-consciousness, he realizes, make him a writer and man. "White is right, clear is dear; cured, I could now abandon all imagined solidarity with the unclear of the world, those whose skin gives them difficulty. And yet, I self-consciously wondered, was not my sly strength, my insistent specialness, somehow linked to my psoriasis?" (74–75).

His imagined solidarity with the unclear of the world is written in the later race chapter. Presented in the form of a letter to the two mixed-race children of his daughter and her black African partner, it begins with a claim about affiliation: "We are all of mixed blood" (164). This is not true to the same degree, as Updike shows, relating his genealogy of mixed European blood against theirs mixed with the blood of Africa. Key is the moment when America is founded on this binary. Updike imagines plantation-owning Updikes, for whom his grandsons would have been slaves and exiled from – though creating – "this American Eden" (189). The binary of history is still existent, racial opposition the defining issue of America, but in the national psyche, deeply buried, manifest and latent, as it is in Updike's works. "Across the politest of exchanges between blacks and whites a shadow falls" (196), he writes, the late twentieth-century equivalent of Du Bois's veil of racial prejudice, and he foresees that his grandsons will be subject to it: "You will each be in subtle (at best) ways the focus of distaste and hatred and fear that have nothing to do with anything but your skins" (196). Although half black, they will be designated black, and his own whiteness, too, will be cause for consciousness. Back in fiction, in *Toward the End of Time* (1997), set in 2020 Massachusetts, even after the American federation has broken down after a Sino-American war, protagonist Ben Turnbull has the same presentiment. He also has two mixed-race grandsons, his daughter having married an African from Togo. He is fascinated by their racial physiognomy, their skin, hair, and eyes: "Where else can I touch an African coiffure?" (*Toward*, 73). But he fears the eventual divide.

And yet in *Self-Consciousness*, Updike hopes for change, which mixed-raceness, this encounter, portends:

> An ideal colorblind society flickers at the forward edge of the sluggishly evolving one. Slim black models pose in *Vogue*, and well-dressed, professional blacks work in the downtowns of the major cities: neither of these things was true of the America I grew up in. Further, the Latinization of North America – the influx of Hispanics – has softened the color line and the singularity of the original black population imported from Africa by pale planters from northern

Europe. America is slowly becoming yours, I want to think, as much as it is anyone's; already, out of the deepest disadvantage, black Americans have contributed heavily to what makes the United States a real country, with a style and a soulfulness no purely white country has. (195–196)

The fact that the whole memoir is dedicated to his grandsons hands his life, if he cannot hand his country, in an act of personal solidarity, to his grandsons.

NOTES

 1. Brian Niro, *Race* (New York: Palgrave Macmillan, 2003), pp. 10, 159, 164–165.
 2. Toni Morrison, *Playing in the Dark: Whiteness and the Literary Imagination* (1992; New York: Vintage, 1993), p. 39.
 3. James Baldwin, *The Fire Next Time* (1963), in *Collected Essays* (New York: Library of America, 1998), p. 340.
 4. bell hooks, *Black Looks: Race and Representation* (Boston: South End, 1992), p. 23.
 5. Edward W. Said, *Orientalism* (1978; London: Penguin, 1987).
 6. Joseph Conrad, *Heart of Darkness* (1902; London: Penguin, 1982), p. 10.
 7. Peter Childs and R. J. Patrick Williams, *An Introduction to Post-Colonial Theory* (London: Prentice Hall, 1997), p. 216.
 8. Susan S. Hunter, *Who Cares?: AIDS in Africa* (New York: Palgrave Macmillan, 2003).
 9. Frantz Fanon, *Black Skin, White Masks* (1952), trans. Charles Lam Markmann (New York: Grove, 1967), pp. 41–82.
10. Claude Lévi-Strauss, *The Elementary Structures of Kinship* (Boston: Beacon, 1969), p. 10.
11. Werner Sollors, Introduction, *Interracialism: Black-White Intermarriage in American History, Literature, and Law*, ed. Sollors (Oxford: Oxford University Press, 2000), pp. 3–16.
12. Dilvo I. Ristoff, "When Earth Speaks of Heaven: The Future of Race and Faith in Updike's *Brazil*," in *John Updike and Religion: The Sense of the Sacred and the Motions of Grace*, ed. James Yerkes (Grand Rapids, MI: Eerdmans, 1999), pp. 68, 64.
13. Renato Rosaldo, "Imperialist Nostalgia," *Representations* 26 (1989), p. 107.
14. Lloyd Schwartz and Sybil P. Estess, eds., *Elizabeth Bishop and Her Art* (Ann Arbor: University of Michigan Press, 1983), p. 312.

GUIDE TO FURTHER READING

Alter, Robert. "Updike, Malamud, and the Fire This Time." *Commentary*, October 1972, pp. 68–74.
Boswell, Marshall. "The Black Jesus: Racism and Redemption in John Updike's *Rabbit Redux*." *Contemporary Literature* 39 (1998), pp. 99–132.
De Bellis, Jack. "African Americans." *The John Updike Encyclopedia*. Westport, CT: Greenwood, 2000, pp. 8–9.
Jackson, Edward M. "Rabbit Is Racist." *College Language Association Journal* 28 (1985), pp. 444–451.

Markle, Joyce. "*The Coup*: Illusions and Insubstantial Impressions." *Critical Essays on John Updike*. Ed. William R. Macnaughton. Boston: G. K. Hall, 1982, pp. 281–301.

Prosser, Jay. "Under the Skin of John Updike: *Self-Consciousness* and the Racial Unconscious." *PMLA* 116 (2001), pp. 579–593.

Ristoff, Dilvo I. "When Earth Speaks of Heaven: The Future of Race and Faith in Updike's *Brazil*." *John Updike and Religion: The Sense of the Sacred and the Motions of Grace*. Ed. James Yerkes. Grand Rapids, MI: Eerdmans, 1999, pp. 64–79.

Robinson, Sally. "'Unyoung, Unpoor, Unblack': John Updike and the Construction of Middle American Masculinity." *Modern Fiction Studies* 44 (1998), pp. 331–363.

6

SANFORD PINSKER

Updike, ethnicity, and Jewish-American drag

I am surely not the only critic who has wondered how much of John Updike went into the making of the Rabbit books, his four-novel series about an average man – Harry "Rabbit" Angstrom – fighting against everything that militates against his self-styled "specialness," and in much the same way, I am hardly the only critic who sees Updike peeking out from under Henry Bech's Jewish skin. Projection accounts for both characters. But to begin before Rabbit first appeared, one needs to meet Fred "Ace" Anderson, the protagonist of "Ace in the Hole," one of Updike's earliest stories (published first in a 1955 issue of the *New Yorker* and then in his 1959 collection, *The Same Door*, 14–26). Ace is a former high school basketball star caught in the gears of adult responsibility: he has a wife, a child, and a dead-end job. His raw sexuality – one of the euphemisms signaled in Updike's pun-riddled title – may have tarnished a bit since his glory days, but as the story's last paragraphs make clear, Ace can still make his wife swoon by dancing her across the floor of their cramped apartment.

"Ace in the Hole" would be regarded as a minor Updike story if it were not for the similarities between Ace Anderson and the more fully developed Rabbit Angstrom. Both know deep in their bones that good looks and a smooth style will trump conventional behavior every time, and that other people will clean up your messes, and possibly even envy you for being daring enough to make them.

Rabbit Angstrom is a character readers love to hate, and in the four Rabbit novels that take him from the 1950s to his ostensible death from a heart attack at the end of the 1980s, we see his life, with all its high-intensity ups and downs, against the backdrop of American culture during the latter half of the twentieth century. Each decade has its distinctive metaphor, whether it be the rhetoric of black militancy during Richard Nixon's presidency (*Rabbit Redux* [1971]) or long gas lines during Jimmy Carter's (*Rabbit Is Rich* [1981]). Updike is at once a healthy arm's length from his protagonist and, at the same time, his closest ally and secret sharer, for Rabbit Angstrom is akin (at least in Updike's imagination) to the life he himself might well have lived – that is, if his mother had not insisted that he leave small-town Shillington, Pennsylvania, behind, attend Harvard University, and, soon after his graduation, become a staff writer on the *New Yorker* magazine.

Enter Henry Bech, the consummate outsider, or, put more fashionably, the ultimate Other. With Bech, Updike tries to imagine (perhaps "impersonate" is the better term) a character as far from himself – and from Rabbit, for that matter – as possible. Whereas Updike is married, a Protestant, and a man who writes book after book in a small Massachusetts town, Bech ends his trilogy (*Bech: A Book* [1970], *Bech Is Back* [1982], *Bech at Bay* [1998]) unmarried, ambivalently Jewish, and a man who nurses his longstanding writer's block in modest digs on Manhattan's Upper West Side. Written in the third person, the books' narrative voice – which is to say, Updike's – describes Bech as "[a] Jew, a modern man, a writer, a bachelor, a loner, a loss" (*Bech*, 124).

At one point we learn that the editors of *Partisan Review* let Bech hang around the office and (on occasion) use an empty desk. But even here Updike's satiric tone makes it clear that Bech is an outsider among outsiders, for if the New York Jewish intellectuals also felt that they lived between a parochial Jewish world long ago rejected and a mainstream culture in no particular hurry to accept them, Bech's alienation is played for laughs. He clings to literary modernism, worshiping Joyce, Eliot, and Valéry long after those names, and their complicated codes of behavior, have given way to postmodernist experimentation and anything-goes performance art.

The woes that Updike's protagonist will endure begin with his name: Bech. The word, ending as it does with a guttural "*ch*" that many American readers find nearly impossible to pronounce, puts poor Henry at a distance even before the trilogy's opening sentence. And the first volume's subtitle, *A Book*, only heightens the undercutting because it comments ironically on the grumbling surprise that "Bech" can acquire if pronounced correctly and with a certain brio. Lilt the last word into a question and Bech's situation worsens, as if it is impossible to imagine a book written by or about him.

Updike's alliterative title is to the letter "b" what "r" is to the Rabbit books, but with this important difference: despite the fact that Bech once wrote an article entitled "The Importance of Beginning with a B: Barth, Borges, and Others" (*Commentary*, February 1962), he is not on the "A" list of "B" writers. And the book that follows his name is dismissively spit out rather than lovingly rolled on the tongue. Even here Bech is the quintessential Outsider, the man who has developed the quip and oddly angled retort into a science. He is, in short, a counterpuncher who imagines blows coming at him from everywhere. Most of his dialogue is taken up with clever rejoinders.

As a contemporary *eiron* – that is, a person defined by his or her generous use of irony – Bech is tight-lipped, always saying less than he knows. Irony drips from such characters (Socrates was one of them), as does a sense that wit and being oppressed are clearly aligned. Bech is forever tonguing the sore tooth of being lionized for books written in the past. In other hands, such a story would crack hearts, but Updike prefers to etch his presumptive Jewish character in the exaggerated strokes of satire. Bech, a man with "thinning curly hair and melancholy Jewish nose" (*Bech*, 49), is one part Bernard Malamud, one part Daniel Fuchs (a writer Bech himself has written about and clearly much admires), and assorted other parts culled from Philip Roth, Saul Bellow, and Norman Mailer. For Updike, Bech represents the Jewish-American literary scene, with its talents and its *tsoris* (trouble) wrapped into a single neurotic ball.

No doubt a certain amount of curiosity about this growing tribe of Jewish-American writers – and their large public successes – drew Updike to create the satiric portraiture he called Henry Bech. Among those who have wondered where the fictional character "Bech" came from is Bech himself. As he writes to Updike, in a letter that stands as the introductory book's foreword, Bech questions "if it *is* me, enough me, purely me" (v). Too many others seem to be part of the mix that ended up, on the page, as him: "My childhood seems out of Alex Portnoy and my ancestral past out of I. B. Singer. I get a whiff of Malamud in your city breezes, and am I paranoid to feel my 'block' an ignoble version of the more or less noble renunciations of H. Roth, D. Fuchs, and J. Salinger?" (v).

Bech is closest to the mark, however, when he ventures the following supposition: there is about the fictional Bech "something Waspish, theological, scared, and insulatingly ironical that derives, my wild surmise is, from you" (v). Even more telling, there are occasions when Bech's style betrays a penchant for lyrical overkill, the kind of airy embellishment that reminds us of none other than Updike himself. The deep connection is especially evident when Bech, warming up to the task, describes

> how in *Travel Light* he had sought to show people skimming the surface of things with their lives, taking tints from things the way that objects in a still life color one another, and how later he had attempted to place beneath the melody of plot a counter-melody of imagery, interlocking images which had risen to the top and drowned his story, and how in *The Chosen* he had sought to make of this confusion the theme itself, an epic theme, by showing a population of characters whose actions were all determined, at the deepest level, by nostalgia, by a desire to get back, to dive, each into the springs of their private imagery. (67)

No doubt Updike could use many of Bech's arguments, especially those centering on countermelodies and lyrically connected deep images, when critics gang up on him for describing, say, a Formica-topped kitchen table in overwritten, all too purple passages. Small wonder, then, that "Bech Noir," the wildest, most delicious story in *Bech at Bay*, is a darkly comic tale about dispatching – quite literally – those critics whose unflattering reviews get under Bech's skin. One of them, an English critic named Raymond Feather-waite (nothing subtle about *that* name!), once said this about Bech's work: "One's spirits, however initially well-disposed toward one of America's more carefully tended reputations, begin severely to sag under the repeated emphatic effort of watching Mr. Bech, page after page, strain to make some-thing of very little" (*Bay*, 156). Everything from the crack about his "carefully tended reputation" to his annoying habit of trying to make much out of pre-cious little suggests that the remarks fall on Updike's shoulders every bit as much as they do on Bech's. Indeed, this self-deprecating attitude on Updike's part (some would call it a very "Jewish" defense mechanism) is part of the trilogy's charm.

As we follow Bech from book to book, something quite amazing happens: Updike warms to his protagonist, not only identifying with his subject but also downright *liking* him. "Bech Noir" offers up a large canvas on which to satirize both his critics and their criticism as well as an opportunity to throw off curmudgeonly assessments about the contemporary art scene:

> He had been to MoMA, checking out the Constructivist film-poster show and the Project 60 room. The room featured three "ultra-hip," according to the new *New Yorker*, figurative painters: one who did "poisonous portraits of fashion victims," another who specialized in "things so boring that they verge on non-being," and a third who did "glossy, seductive portraits of pop stars and gay boys." None of them had been Bech's bag. Art had passed him by. Literature was passing him by. (155)

Updike is hardly Henry Bech when it comes to dishing the dirt about con-temporary artists or competing writers. He is widely regarded as possessing a sharp eye and a generous heart – at least in public print. True enough, when Updike reviews, say, V. S. Naipaul, his assessments tell us a good deal about Naipaul but even more about himself. This is because, as the poet-critic T. S. Eliot pointed out long ago, writers tend to use literary essays and reviews as occasions to justify what they have written in the past or what they are work-ing on at the moment. How, pray tell, could it be otherwise? What *Bech at Bay* does is give Updike a persona, a mouthpiece that is simultaneously him and not him. Thus he can peek out at a world that gave High Modernism the raspberry and that now coarsens the atmosphere with self-indulgent junk.

In much the same way, he can peek out at an America that has changed beneath his very eyes – for the worse – and, much like an aging Rabbit Angstrom, rail against a society in which political correctness would seem to have trumped political astuteness. Poor Bech has a nasty habit of putting his un-PC foot into his old-fashioned, un-PC mouth. Updike, who conducts himself with WASP decorum, clearly enjoys the chance to sound off inside Bech's skin. For example, Bech runs into a potentially angry confrontation when asked, point-blank, by a college student if he isn't, "now and then, somewhat racist" (*Bech*, 113). His antagonist, a girl with an "Afro hair-do cut like an upright loaf of bread," has his 1955 novel *Travel Light* in mind and the fact that Roxanne, one of the book's characters, is called a "Negress" (113). "But she was one," Bech replies, caught offguard by the accusation (113). What, he no doubt wonders, could be wrong with using a well-traveled word such as "Negress"? The answer, at least in the here-and-now of the story, is *plenty*. "The fact is," his Afro-headed antagonist continues, "the word has distinctly racist overtones" (113). No doubt there are any number of ways to defuse this situation, but Bech will have none of them – not, that is, if language is to be used precisely: "Calling you a black woman is as inexact as calling me a pink man" (113).

It doesn't take long before race cards of all sorts get played. "Calling me a Negress is as insulting as calling you a kike," the student argues ("Bech liked the way she said it. Flat, firm, clear" [113]), and goes on to ask him how he feels about the word "Jewess." Bech, who winces at the word, manages to keep his cool and throw off this retort: "Just as I do about 'duchess'" (114). That Bech offers up this rejoinder in something of the same spirit that the sociologist Daniel Bell once pointed out the important differences between terms like "socialist" and "socialite" is true as far as it goes. Bech and Bell share an interest in precision, but it is also clear that Bech, given his socialist, red-diaper upbringing, has little fondness for duchesses. "Jewess," however, rankles because it is a word that snotty non-Jews like to throw around. One could, of course, argue that "Negress" offends blacks in much the same way. Bech may not see the irony here, but surely Updike does – indeed, that is one of the dimensions that makes his cross-dressing in Jewish-American drag so interesting.

It is the ventriloquism that accompanies such cross-dressing that proves more controversial. In much the same way that Bech relied on secondary reading rather than raw experience to write an extended fantasy of motor-cycling into the heart of America in *Travel Light*, Updike fashions his vision of Bech from digesting large heaps of Jewish-American fiction. Small wonder, then, that Cynthia Ozick, a first-rate fiction writer, essay-ist, and scold, should take Updike to task for giving us the altogether predictable, which is to say "ethnic," Henry Bech. His "Jewishness," Ozick argues, exists entirely on the surface where wit replaces Jewish learning and a pervasive shivering in the face of modern life is passed off as Jewish belief. The result is that Bech-as-Jew has no existence, is not *there*, because he has not been imagined: "Bech-as-Jew is a switch on a literary computer. What passes for Bech-as-Jew is an Appropriate Reference Machine, cranked on whenever Updike reminds himself that he is obliged to produce a sociological symptom: *crank*, *gnash*, and out flies an inverted sentence."[1]

As Ozick would have it, Bech is a compendium of a "soi-distant Jewish novel," one fashioned from adjectives such as *zoftig*, nouns such as *shikse*, and generous sprinklings of exclamations such as *oy*. That the habit puts Updike "about even with most indifferent disaffected de-Judaized Jewish novelists of his generation" is a fact Ozick rightly acknowledges, but the *fact* does not make Bech an authentically Jewish character: "because Bech has no Jewish memory, he emerges with less than a fourth-grade grasp of where he is . . . In your uncles' back rooms in Williamsburg you learned zero: despite your Jewish nose and hair, you are – as Jew – an imbecile to the core. Pardon: I see, thanks to the power of Yuletide, you've learned of Hanukkah."[2]

True, all true, as Bech himself would no doubt admit; after all, he makes no bones about his early alienation from everything Ozick holds dear: "his little family world was an immigrant enclave, the religion his family practiced was a tolerated affront, and the language of this religion's celebration was a backwards-running archaism" (*Bech*, 173).

To call the Hebrew language "a backwards-running archaism" is enough to spike the blood pressure of Jewish-American critics who join Ozick in feeling that ethnicity of the sort that oozes from earlier books such as Philip Roth's *Portnoy's Complaint* (1969) and from the Bech series is demeaning to authentic Jewish literature and delimiting to their putatively "Jewish" authors. Predominantly Jewish neighborhoods in Brooklyn or Newark, with their distinctive foodstuffs, Yiddish flavorings, and guilt-producing mechanisms, ultimately make for thin goods. Add ethnic details by the boatload and, at best, what one gets is sociological "atmosphere" rather than a serious (Jewish) vision. Bech knows that Jewish history is a series of ugly persecutions (when provoked he can tick them off), but knows less about the laws received at Sinai and still less about the Talmudic discussions those laws inspired. As such, the Bech that Updike brings to life on the page is not defined by a covenantal relationship to the Jewish God or by his deep acquaintance with Jewish history and thought, and for Ozick the result can only be an empty, and unsatisfying, pseudo-Jewish character.

Granted, Bech is neither more – nor less, I would argue – than a literary Jew, and if this means that he is not a member in good standing of Ozick's synagogue, so be it. This does not suggest, however, that Bech does not have his own pantheon of stern gods, only that they arrived in 1922, a year that began with Joyce's *Ulysses* and ended with Eliot's *The Waste Land*. In many respects this is the result of his odd career, one that Updike chronicles in *Picked-Up Pieces* (1975), a gathering of assorted articles and book reviews. Bech began, Updike tells us, "as a kind of war correspondent, a soldier who wrote stories with gung-ho titles for magazines like *Liberty* and *Collier's*. He was intellectualized in New York in the post-war period. And now he has fallen into silence" (*Picked-Up*, 507). Being "intellectualized" in New York refers to the various ways that the *Partisan Review* crowd and the High Modernism they applied to their marginalized condition influenced (yea, *formed*) Bech. And "silence" is one of the weapons (the others are "exile" and "cunning") that the pinched-faced Stephen Dedalus of Joyce's *A Portrait of the Artist as a Young Man* (1916) permits himself to use. Caught as he is among the nets of family, church, and state, Stephen gives his all to Art, or what he, at the time, regards as Art. "Silence" separates a writer from a noisy, corrupting world and allows an artist the monkish environment that creative work requires.

Meeting the early, altogether human Leopold Bloom in *Ulysses* will presumably alter this overly romantic view, at least for Stephen. Bech, alas, is another matter, and it is not until the final pages of *Bech at Bay* that he seems at last connected to another human being – namely, his infant daughter. Moreover, a fatal attraction to the pubs of Dublin, where his ebullient father told stories, sang songs, and drank away his life, notwithstanding, Joyce knew that he could only write about Dublin by not being there. By contrast, Bech keeps his silence in Manhattan. He does not, interestingly enough, feel any bond with the Jewish Leopold Bloom. It is as if Bech had stopped his Joycean reading with *A Portrait*. He knows about the artistic manifestos that Stephen loves to spout but badly misses Joyce's point, made over and over again in *Ulysses*, about the importance of love.

In the final analysis Bech's silence is much closer to that of Daniel Fuchs, one of the writers Bech encounters during his intellectualizing New York period. He was not the only Jewish-American writer to (largely) abandon his fledgling career as a fiction writer for the attractions – and, let's face it, the big paydays – that Hollywood offered. In Fuchs's case, his *Williamsburg Trilogy* (written during the mid-1930s) had been, at best, a modest success and he left for Hollywood in 1937 to, as Updike/Bech puts it, "write scripts for Doris Day" (*Bech*, 6). And there is more: "To Bech [and Updike as well], it was one of history's great love stories, the mutually profitable romance between Jewish Hollywood and bohunk America, conducted almost exclusively in the dark" (6).

Bech writes brilliantly about the deep psychic appeal of the silver screen at the same time that he is suspicious of its power and knows in his bones that, for many, celluloid images will beat those on the printed page every time. Still, as Bech soon realizes, speculations of this stripe are "for graduate students, neither here nor there" (6). As he steps off the Aeroflot jet that has landed him in post-Cuban Missile Crisis Russia, he discovers that he is awash with rubles from sales of the recently translated *Travel Light*. Go figure. Go know. Bech is not only famous but rich into the bargain.

Yet in the same way that the nineteenth-century essayist Ralph Waldo Emerson warned that we take our ghosts with us when we travel, Bech lugs his defining "silence" along with him as if it were a toothbrush. That he falls into silence after what can only be called a so-so career is an understandable American phenomenon; he is constantly in danger of being a literary personality rather than a working author, somebody famous for being famous. Silence is a condition that he shares with Melville, an abiding presence in Bech's literary pantheon – despite not being able to get all the way through *Pierre*. Silence also makes for slyly satiric moments as when Bech is awarded the Melville Medal for "the most meaningful silence" or when he turns an earnest discussion about "fascists *manqués*" into one of his most celebrated quips: "*Manqué* see, *manqué* do" (90). And it is silence, albeit of a highly qualified sort. About his kvetches it can be accurately said that Bech hardly suffers in silence. More to the point is his shaky status as an artist. Bech writes (or, more correctly, *tries* to write) as he talks; and so inverted sentences easily outnumber those uttered (or written) in what we take to be the normal order of subject, predicate, object.

Bech may well be alienated – and his silence the result of that condition – but he is not alienated in the same way that a wag at the *New Yorker* once quipped that *Partisan Review* writers had typewriters that could punch out the word "alienation" in a single stroke. Israel, the land where three religions were born, brings his underlying religious ambivalence to a boil. His new wife, the former Bea Lachett Cook, insists on calling Israel "the Holy Land." For her, every step along the Via Dolorosa is packed with significance and a reason to swoon. By contrast, Bech keeps his eye on the irrelevant: "the overlay of commercialism upon this ancient sacred way fascinated him – Kodachrome where Christ stumbled, bottled Fanta where He thirsted. Scarves, caftans, olive-wood knickknacks begged to be bought" (*Back*, 66–67). Moreover, Israel has no sentimental significance for him:

his father, a Marxist of a theoretical and unenrolled sort, had lumped the Zionists with all the *Luftmenschen* who imagined that mollifying exceptions might be stitched into the world's cruel and necessary patchwork of rapine and exploitation. To postwar Bech, busy in Manhattan, events in Palestine had passed as one more mop-up scuffle, though involving a team with whom he identified as effortlessly as with the Yankees. (69–70)

One suspects that Updike felt an obligation to schlep Bech to Israel because his portrait of the Jewish-American writer could hardly be complete without it. After all, as one Israeli writer dryly (and accurately) points out – during one of those equally obligatory dinners arranged for distinguished visitors spending time at Mishkenot Sha'ananim (Israel's swank writers' retreat) – "Henry Bech will go back and write a best-selling book about us. Everyone does" (85). But Bech is not Saul Bellow, who wrote about the complexities of Middle Eastern politics in *To Jerusalem and Back* (1976); nor is he Philip Roth, who brings his special brand of playfulness to Israel in books such as *The Counterlife* (1986) and *Operation Shylock* (1993).

There is no reason to fear that Bech will write about Israel because his all-consuming writer's block is more reliable than his ability to put scattered observations into paragraphs. If it is true that Bellow, an absolutely first-rate Jewish brain, did no better than anybody else in terms of "solving" the Middle East dilemma or that Roth's dazzling postmodernist techniques are longer on style than on content, the best that Bech can muster up is the less than breathtaking observation that "Arabs . . . are the blacks of Israel" (83). Such a notion would surely strike some as racist and others as simply accurate. Either way, the remark is "off the record" – as it probably should be – in a country deeply divided, then and now, about what to do about the "Palestinian question." (Ironists will point out that in nineteenth-century Europe it used to be the "Jewish question.") Here Bech and Updike seem to be cut from the same cloth. Neither wants to get tangled up in the brouhaha of politics – Bech because he is the product of an apolitical modernism, Updike because he has no taste for the passions of political correctness. What matters to both is the permanency of art. By contrast, those American writers, Jewish or otherwise, who have tried to unlock the mystery of Jerusalem have had only limited success (one thinks of, say, Robert Stone's *Damascus Gate* [1998]), largely because the material is too volatile, too "crazy" for even the wackiest postmodernist experimentation.

So while Bellow balances the best arguments of Israelis against similar efforts by the Palestinians, and Roth gives his kaleidoscopic vision of the Middle East ever more interesting turns, Bech pretty much plays dumb. After all, he is not interested in fictions such as *Operation Shylock* in which a

shape-shifting character named Philip Roth is revealed to be an agent of the
Mossad and, moreover, the man who saved Israel from a second Holocaust.
Roth craves exactly this sort of adulation from the Jews who have scolded
him (and worse) since his earliest days as a writer. That is why he has a fantasy
of marrying Anne Frank in *The Ghost Writer* (1979) (*that* will shut up his
parents) and why he gave tear-jerking public readings of *Patrimony* (1991), a
nonfiction account of his father's slow, agonizing death. By contrast, Bech is
his own sharpest critic, and, as such, he does not need others to tell him how
good – or how bad – his books are. And when he visits Israel, he does not
feel the necessity, as Bellow did, to pontificate. He is, after all, an imaginative
writer, not a member of "The Capital Gang."

The irony, of course, is that Bech feels as uncomfortable in Israel as did the
infamous Alexander Portnoy. Granted, Portnoy is much more than merely
"uncomfortable"; Israel causes him to be struck impotent. Bech, on the other
hand, is coming to grips with advancing middle age and with his disastrous
marriage to a Christian. When he muses, at the end of the story, about the
meaning of his experiences, the "words" might be his, but the essential *music*
is Updike's: "The holy land was where you accepted being. Middle age was
a holy land. Marriage" (89).

Surprisingly, Bech finds a measure of happiness in, of all places, Scotland:

> In this serene, schizophrenic capital – divided by the verdant cleavage of a loch
> drained in 1816 – he admired the biggest monument ever erected to an author,
> a spiky huge spire sheltering a statue of Sir Walter Scott and his dog, and he
> glanced, along the slanting Royal Mile, down minuscule alleys in the like of
> which Boswell had caught and clipped his dear prostitutes. "Heaven," Bech
> kept telling Bea, who began to resent it. (91–92)

That Updike has ironic reversals in mind – a Christian who goes ga-ga in "the
Holy Land," a Jew who waxes rhapsodic amid the Scots – is clear enough,
but one wonders if there is not a more serious subtext churning just beneath
the satiric waters. For if, say, Philip Roth has taken some pains to suggest
just how infuriating the snobbish anti-Semitism of British "Christendom"
can be (one thinks of novels such as *The Counterlife* and *Deception* [1990]),
Updike means to suggest precisely the opposite – namely, that prejudice and
hypocrisy flourish in Israel as perhaps nowhere else. Thus the Israeli writers
that Bech meets are at once condescending and ultracritical; they know that
the place to "make it," the place that matters for writers, is New York (as the
song would have it, "If I can make it there, – / I'd make it anywhere"), not
Tel Aviv. Even more important is the take-no-prisoners attitude that many
of the Israelis whom Bech meets exhibit. Despite their efforts to put a good
face on what has happened to the country since the '67 war, Bech cuts to

the quick when he tells Bea that "I've spent my whole life trying to get away from them, trying to think bigger" (88). Granted, this is a country under steady siege; niceties do not matter as they might in other places.

"Bech Wed" moves Bech back to America and Bea's mock-Tudor house in Ossining, New York. There he continues his longstanding fantasy of having "made it" (in a fashion) in the WASP world. But poor Bech can never quite get used to the house's sheer size and its Gatsby-like opulence. The result is his feeling of being "installed" in Bea's mansion "like a hermit crab tossed into a birdhouse": "The place was much too big; he couldn't get used to the staircases and the volumes of air they arrogantly commandeered, or the way the heat didn't pour knocking out of steam radiators . . . he had never in his bones known before what America was made of: lonely outposts, log cabins chinked with mud and moss" (105).

More to the point, Bech has not known that a blank page could be conquered in much the same way that an American spirit once plunged, head-long, into the western frontier. But Bea argues, and in ways of which the prolific John Updike might approve: "What you must do . . . is go up there [his upstairs study] first thing every day and write a certain number of pages – not too many, or you'll scare yourself away. But do that number, Henry, good or bad, summer or winter, and see what happens" (107).

Not surprisingly, Bech finds the idea preposterous: "Good or bad?" he asks, making it clear that, first, there *is* a difference, and, second, he knows, and cares, about the distinction. Bea, however, sticks to her guns, and uses one of Bech's favorite writers, none other than Franz Kafka, to make her point: "Who can tell anyway, in the end? Look at Kafka, whom you admire so much. Who cares now, if *Amerika* isn't as good as *Das Schloss*? It's all Kafka, and that's all we care about. Whatever you produce, it'll be Bech, and that's all anybody wants out of you. *Mehr Licht; mehr Bech!*" (107).

For Bea, Kafka is a brand name, and so, she argues, is Bech; whatever he writes will be fine. What she misses, of course, is everything that makes Kafka such an important figure for a Jewish-American writer such as Bech. Kafka is, first and foremost, *the* alienated modern man. Bech's generation discovered in this *angst*-ridden, extremely nervous type the prototype of its own condition, albeit magnified exponentially. For Bech, Kafka's strange, unrelenting characters – the "guilty" Joseph K., the beetle-like Gregor Samsa, the odd hunger artist – are all aspects of himself and his isolated condition. Whatever else Kafka may be, however, he is *not* an easy fix for Bech's persistent writer's block. Indeed, his very life counsels just the opposite. Ironically enough, Bea's just-get-it-down-for-God's-sake advice results in *Think Big* (1979), the sexy novel that soars up the bestseller list and that reminds us of Updike's own success with *Couples* (1968).

Bech's induction into the Academy of Arts and Sciences (at the end of *Bech: A Book*), a society filled, as he finds to his dismay, with third-raters, is a comic foreshadowing of greater debacles to come. Flash forward to the announcement (at the end of *Bech at Bay*), wrapped in an even larger amount of shocked amazement than usual, that Bech has been singled out for the 1999 Nobel Prize in Literature. What must Updike have thought as he composed these paragraphs about Bech? After all, unlike Bech, Updike is a prolific writer who, . . . well . . . *writes*. By contrast, Bech is most identified by the exquisite way he suffers from a protracted bout of writer's block. Small wonder, then, that *silence* is the motif that runs through each of the books or that a good deal of Updike's satiric comedy revolves around Bech's misadventures as a lecturer/goodwill ambassador. When Bech at last nabs the Nobel Prize, he proves the underground adage that unworthy guys finish first.

Updike uses Bech's sudden, unexpected ascension to center stage in Stockholm as a springboard to comment on those curious types who year after year find a way of fitting the Swedish Academy's profile: writers more notable for their political views than for the shape and ring of their paragraphs, and writers largely unfamiliar to an American audience. Granted, Bech does not come from a tiny country nestled near the Arctic circle or deep inside sub-Saharan Africa; nor does he write books in a language nobody bothers to translate into English. Nonetheless, Bech might as well have dropped down from another planet, so obscure is he to the wide American public as well as to those journalists who scramble to find something duly appropriate to say about him, all of which makes the headline about Bech in the *New York Daily News* all the funnier: "BECH? WHODAT???" (*Bay*, 210).

In addition, Updike uses Bech's acceptance speech as an opportunity to turn the solemn ceremony on its ear, and to give Bech's prolonged "silence" – and the Bech series itself – a fitting conclusion. "My life has been spent," Bech confesses early, "attending to my own inner weather and my immediate vicinity" (239). Thus, he goes on to say, "I represent . . . only myself; in citizenship I am an American and in religion a non-observant Jew, but when I write I am nothing less than a member of my triumphant but troubled species, with aspirations it may be to speak for the primates, the vertebrates, and even the lichen as well" (240). Our most important writers tend to their own inner weather, not concerning themselves about the vagaries of fashion. What Bech adds, however, is a sense that he hopes to speak for the entire planet as well as to humanity's troubled condition.

Grand stuff, all right, and it reminds me of nothing so much as the way that Alan Lelchuk's *roman á clef*, *Ziff: A Life?* (2003), ends with Ziff, a dead ringer for Philip Roth, getting the nod from the Swedish Academy.

As with Bech's announcement, people are incredulous, but not because Ziff is a nobody. Rather, he is a somebody who had long been regarded as a self-hating Jew and, worse, as a danger because of the way he hung dirty linen on public lines. Anti-Semites would, the argument went, take aid and comfort from Ziff's satiric portraits and sexual romps. But a new biography, *Ziff: A Life*, changes these old perceptions. Readers learn, for example, that Ziff gave generously to Holocaust survivors (in exchange for hearing their stories). When Ziff publishes his Holocaust masterpiece, *The Wallenberg Wars*, in 2002 (the same year that the eye-opening Ziff biography appears), he is a shoo-in for the Nobel Prize.

After announcing the scope of his imagination (interior for the most part, but presumably beamed out as well to lichens everywhere), Bech tells the audience that he has developed a speaker's block – what else is new? – and has asked his ten-month-old daughter to speak on his behalf. After all, Bech points out, she will "enjoy her first birthday in the new millennium" and can get to the essence of the address's title – "The Nature of Human Existence" – far better than he can (240). And then Bech

> shifted their child to his other arm, so that her little tooth-bothered mouth came close to the microphone – state-of-the-art, a filigreed bauble on an adjustable stem . . . Into the dear soft warm crumpled configuration of her ear he whispered, "Say hi."
> "Hi!" Golda pronounced with a bright distinctness instantly amplified into the depths of the beautiful, infinite hall. Then she lifted her right hand, where all could see, and made the gentle clasping and unclasping motion that signifies bye-bye. (241)

On these minimalist notes – "hi" and a wave goodbye – *Bech at Bay* concludes. Whatever reasons may have prompted Updike to invent an antiself, it is clear that he brought Bech back for a second and then a third volume because he grew rather to "like" him in something of the same way that he came to "like" Rabbit. My hunch is that Updike must have toyed with the idea of allowing Rabbit to recover from his heart attack and, in the New Age of Viagra, to ride off once again into the sunset as a sexual outlaw. But Updike thought better of the idea and, instead, allowed his readers to "remember" Rabbit as the ghost who hovers around his wife's reconstituted house.

About Bech there was little to prompt the making of a fourth book. For Updike, the steady march into the twenty-first century is a graph of diminished returns; exhaustion is setting in – for characters like Bech, for the Jewish-American novel, and possibly for the country itself. Whatever else Updike may do in the years left to him – and I hope it is a great deal – he will write about America, the literary scene, the art world, and whatever else strikes his fancy without the props that poor Henry Bech provided. For a writer as clever as Updike, prancing around the pages in Jewish-American drag turned out to be easy, perhaps *too* easy, especially since the next generation of literary Jews seemed so predictable. Any mimic worth his or her salt can learn to ape, say, Jackie Mason's heavy Yinglish accent or to imagine a character who carries the burdens of a Brooklyn childhood on his or her narrow shoulders. Bech was more, much more, than this, and that is why I shall miss him terribly.

NOTES

1. Cynthia Ozick, "Bech, Passing," in Ozick, *Art & Ardor* (New York: Knopf, 1983), p. 115.
2. Ibid., pp. 116–117.

GUIDE TO FURTHER READING

Hamilton, Alice and Kenneth. "Metamorphosis Through Art: John Updike's *Bech: A Book.*" *Queen's Quarterly* 77 (1970), pp. 624–636.

Luscher, Robert M. *John Updike: A Study of the Short Fiction*. New York: Twayne, 1993, pp. 64–88.

Miller, D. Quentin. *John Updike and the Cold War: Drawing the Iron Curtain*. Columbia: University of Missouri Press, 2001, pp. 115–127, 178–180.

Ozick, Cynthia. "Bech, Passing." *Art & Ardor*. New York: Knopf, 1983, pp. 114–129.

Pinsker, Sanford. "John Updike and the Distractions of Henry Bech, Professional Writer and Amateur American Jew." *Modern Fiction Studies* 37 (1991), pp. 97–111.

Plath, James, ed. "Bech Meets Me" (1971). *Conversations with John Updike*. Jackson: University Press of Mississippi, 1994, pp. 55–58.

Pritchard, William H. *Updike: America's Man of Letters*. South Royalton, VT: Steerforth, 2000, pp. 149–155.

Schiff, James A. *John Updike Revisited*. New York: Twayne, 1998, pp. 112–121.

III

AMERICAN CHRONICLES

7

EDWARD VARGO

Updike, American history, and historical methodology

As a young writer, John Updike imagined paying homage to his native state of Pennsylvania with "a tetralogy, of which the first novel would be set in the future, the second in the present, the third in the remembered past, and the fourth in the historical past."[1] So he began, respectively locating his first three novels – *The Poorhouse Fair* (1959), *Rabbit, Run* (1960), and *The Centaur* (1963) – in the time frames of future, present, and remembered past. Three more novels followed during the next decade, none situated in the historical past. Finally, in 1974, Updike revealed that an uncharacteristic play, *Buchanan Dying*, was originally meant to be the fourth novel in his youthful tetralogy. It took eighteen more years before he found a compelling way to write historical fiction.

The afterword to *Buchanan* gives ample evidence that Updike sought out the facts as meticulously as any traditional historian would. He did massive research in a twelve-volume collection of James Buchanan's writings as well as in dozens of nineteenth- and twentieth-century histories, biographies, articles, and original documents (*Buchanan*, 183–214). Although he occasionally "touched something live" in his research, he simply could not bring a plot to life (256). Again and again, his efforts to enter into the life of the fifteenth president of the United States were stymied: "[R]esearched details failed to act like remembered ones, they had no palpable medium of the half-remembered in which to swim; my imagination was frozen by the theoretical discoverability of *everything*" (259). He decided to abort the novel, salvage what he could, and form it into a play; perhaps actors, set designs, and period costumes could bring the story alive onstage. Commenting on his "failure" at a later date, Updike admitted his fictional imagination's dependency on the "present-ness" of things: "Never having lived in a log cabin, I found myself inhibited about describing one; never having participated in a Washington 19th-century political parley, I found myself at a loss to imagine exactly what went on."[2]

Blind-sided by his fidelity to historical accuracy, Updike created a closet drama. Although he provided an "eagle's-eye view" of Buchanan's life by centering the scene on his deathbed, the many characters that parade through the room produce an unchronological mishmash of confrontations, threats, prevarications, and betrayals. The linkage of private disaster and public perfidy – Buchanan's fiancée Ann Coleman breaking off their engagement and his Southern friends deserting him as South Carolina moves to Secession – is unconvincing. Only with a return to these same materials some two decades later could Updike enliven his historical characters and generate resonating oscillations between public and private. By then, postmodern theory had problematized the verities of historical discourse.

Meanwhile, Updike was busy creating a body of work that, with its detailed focus on the present and the remembered past, with its accurate depictions of social mores, offers us a "living" history of the United States during the second half of the twentieth century. Preeminent in this regard are the Rabbit novels. Before Updike published *Buchanan Dying*, he had already produced *Rabbit, Run* and *Rabbit Redux* (1971), the first two of four novels that would evolve spontaneously into a tetralogy to provide "a kind of running report" on the state of the Union from 1959 through 1989 (*Tetralogy*, ix). By the time Harry Angstrom's life and the tetralogy both come to a close in *Rabbit at Rest* (1990), Rabbit has become an emblem of his age. The macroworld of the nation plays itself out within the microworld of one family, the Angstroms. Updike's "metaphorical prose," rooted in "that old American transcendentalist desire that the things of this world should stand for something," configures *Rest* into a significant piece of cultural history: "Rabbit's memory, which cuts a deep, narrow slice into the American past, fuses with the narrative's metaphors to make an elegy for our world."[3] As Harry ages from the first to the last Rabbit novel, a sense of history grows stronger in his own consciousness and in the narrative as a whole.

Most obviously, extensive quotations from Harry's bedtime reading – Barbara W. Tuchman's study of the American Revolution, *The First Salute* (1988) – introduce formal historical discourse into the complex mix of the narrative in *Rabbit at Rest*. Harry's reading often impinges upon his personal preoccupations. Thus, for example, on the night before his fatal heart attack, an account of "British atrocities around Williamsburg" agitates him deeply; the Revolution was not a "gentlemen's war" after all, as he had always imagined (*Rest*, 499). At first, the images stir nightmarish waking dreams and a fear of death that cause him to sleep fitfully. Eventually, his dreams settle into a blend of happy scenes from his own personal history in *Run* with a fantasy of meeting his grandchild Roy as a grown man in the future. Harry wakes from this meld of past, present, and future with "a smile of greeting dying on his face" (500), and we, too, can experience with him the shimmering fragility of several time levels coming together in memory and dream.

The manner in which Updike developed *Rabbit at Rest* – intertwining macro- and microworlds, configuring memories into an elegy for the past through metaphorical prose, introducing formal historical discourse into his fiction, fusing time streams – prepared the ground for solving the writerly problems that troubled him in *Buchanan Dying*. In his next novel, *Memories of the Ford Administration* (1992), Updike discovered a way to bring the historical past to life by placing it within the context of the remembered past. When, in the early 1990s, a scholarly journal asks the historian-hero Alfred Clayton to recount his memories and impressions of the Ford Administration (1974–77), he does not opt for a standard interpretation of his assignment. Instead, Alf focuses on two events most important to *him* personally during that era – his attempts to move from an old to a new marriage and to compose a biography of James Buchanan. In doing so, he links the emotions of his twentieth-century marriage's blow-up with the disastrous nineteenth-century end to Buchanan's hoped-for marital union and the breakdown of the pre-Civil War national union at the end of his term in office. As in *Rest*, throughout *Memories* Updike intertwines macro- and microworlds, fuses time streams, and conveys an elegiac sense of irrecoverable loss. Here, however, he also raises questions about historical methodology through Alf's running comments to his editors on the process of writing history and through his use of a conditional discourse to expose the patchy quality of memories. From the start, the narrative is filled with suppositious and hypothetical phrases like "let's say," "as if" (*Memories*, 9), "[i]f this was . . . , there must have been," "let us suppose she said" (140). Such conditional discourse accentuates indeterminacy in what we take as reality, a sense that what is being put forth as true is based on inconclusive grounds or on what-could-have-been-but-never-came-to-be. To appropriate Roger D. Sell's words, Alf's remarks suggest that we "make" or "write" history by constantly "pulsing between deconstruction and reconstruction" of events or texts.[4]

In the rest of this essay, I will examine what the title, epigraphs, and form of *Memories* already reveal about its content. Then I will explore how Updike works history and fiction to create what Linda Hutcheon might call a multi-layered "historiographic metafiction."[5] Does history consist simply of texts that are nothing but "documents shredded, pulped, compacted, [and] abandoned to the cleaning crew," as Alf's colleague Brent Mueller insists? (110). Or must a writer "quit the clearly demarcated limits of historic inquiry" and allow fiction to "replace history at precisely that point where experience is sufficiently emotional, spiritual, psychical, moral, existential, or supernatural," as Norman Mailer claimed?[6] Updike's text answers these questions through code switching and an approach to the tripartite structure of temporality similar to that of Paul Ricoeur or Hayden White. This configuration includes "within-time-ness" with its focus on events happening "in" time, "historicality" with its study of events from the past, and "deep temporality" with its attempt to grasp "the plural unity of future, past, and present" in relation to "the enigma of death and eternity."[7] My conclusion will primarily concern the significance of deep temporality for the production of meaning in *Memories*.

With its dry, quasi-historical taste, the title *Memories of the Ford Administration* gives only the slightest of clues to the complex interweaving of the marital, political, and methodological indicated above. The trace of things to come lies in the word *Memories*. If this were a traditional history text instead of the mixed genre that it is, one could expect a more formal title – *Chronicle*, *Annals*, *History* – as in Henry Adams's grand *The History of the United States of America during the Administrations of Thomas Jefferson and James Madison*, written a century earlier (1889–1891). Settling upon *Memories* implies bringing forth things remembered, possibly with less than academic rigor. It leaves the field open to a subjective presentation of both public and private events. Indeed, when historian-narrator Alfred Clayton seems to stray from his assigned topic, he reminds his editors that he is giving them what they asked for – not a standard rehash of well-documented facts, but the "*living* memories and impressions" of a witness who has survived the age (9).

The novel's two epigraphs, placed in counterpoint, suggest that the text to follow is both "a vehicle for the transmission of information about an extrinsic referent" *and* "an apparatus for the production of meaning."[8] The first heralds Updike's intent to provide "facts," the traditional data of history, whether wanted or not: "I am well aware that the reader does not require information, but I, on the other hand, feel impelled to give it to him." Since the quotation comes from Rousseau's *Confessions*, one can expect many of the facts to be quite personal. The second epigraph – from Heidegger's *The Question of Being* – provides a metaphysical slant: "Man in his essence is the memory [or 'memorial,' *Gedächtnis*] of Being, but of ~~Being~~." This quotation undercuts the certain, logocentric knowledge promised in the first epigraph. A fussily academic footnote indicates that Updike is quoting not from Heidegger's original text but from "the preface to *Of Grammatology*, by Jacques Derrida, by the translator from the French, Gayatri Chakravorty Spivak." His tongue-in-cheek pedantry problematizes Alf's unequivocal objections to postmodern theory, as well as his devious exploitations of it, before we even encounter them.

The form for the text proper is that of a "Memo" *From:* "Alfred L. Clayton" *To:* the "Northern New England Association of American Historians" *Re:* its request for a contribution about the Ford Administration "for Written Symposium on Same to Be Published in NNEAAH's Triquarterly Journal, *Retrospect*" (3). The choice of this convention recalls the 1918 Editor's Preface to *The Education of Henry Adams* (1906), in which "Henry Cabot Lodge" presented Adams's text to the public under the auspices of the Massachusetts Historical Society. In both cases, placing the text under the umbrella of a professional organization provides a comforting sense of scholarly authority. In fact, Adams himself wrote the Editor's Preface for Lodge's signature. Updike goes even further in fictionalizing author, learned society, and memo.

The entire novel holds to this form. With no chapter divisions to mark the narrative's major shifts – only space breaks – the nineteenth- and twentieth-century texts stream together into one majestic river, sometimes placid, sometimes surging or churning up like rapids. (Memo)ries from the administration of the thirty-eighth president alternate with episodes from Alf's never-completed study of the fifteenth president of the Union. Out of a total of 369 pages, 183 pages relate to Buchanan and 186 pages to the Ford era, ten installments apiece comprising the bulk of the work. In effect, *Memories* contains a book within a book, a history within a fiction. The most obvious impediments to the free flow of these two narrative currents are abrupt intrusions of direct address to the *Retrospect* editors or Alf's fellow historians. Usually put into brackets, sometimes inserted directly into the text, these comments most clearly fit the kind of discourse one expects in a memo. They consciously draw attention to the writerly aspects of the text and create the illusion that we are reading what is still a work-in-progress. Supposedly meant for a small circle of professional readers, these remarks turn us into voyeurs gazing at the underbelly of writing history, not to mention Alf's hyperactive sexual life.

In the first such writerly intrusion, Alf asks the editors not to "chop up my paragraphs into mechanical ten-line lengths" (5). In those that follow, he presents further editorial suggestions, puts his personal behavior into historical perspective, offers alternative interpretations to those in the text proper, discusses the nature of historical methodology, and addresses his own difficulties with the process of writing history. By the end, he chats with the editors as with old friends. One might argue, as Hayden White does for *The Education of Henry Adams*, that the form of *Memories* "can be seen, from a semiological perspective, as the specifically ideological content of the text as a whole," the "place where it does its ideologically significant work."[9]

One of the ways in which the form "does its ideologically significant work" in *Memories* is through figurative couplings of literally separate episodes from the Buchanan biography and Alf's love life. In the first of these couplings, an episode in which Alf's lover Genevieve Mueller informs him that she is now free to marry him immediately follows one in which James Buchanan delays his marriage to Ann Coleman. What links the two episodes figuratively, aside from the courtship settings, is that in both the man is not ready to settle down. Comparable linkages occur in each of the subsequent alternating episodes. Thus Buchanan and Alf have harmless enough visits with women – Grace Hubley and Jennifer Arthrop – that lead to negative consequences for both. Despite the literal gap of more than a century, similar emotions figuratively join otherwise dissimilar movements of plot as, for example, in the sexual dance of Buchanan with the Czarina of Russia and of Alf with the Rubenesquely fulsome Mrs. Arthrop. The figurative coupling of episodes becomes an effective protocol for bringing dead facts to life.

The switching of codes that allows the reader to assign "possible meanings" to this narrative moves primarily between the literary codes of historical and fictional discourse, the methodological codes of reconstruction and deconstruction, and the social codes of sexual mores and politics. First and foremost, *Memories* pulses between Updike's ingrained tendency toward the representation of things as they really are and his sensitivity to late twentieth-century views on the indeterminacy of facts. Throughout the novel Updike exults in minute details of setting, architecture, clothing, personal characteristics, and suchlike – what many criticize as his excessive devotion to the paraphernalia of realism. Alf calls it "decor" and justifies its presence as a "part of life, woven inextricably into our memories and impressions" (8). Concomitantly, there is a steady movement from a naïve trust in "objective certitude" to the more worldly, "fallen" knowledge of postmodern theory, from a historical discourse innocently grounded in the study of original documents, eyewitness accounts, and previous interpretations to a discourse recognizing history's tainted indeterminacy.

During one of Alf's first stalemates with his scholarly writing, a new colleague at Wayward College, the "deconstructionist" Brent Mueller, claimed that "there is no Platonically ideal history apart from texts, and texts are inevitably indefinite, self-contradictory, and doomed to a final aporia" (35). If all texts share in such indeterminacy, Alf thought, then *his* text does as well. He attempted to write accordingly, "to overcome my mistaken reverence for the knowable actual versus supposition or fiction, my illusory distinction between fact and fancy" (35). As a sample of the result, Alf offers to his fellow historians the episode in which Buchanan told Ann Coleman that they must once again postpone their marriage. The later episode recounting

Buchanan's visit with Grace Hubley is another conscious attempt "to work into the fabric of reconstruction the indeterminacy of events" (75).

But by the time Alf gets to his long account of the desertions from Buchanan's Cabinet during his last month in office, the impossibility of keeping a straight, ordered line in his narrative exasperates him. He cuts off a false start with an outburst: "I *hate* history! Nothing is simple, nothing is consecutive, the record is corrupt" (307). When reconstructing the especially rancorous Cabinet session of 27 December 1860, Alf expresses dismay that "at this climactic crisis of my tale and of Buchanan's life" he has nothing to build on "but dried old words, yards of them strung together from accounts of suspect authenticity" (331). In the end, Alf's opus, and perhaps Updike's original project as well, caved in under the "growing weight" of its own methodology – "all that comparing of subtly disparate secondary versions of the facts, and seeking out of old newspapers and primary documents, and sinking deeper and deeper into an exfoliating quiddity that offers no deliverance from itself, only a final vibrant indeterminacy, infinitely detailed and yet ambiguous" (360). The old way of writing history, with its naïve trust in facticity, no longer works. Yet the new history's embrace of indeterminacy is more than Alf can handle.

He has certainly tried, writing his biography in the spirit of the Norman Mailer citation. That is to say, where historical discourse bangs against its limitations, fictional expansions fill in the gaps to deepen the reconstruction of past events and to enliven flat facts. Three examples can demonstrate how Alf brings fiction to the rescue of history. In the first instance he provides motives for events without textual evidence. He considers the few surviving texts related to the mysterious death of young Ann Coleman to be "pieces of a puzzle that only roughly fit. There are little irregular spaces between them, and through these cracks, one feels, truth slips" (165). To cross over the "fault-lines," Alf presents Ann as feeling trapped between the two impenetrable walls of her father and Buchanan, "doomed to the cosmic forgetting, a minor historical figure, with but one little footnoted life to contribute to the avalanche of recorded events" (112). Then he stops dead in his tracks with a wonderfully satiric deconstruction of his own writing: "[N]o, this is too much *my* terror, my hysteria – my h(i)st(o)ria, the deconstructionists might say, if they, too, and their anti-life con(tra)ceptions were not now becoming at last passé and universally de(r)rided." Yet "this void where history leaves off" will not let him rest, so he begins again, settling upon an imagined conversation between Ann and her younger sister Sarah (112).

Alf also embellishes dialogue reported by multiple sources, as in the "open-air conversation" between the cautious rising politician Buchanan and the fiery General Andrew Jackson in 1824. Two years later, this exchange became

EDWARD VARGO

implicated in "the 'bargain and sale' controversy tainting [John Quincy] Adams's Presidency" (188). Various written charges forced Buchanan to write his own version of the meeting for the Lancaster *Journal*. Alf indicates that he based his own account on this document, but that he invented Jackson's remarks about his life and philosophy. What Alf remarks about the writing is also true of the reading: "In that curious way of fiction and reality, it came to life as nothing in the reported conversation did" (190).

Finally, Alf engages in the outright fabrication of alternative scenarios that go against the public record. He picks up his cue from the claim of an "untrustworthy source" that Buchanan *did* pursue Ann to Philadelphia after their break-up instead of remaining in Lancaster, contrary to the evidence of more reliable documents (118). He goes with it to create a narrative in which Buchanan was reconciled with Ann, married her, and turned his back on politics. As a result, in 1856 Stephen A. Douglas was elected president of the United States in his stead and pursued policies that led to the demise of slavery through bloodless, democratic means. In 1860 Douglas defeated the little-known Abraham Lincoln for a second term, and the Civil War never came to pass. By this time, "both the United States and Mr. and Mrs. James Buchanan – forty years wed – had all but forgotten" the passions and furies of the previous decades (121). Alf ingeniously fuses the vagaries of personal and national life through the creative use of what medieval scholastic philosophers called *futuribilia*: imagined events that contain some mysterious element of reality in them because they could have happened if different choices had been made earlier. That said, Alf returns to the sadder actual scenario.

In addition to the code shifting between historical and fictional discourse considered above, there is also significant shifting between the social codes of sex and politics. Updike uses the sexual mores of America during the Ford era as a gauge for observing, representing, and assessing the decades of Alf's adult life. The transitional Ford years were the heyday of the sexual revolution between the breaking down of sexual barriers in the 1960s and the fear of deadly viruses transmitted through bodily fluids in the 1980s and 1990s. Updike also places the sexual mores of the twentieth century against those of the nineteenth century. For instance, Alf contrasts the sexual behavior of American men in the two centuries by asking whether Buchanan loved Senator King of Alabama, his roommate and closest of friends for many years in Washington. In the climax to this episode, Alf reconstructs the impassioned pro-South speech that Buchanan delivered to Congress in 1838 as "a love song to King" (233). However, what joined this Northerner and Southerner together was not a homosexual liaison, but their love for the Union and their espousal of a rational, gradualist approach to eradicating slavery, a position becoming more and more difficult to maintain. The subtext to this political speech is the domestic passion, the yearning for union, the impending disaster that Alf is beginning to sense in his relationship with his own beloved – Genevieve.

Buchanan's absorption in national politics and Alf's engagement in sexual politics share a similar dynamic in their confrontations, prevarications, compromises, wheeling and dealing. During Buchanan's time the storm around the question of slavery pitted the Abolitionists' view of its debasing immorality against the Southern fire-eaters' view of its sacred nature for political and economic as well as religious and ethical reasons. During Alf's lifetime feminism restructures the patriarchal meaning of sex for both ethical and political ends. Alf faced the sexual politics head-on in Jennifer Arthrop's dead-serious use of feminist argument in her term paper on American imperialism during the McKinley and Roosevelt eras. In the end, when he realized that the real purpose of her consultation was to seduce him, Alf "unwomaned her" with a wickedly outlandish reversal of her feminist deconstructions of history (84). More than a year later, Alf met Jennifer with her mother. His former student engaged him in a humorless debate over sexism in the classic Greek comedy *Lysistrata* while Mrs. Arthrop entered into the gamesmanship of flirtation. Alf found her sexy mother more attractive than Jennifer, "contaminated" as she was by Brent Mueller's "anti-canon deconstructionist chic, which flattened everything eloquent, beautiful, and awesome to propaganda baled for the trashman" (201). It was precisely from this "ideological Flatland" that he wanted "to rescue Genevieve" (201).

Both history and fiction are, according to Bernd Engler, "*discourses of desire*," expressing the insatiable urge for "control in a world which seems to constantly unmask man's illusions."[10] Thus questions of methodology in Updike's book correspond to questions of domesticity: specifically, whether Alf should stay with the wife or opt for the mistress he imagines as the "Queen of Disorder" and the "Perfect Wife" respectively. These *topoi* of order and disorder, perfect and imperfect, are active throughout the novel. After the break-up with Genevieve, they culminate in Alf's realization that his attempts to bring closure to his book and to marry the Perfect Wife "had been aspects of a single vain effort to change my life," to put order into his academic research and to escape a disorderly domestic life (303). He returns to his imperfect wife Norma and drops his disordered project. While Alf judges his book as an unsatisfactory *product* – a failure in achieving his grand design, in reconstituting the sober facts, in bringing the historical characters to life – Alf's comments to his editors successfully invite reflection upon the *process* of history. Although Alf's biography of Buchanan does not meet his own standards of the "perfect," his imperfect reconstruction raises key issues about historical methodology.

The previous discussion of code shifting between history and fiction, reconstruction and deconstruction, sexual mores and politics reveals how the text illuminates its context and how "the context is already in the text."[11] Updike inscribes into Alf's text the limitations or freedoms that context imposed upon *himself* as well, in both the 1970s and the 1990s. When "Alf" was composing Buchanan's 1838 pro-South speech to Congress, "in the centennial-year struggle of Ford versus Carter," he came to realize how out of sync his project was with its context. He was writing in an era when American history was turning "to the rescue from obscurity of the women and slaves patriarchal historians had hitherto consigned to the shadowy margins" (242). In such a context, how could any "but the most perversely patient of historians" empathize with a political leader who produced so many statements sympathetic to slavery? (243). His context worked against Alf's attempt to rehabilitate Buchanan not only culturally but also personally, since his relationship with Genevieve was unraveling at the same time. In the 1990s, when "Alf's" text was inserted into Updike's second book on Buchanan, the climate was different. He could now do parodies of deconstruction not possible eighteen years earlier. He could also state, in his final word on both Ford and Buchanan, that the good intentions of all presidents are constrained by their context, by the "assumptions and pressures that have melted into air, that were always air – *Zeitgeist, Volksgeist*" (366). By the 1990s, as *Memories* illustrates so vividly, an increased awareness of how histories and novels complement each other encourages a great scumbling of the line between real and imaginary events.

In this final movement of my essay, I will suggest how *Memories* also deals with a metaphysical concern common to both types of symbolic discourse. Updike's novel finds its own significance by representing the "drama of the human effort to endow life with meaning" in the face of "the corrosive power of time." The drama is necessarily tinged with a tragic vision of human life even if the comic is often near the surface. This is so, as Hayden White argues in his presentation of Paul Ricoeur's philosophy of history, because time's passing inevitably leads beyond within-time-ness and historicality to "the enigma of death and eternity" at the heart of deep temporality.[12] *Memories* is also an excellent example of how people construct what Fred Weinstein calls imaginative "versions of the world in terms of their own needs and interests."[13] For Alf, those interests center on the fleeting quality of happiness and the accumulating sense of loss and shame that develops in time.

In the very first scene of the novel, watching the national scandal of Nixon's resignation on television with his "abandoned children" temporarily distracts Alf from the "irrecoverable loss" that he feels for his domestic scandal (3, 4). While this pain at what his search for personal happiness with Genevieve does to their children remains a subcurrent throughout, the admixture works itself out in other ways as well. When Alf recalls the night his mother spent in his Adams apartment after an asthma attack that he has had, his fusing of past, present, and future points to the enigma at the heart of deep temporality. The two of them chat about his childhood years during President Roosevelt's second term (1936–40), laughing with delight at "having defeated time" whenever they recover a lost memory (159). But Alf wraps up the scene with his mother's death in 1978, in the future with reference to the Ford era. With her gone, Alf has no one left in the world to share childhood memories with him. He is left behind with a single "great lesson, which we are loathe to learn: we too will die" (160).

Alf tries to work the *topoi* of loss, shame, and happiness into his biography of Buchanan as well. Early on, when Genevieve suggests that he break an impasse by deconstructing some troublesome facts, as her husband Brent would do, Alf rejects the idea on moral grounds: "[I]f you deconstruct history you take away its reality, its guilt, and for me its guilt is the most important thing about it – guilt and shame, I mean, as a final substratum of human reality" (103). In fact, "SHAME" was supposed to be the great theme of the biography; for that reason Alf directs his attention to episodes of embarrassment, disgrace, and loss in Buchanan's life (322). But Alf also "wants to imagine Buchanan happy," and diary entries from his term as ambassador to Russia make that possible (212). To conclude his description of Buchanan's last enjoyable days there, Alf offers a bittersweet riff on happiness. His eschatological and semiological language highlights how ephemeral our sorrows and our joys are. We can find happiness in the simplest of things, and we want to live happily ever after, but happiness leaves "as little residue in the memory as pain. We have in the end only a few flat images painted in calcium on the wet stuff of brain cells, a set of signs no more enduring than a fresco sunk in crumbling plaster." For the moment, "Buchanan was happy, whirling in the rosy rounded arms of Aleksandra Fedornovna" (215). So, too, in the next episode, Alf and Mrs. Arthrop "sought, in the approved manner of the Ford era, to give each other happiness, for a stolen interim" (216). But a gnawing guilt fills Alf immediately after they have sex. His thoughts turn again to the fragility of happiness and to the speed with which the present transmutes into the past: "The present is Paradise, yet our brain forbids our living in it long. Past and future conspired to diminish this treasure beached beneath me, lightly panting" (219).

Near the end, smarting from his loss of Genevieve, Alf identifies with Buchanan's loss of his friends as the Union moved towards dissolution, even wondering whether the lost happiness that he was mourning had any reality: "When loved ones kiss us off, the question arises, did they ever love us? Or has it all been illusion and cool scheming?" (340). Personal and national disasters invite consideration of a still larger void in the universe: "The floor of things: the worse things get, God draws closer, a sublime absence we conjure from the void, from beneath the floor" (341). Alf imagines both Buchanan and Ann Coleman suffering this absence. All his life, doubting Buchanan felt only silence as God's response to his "hours of prayer" (70). When Ann turned to God for solace on the last day of her life, "her grip closed upon nothing, nothing but the silence of absence wrought by her old mocking spirit" (122). Alf's hold on his writing is just as illusive: "Modern fiction – for surely this reconstruction, fifteen years later, is fiction – thrives only in showing what is *not* there" (296). With Alf's return to his imperfect wife coinciding with his decision to leave his Buchanan biography unfinished, his demands for closure and moral order have come to nothing. The transitional years of the Ford Administration signal a brave new world in which "God is not there, nor damnation and redemption, nor solemn vows and the sense of one's life as a matter to be judged and refigured in a later accounting" (296). Recalling his painful loss of Genevieve brings Alf in touch with an even deeper loss: "The sense of eternal scale is quite gone, and the empowerment, possessed by Adam and Eve . . . , to dispose of one's life by a single defiant decision" (296). God is silent in the movements of history and of the heart, and Alf feels it keenly.

Yet the very final memory that Alf recounts is a happy one of an exhilarating ski run during the Ford Administration. When he swoops to the bottom of the slope, all his "life's companions" are there waiting for him, smiling at his skiing prowess (368). He is still young, "a fabulous creature, wiry and rapacious" (369). But now he cannot remember on what holiday break this took place, on what mountain, in what year, why his wife Norma and his mistress Genevieve were both there together. The gaps in his memories blight his recollection, as he admits at the close of his *Retrospect* memo: "I had descended the mountain into bliss; this lengthy response to your provocative query seems to have delivered me into darkness. The more I think about the Ford Administration, the more it seems I remember nothing" (369). And so the text ends. The poignancy of passing time has gotten to Alf, the way our lives fade into the haze of history, into the darkness of cosmic forgetting. Perhaps the deconstructionist Brent Mueller had it right after all. The center does not hold. The reconstruction of the past in which Alf has engaged yields only the "ideological Flatland" that he feared. We had better enjoy our moments of happiness before they meld into history. The only other tenable stance in this age is an honest acceptance of one very bleak reality: the ruthless passing of time inevitably leads to death.

But is it possible for a John Updike novel to end so unambiguously – without the "yes, but" quality that he himself has ascribed to his novels?[14] *Yes*, Alf is overcome by the relentless action of time upon human memory and life itself. He looks into the maw of a world of absence, silence, and cosmic forgetting only to see oncoming death. *But* he has been able to imagine an alternative vision for the star-crossed nineteenth-century lovers in their own moments of deepest darkness. At the moment of Ann's sinking into death, at the height of Buchanan's crisis with his Cabinet over the secession of South Carolina, silence becomes a mystic answer.

When Ann actively sought rest in the "giant hands" of God, nothing happened (132). Only when she was on the cusp of death, going under to an overdose of laudanum, did the divine presence come uninvited, unannounced, out of nowhere. She wondered "that a fact so blazingly obvious – God's tireless inexhaustible love – should be hidden from us in all but a few moments of our earthly lives." Then she died. The last experience of her doubt-plagued young life was "the lucid perception of goodness" (135). As for weary old Buchanan, when he moved from waking to sleeping after the contentious late-night Cabinet meeting of 29 December, Alf imagines that the "half-formed words" of his prayers for the nation were met with the usual silence (346). On that night it did not trouble him. Rather, he realized that from the vantage point of eternity, human disasters were of no great concern: "[W]ithin the beautiful dispassion of God these cataclysms had been cradled, and now slept unremembered but by a few." At last he "appreciated that the silence *was* an answer, the only answer whose mercy was lasting, impartial, and omnipresent" (346). On these inner reassurances Buchanan "sank on a sustained note of praise into the void and woke with surprise into a still-stormy world" (347). At the break of day, his vision leaves him as quickly and quietly as it came. With more threats of resignations in his Cabinet, "the unfathomable *shame*, the daily small losses that mask great loss" returned to his consciousness (348).

A skeptical age can dismiss such visions as drug-induced hallucinations or fantasies aggravated by exhaustion, just as, in Alf's argument, "only our coarse materialist imaginations seek to de-Platonize the masculine romances of the previous century" (231). Notwithstanding, Updike has planted some seeds of light in Alf's darkness. Reflecting on the erasures and aporias that make reconstructing history so difficult, Alf writes a riff on within-time-ness, historicality, and deep temporality that exposes an unquenchable human drive to crack the enigma of eternity and death: "The past is as illusory as the future, and we exist in the present numbly, blind to the cloud formations, deaf to the birdsong. Yet there is something sacred about life that leads us to keep trying to resurrect it" (313).

Alf does not have any illuminating experience like the ones he has imagined for Ann and Buchanan. Rather, he learns that it is impossible to bring the reality of the past back to life in all its fullness, whether for a single individual or an entire age. It is impossible to remember everything that has happened even in one's own lifetime. It is impossible to staunch the hemorrhaging flow of time. There are many losses, small and large, for which to mourn. Yet the very process of reconstructing and deconstructing history, tied in as it is with reflections on deep temporality, is of value in itself. Although Alf the narrator may not fully understand, Updike the orchestrator seems to realize that the *via negativa* paradoxically leads the way out of darkness. Updike is once again revealing his preference for the "dark, tangled, visceral" faith that modern readers find so hard to accept (*Run*, 237). All that has been said and imaged about God, damnation, redemption, and the rest is merely a set of signs. Emptiness, silence, the absence of God do the cosmic work of deconstructing our flawed conceptualizations. By entering more trustfully into the ensuing darkness, one might ultimately go through to gladness.

NOTES

1. John Updike, Afterword, *Buchanan*, p. 252.
2. John Updike, "Why Rabbit Had to Go," *New York Times Book Review*, 5 August 1990, p. 24.
3. Hermione Lee, "The Trouble with Harry," review of *Rabbit at Rest* by John Updike, *New Republic*, 24 December 1990, p. 36.
4. Roger D. Sell, *Literature as Communication: The Foundations of Mediating Criticism* (Amsterdam: John Benjamins, 2000), p. 139.
5. Linda Hutcheon, *A Poetics of Postmodernism: History, Theory, Fiction* (New York: Routledge, 1988), p. 5.
6. Norman Mailer, *The Armies of the Night: History as a Novel/The Novel as History* (New York: Signet, 1968), p. 284.
7. Hayden White, *The Content of the Form: Narrative Discourse and Historical Representation* (Baltimore: Johns Hopkins University Press, 1987), pp. 51, 184.
8. Ibid., p. 42.
9. Ibid., p. 204.
10. Bernd Engler, "The Dismemberment of Clio: Fictionality, Narrativity, and the Construction of Historical Reality in Historiographic Metafiction," in *Historiographic Metafiction in Modern American and Canadian Literature*, ed. Bernd Engler and Kurt Müller (Paderborn: Ferdinand Schöningh, 1994), p. 27.
11. White, *The Content of the Form*, p. 212.
12. Ibid., p. 181.

13. Fred Weinstein, *History and Theory After the Fall: An Essay on Interpretation* (Chicago: University of Chicago Press, 1990), p. 9.
14. Charles Thomas Samuels, "The Art of Fiction XLIII: John Updike," *Paris Review* 45 (1968), p. 100.

GUIDE TO FURTHER READING

Boyer, Paul. "Notes of a Disillusioned Lover: John Updike's *Memories of the Ford Administration*." *Novel History: Historians and Novelists Confront America's Past (and Each Other)*. Ed. Mark C. Carnes. New York: Simon and Schuster, 2001, pp. 45–57.
Vargo, Edward. "Corn Chips, Catheters, Toyotas: The Making of History in *Rabbit at Rest*." *Rabbit Tales: Poetry and Politics in John Updike's Rabbit Novels*. Ed. Lawrence R. Broer. Tuscaloosa: University of Alabama Press, 1998, pp. 70–88.
Veeser, H. Aram, ed. *The New Historicism*. New York: Routledge, 1989.
Weinstein, Fred. *History and Theory After the Fall: An Essay on Interpretation*. Chicago: University of Chicago Press, 1990.
White, Hayden. *The Content of the Form: Narrative Discourse and Historical Representation*. Baltimore: Johns Hopkins University Press, 1987.
Tropics of Discourse: Essays in Cultural Criticism. Baltimore: Johns Hopkins University Press, 1978.
Young, Robert. *White Mythologies: Writing History and the West*. London: Routledge, 1990.

8

JAMES PLATH

Updike, Hawthorne, and American literary history

Shortly before fame first came to John Updike in 1968 – his impish face cele-brated on the cover of *Time* as the author of that sensational wife-swapping novel, *Couples* – the 35-year-old was asked by the *Paris Review* if he con-sidered himself part of an American literary tradition. Pressed further to comment on Nathaniel Hawthorne, Herman Melville, and Henry James, Updike responded, tellingly, "I love Melville and like James, but I tend to learn more from Europeans because I think they have strengths that reach back past Puritanism." [1]

By avoiding mention of Hawthorne, yet referring to that rigid religion associated as much with the author of *The Scarlet Letter* (1850) as with New England itself, Updike could not have been more in denial than if he had climbed upon Reverend Dimmesdale's midnight scaffold. That is ironic, considering all that we know, now, of Updike's longstanding fascination with the first American author to write a novel that Henry James proclaimed worthy of export, "as exquisite in quality as anything that had been received" from Europe. [2] While the young Updike clearly felt it premature to allow himself to be linked to Hawthorne and an American literary tradition, an older Updike more at ease with the notion would simply say that "one would love even to aspire to be as good as Hawthorne." He may have learned more from Europeans, but Updike did not hesitate to embrace Hawthorne later as an influence, even on *Couples*, which he described as being consciously set in "Hawthorne's territory," a novel as much "about New England and the Puritan faith" as it was about marital infidelity in the early 1960s. [3]

The long shadow that Hawthorne cast on American literature has not escaped critics, [4] nor, certainly, Updike, who observed that the "Protestant villages of America, going back to Hawthorne's Salem, leave a spectral impression in literature: vague longing and monotonous, inbred satisfac-tions are their essence" (*Odd*, 307). That description also applies to the restive maladies that plague Updike's own fictional heroes – earnest but con-flicted characters such as Rabbit Angstrom, Piet Hanema, Richard Maple, and Jerry Conant, whom Alice and Kenneth Hamilton, authors of the first book-length study on Updike, quite accurately saw as "pilgrims faltering toward divorce" in pursuit of Eros.[5] As Updike would later affirm, "My subject . . . is the American Protestant small-town middle class" and the "sexual *seethe* that underlies many a small town."[6]

Although Updike said that he discovered Hawthorne relatively late in life, reading *The Scarlet Letter* for the first time at the age of thirty, he admitted that it "sticks in my mind as the first American masterpiece," and the more he reads it the more he is "struck by how 'right' everything is."[7] No anxiety of influence sufferer, Updike has revealed that he almost always begins one book with another in mind, and the text that has served as his most extensively employed source is, in fact, *The Scarlet Letter*. Updike has said that this "novel of religious conscience and religious suffering" was of interest to him primarily because Hawthorne is "the only classic American author who talks about sex,"[8] and because *The Scarlet Letter* is "the one classic from the lusty youth of American literature that deals with society in its actual heterosexual weave" (*Hugging*, 73; *Odd*, 858). "Let's take coitus out of the closet and off the altar and put it on the continuum of human behavior," he told his *Paris Review* interviewer[9] – an attitude that marked Updike as a pilgrim himself, one who, with *Couples*, was partly responsible for introducing graphic sex into the American literary mainstream. As the novelist Nicholson Baker wrote in a wry tribute, "Updike was the first to take the penile sensorium under the wing of elaborate metaphorical prose."[10]

Shortly before Updike was first encountering Hawthorne's masterwork, he discovered Denis de Rougemont's *Love in the Western World* (1939; English translation 1956) and its persuasive argument that passion and marriage are virtually incompatible, according to the principles of courtly love and the archetypes for the adulterous triangle: Tristan/Iseult/King Mark and Lancelot/Guinevere/King Arthur.[11] In an act of unprecedented intertextuality, Updike has forever linked himself to Hawthorne and that adulterous archetype, as it was famously transplanted to American soil and grafted onto Puritanism, by retelling the story of Hester Prynne, her estranged husband Roger Chillingworth, and her minister-lover Arthur Dimmesdale in three separate novels and from the point of view of each major character in *The Scarlet Letter*: Dimmesdale, in *A Month of Sundays* (1975); Chillingworth, in *Roger's Version* (1986); and Hester, in *S.* (1988).

At the center of both Hawthorne's novel and Updike's fictional reconsiderations is what D. H. Lawrence described as a dualism responsible for the "diabolic undertone of *The Scarlet Letter*" – the conflict between "blood-consciousness" and "mind-consciousness,"[12] or what Updike has termed the battle between "Earth-flesh-blood versus Heaven-mind-spirit"

(*Hugging*, 78), which is prevalent not only in Hawthorne's fiction, but also, as nearly every critic has observed, his own. In a talk on "Hawthorne's Creed" (1979), Updike noted that "Hawthorne's instinctive tenet is that matter and spirit are inevitably at war," and that the conflict between spirit and the flesh is exacerbated when organized religion imposes additional constraints – at which point it also becomes a conflict between the self and society (77).

A traditional reading of *The Scarlet Letter* certainly supports that observation. The novel begins with a description of the prison and a throng of people waiting outside in their "sad-colored garments" for Hester Prynne to endure "the whole dismal severity of the Puritanic code of Law."[13] She emerges with a baby in her arms and a scarlet "A," for adulterer, embroidered on the breast of her gown. The novel, or "romance," as Hawthorne preferred, ends with Hester, however punished or penitent, isolated from society and living out her days as an angel of mercy. Her lover, Reverend Dimmesdale, dies on the scaffold after finally confessing his sin with Hester, coaxed (or goaded) out of him in part by the evil machinations of the cuckolded husband, physician Roger Chillingworth.

In a traditional reading Dimmesdale is overpowered by desires of the flesh, as is Hester. She endures public humiliation and ostracism because of the illegitimate baby born to her, while the minister who refuses to confess his part suffers the greater burden of a secret sin and the torment of guilt. Yet, as Hawthorne's biographer Newton Arvin has astutely observed, neither Hester nor Dimmesdale "is represented as the greatest sinner of the drama, and their punishments are less terrible" than those of the aged scientist, who tries "to bring warmth into his own benumbed existence by attaching to himself the radiance and vigor of Hester's youth."[14] Updike has also sensed this, observing that Dimmesdale and Hester are guilty of nothing more than "flashing out momentarily" against what Hawthorne called "'the moral gloom of the world'" (78). "I don't claim to be a proponent of the nuclear family," Updike has said, preferring relationships that recognize "there are areas of each other that we cannot possess and that each person should be given the divinity of certain kinds of freedom – and that includes spouses."[15]

Lawrence links the conflict between the flesh and spirit to Original Sin. After Adam and Eve partook of the apple, "they peeped and pried and imagined," concluding that the sin was in the act, when, Lawrence argues, it was really in "the self-watching, self-consciousness." His view of Hawthorne's triangle is that Hester, like Eve, was the seductress, while Dimmesdale gave in willfully, after which the two of them would "hug their sin in secret, and gloat over it, and try to understand. Which is the myth of New England."[16] Adam and Eve's descent into sin is paradoxically, for Updike, an ascent into the realm of knowledge and the intellectual self-awareness that separates humans from animals. "Unfallen Adam is an ape," Updike told one interviewer, adding that "to be a person is to be in a situation of tension, is to be in a dialectical situation."[17]

Although Updike, like many before him, assumes that the guilt so predominant in *The Scarlet Letter* was based in part on guilt which Hawthorne felt for an ancestor who took part in the Salem witch trials (*More*, 478),[18] no less an authority than James, whose life overlapped Hawthorne's by twenty-one years, maintains that the "passionless quality" of *The Scarlet Letter*, "its element of cold and ingenious fantasy, its elaborate imaginative delicacy," is a reflection of the author's interest in narrative artifice rather than reality or the simple depiction of adulterers.[19] That is also the case with Updike's fictional dualism, which has both taunted and daunted readers. In his review of *Love Declared* (1961; English translation 1963), Updike took exception with de Rougemont's claim that "happy love has no history" because passion is, in part, dependent upon there being obstacles to love, which in turn generates a state of exquisite anguish that comes from desiring that which cannot be easily obtained. "Happy love, unobstructed love," Updike countered, "is the possibility that animates all romances; their plots turn on obstruction because they are plots" (*Assorted*, 289). Nevertheless, Updike is also conscious of the powerful residual effects of Puritanism. In a tribute to fellow writer John Cheever, Updike wrote that "[b]eing back in New England has activated dormant devils in him," and that "[t]he Puritan admonition to look into the darkness of our hearts was not lost on him" (*Odd*, 112, 111). It is through the act of deep introspection, of course, that one discovers a divided and often contradictory self.

The divided self occurs in Updike's fiction almost from the beginning – most notably in *Rabbit, Run* (1960), in which Rabbit Angstrom feels conflicted about his life and his liaisons with an aging prostitute. Yet Updike begins his Hawthornian explorations in earnest in *Couples*, a novel that generally has not been considered by critics in the context of Updike's *Scarlet Letter* trilogy. A close reading not only reveals that in it Updike laid the groundwork for the more detailed allusions to Hawthorne's text that would inform the later trilogy, but also sheds light on the apparent evolution of Updike's attitudes toward Hawthorne's primary theme of guilt.

Ostensibly, *Couples* concerns a group of comfortably liberated couples in Tarbox, a fictional community whose name alludes to a Brer Rabbit fable about entrapment. Within this prototypical novel, Foxy Whitman, like Hester, experiences a pregnancy that exposes her adultery. Her lover Piet Hanema is, like Dimmesdale and Updike's other straying ministers, a chronic adulterer. And her husband Ken is, like Chillingworth, a learned man of science, an "icy" academician who is resented by Foxy for his endless education

(*Couples*, 210), who speaks about people "as of chemical elements, without passion" (410), and who anticipates one of the themes of *Roger's Version* when he remarks, "If a clever theologian ever got hold of how complex [chemistry] is, they'd make us all believe in God again" (33).

Despite the casual attitude in Tarbox toward sex and adultery, however, guilt is still prevalent – in part because the gates to the "*post-pill paradise*" have only recently been opened and the idea of sexual liberation is still new (52), and in part because the guilt arises from a familiar Hawthornian source: secrecy. As free as the couples are with their cheating, they experience the same self-consciousness that caused Adam and Eve to shrink from God, and they try to conceal their affairs from their spouses. Although adultery "lit her from within" (204), Foxy nonetheless has an experience that parallels Dimmesdale's having to endure Chillingworth's hovering in-house presence. Troubled by her secret and the "two hidden burdens" that have grown parallel – pregnancy and her adultery – she "felt that her mother's presence in the house formed a dreadful, heavensent opportunity to confess that she had a lover" (274), even though the mother only benignly pries into her daughter's life.[20] The secret of adultery affects Piet more dramatically; in him the need to confess "rose burning in his throat like the premonition of vomit" (273). It is only through the sharing of blame – something that Dimmesdale and Hester are unable to achieve together – that Piet approaches a state of grace. After he has intercourse with the pregnant Foxy, "in their accepting the blame together, their love had exercise and grew larger" (202).

Such prying into the secrets of adultery is not only experienced by Foxy and Piet. In a further echo of Chillingworth, the slightly demonic Freddy Thorne "knows" about his wife's infidelity but is "saving" that knowledge to use later (51). He tries to get at the identity of Foxy's lover, and draws out the secret of Piet's earlier affair with his own wife Georgene, then uses his knowledge of Foxy's second pregnancy by Piet to obtain a night with Piet's wife. Foxy plays "the devil's advocate for a while" (418), and Piet complains about his wife Angela's psychiatrist in language that again recalls Chillingworth's opportunistic prying into Dimmesdale's heart: "[t]he more miserable you are, the deeper he'll get his clutches in" (415). He tells Angela that psychiatry is "witchcraft, and a hundred years from now people will be amazed that we took it seriously. It'll be like leeches and bleeding" (415).

Yet the guilt that forces characters to conceal their affairs (sexual and otherwise) no longer stems from religious transgression. In *The Scarlet Letter* "religion and law were almost identical," a pervasive presence that penetrates every bit of the social fabric.[21] By the time of *Couples*, set during the Camelot era of the Kennedy White House, religion has lost its preeminence, while sexual liberation has brought intercourse into the public discourse. Sex and a small circle of like-minded friends have become so central that the couples have "made a church of each other" (7) – though not without problems. Their stripped-off clothes are "tarpaper" and sure to ensnare them in Tarbox, "an outer limit" of Boston (54, 43). Instead of a letter branding the wearer a deviant from society, the women in *Couples* coin the term "big H" to signify the opposite: all the ridiculous "horsey" people who "did all the right things" in Tarbox society (106). Two of the women among the couples, Marcia and Janet, anticipate *S.* with notes of their own to men in their lives, each signed with a simple monogram (133–134, 169). The scarlet letter even makes a wickedly ironic appearance: Foxy's "coral cunt, coral into burgundy, with its pansy-shaped M, or W, of fur" (435).

Ironized in this manner, the decline, decay, and degeneration that are already underlying themes during the period in which *The Scarlet Letter* is set come to fruition in a contemporary present in which "Puritanism [had] faded into Unitarianism and thence into stoic agnosticism" (*Hugging*, 66). Updike's fictional Tarbox is located on once-sacred ground, albeit an American Indian site (84) – which suggests that Tarbox is founded on what would have been moral wilderness in *The Scarlet Letter*. In the end, the Congregational Church, with its "Pilgrim hymnals" and "Gothic-tipped hymnboards" (18, 442), is struck by "God's own lightning" and burns down (441), and Piet, whose adultery earns him the same measure of isolation as Hester, despite the seemingly loose and accepting morality, is shunned by the couples, who "quickly sealed themselves off from Piet's company" (456). Yet Piet is relieved "that at least he had been redeemed from Freddy Thorne's spell" (407), just as Dimmesdale is redeemed from Chillingworth's spell at the climax of Hawthorne's novel.

While the protagonists in Updike's *Scarlet Letter* trilogy often feel conflicted about their actions, they are not nearly as weighed down by a sense of morality and guilt as those in *Couples*. This is especially the case with respect to those fictional reworkings of Dimmesdale, the character whose health, in Hawthorne's work, has already deteriorated from guilt that is gnawing away at him before Chillingworth ever appears. In *A Month of Sundays* the Reverend Thomas Marshfield's unhappiness comes not so much from guilt as from annoying speculation. When his mistress questions whether being a minister is still Marshfield's "thing," he snaps, anticipating her criticism, "Because I keep fucking you? And being a hypocrite?" Alicia says that she does not mind the hypocrisy, only his unhappiness (*Month*, 65) – which, ironically, is caused by Marshfield's own jealousy over an affair he imagines his protégé Ned Bork to be having with his wife and jealousy over Bork's affair with their mistress-in-common Alicia. Likewise, in *Roger's Version* Dale (a diminutive of Dimmesdale) might have gone happily about his business if not for the jealousy-motivated prying of Roger Lambert. Dale is smug at the beginning of the novel, passionate about his computer-programming experiments to try to prove the existence of God, and so excited by his theorems that one has to wonder whether he is even capable of having the affair with Roger's wife Esther that Roger describes. It is only when Roger plays devil's advocate (pun intended) and deliberately manipulates discussions in order to precipitate a crisis of faith that Dale begins to despair, even verging on a confession about his personal life that Roger is certain will turn out to be that imagined affair with Esther.

The Dimmesdale figure in *S.* feels even less discomfort over his many affairs, having founded an Eastern religion to preach that prescribes Tantric sex and multiple partners. His only annoyance comes from jealousy over Sarah's husband, despite Charles's living hundreds of miles away. Even in *The Witches of Eastwick* (1984), which was written between the first and second volumes of Updike's trilogy, and which James A. Schiff has called "Updike's most Hawthornesque work,"[22] guilt is never much more than a few fleeting thoughts of how the witches' actions may or may not have been related to the deaths in the novel or to nature. Updike's witches have no real guilt, because, as Alexandra explains, a "natural principle" is that "[w]e must lighten ourselves to survive" (*Witches*, 97–98), and that includes blame, or guilt. In so rewriting *The Scarlet Letter* from the perspective of Satan and the witches, Updike sends typically mixed messages: he suggests that Lawrence's revisionist view of Hester as an evil force may be interesting, but he also seems to believe what Hawthorne is too timid to state outright – that Nature ultimately absolves everyone of blame or guilt.

To a certain extent, such absolution reflects the fact that by Updike's time, adultery has become so common that a "tell-tale heart" treatment would be nothing short of anachronistic, even comic. As Updike told Donald J. Greiner, "the primary purpose behind *A Month of Sundays* with its fitful Hawthornian echoes was to show how radically American attitudes have changed in regard to adulterous clergy," with modern clergymen "quite unapologetic about where their bodies take them."[23] Despite the comic characteristics of Updike's trilogy, then, the novels are less a parody of Hawthorne's work or an indictment of Hawthorne's time and values than a critique of American society.

To a larger extent, however, their rejection of guilt reflects Updike's belief that the adulterous triangle may be more natural than the bond of two people who enter into marriage: "Things fall into threes. And magic occurs all around us as nature seeks and finds the inevitable forms . . . the isosceles triangle being the mother of structure" (*Witches*, 5). The myth of the adulterous triangle operates, according to de Rougemont, "wherever passion is dreamed of as an ideal instead of being feared like a malignant fever."[24] Lawrence likewise believed that myth was concerned with "the onward adventure of the integral soul," which made Hester, by virtue of her choosing to follow her individual desires, a mythic pilgrim, venturing into the moral frontier, ultimately living apart from society where her "intellect and heart had their home" and roaming "as freely as the wild Indian."[25] This moral hero will eventually give way to the much-celebrated Western hero, that knight on horseback who is moral despite living outside the laws of civilized society. In Updike's updating it is the minister who revels in the next sexual conquest rather than dwelling on some abstract "sin" connected to his previous encounters who assumes the role of hero in the chivalric tradition. As Marshfield rhetorically remarks, "Wherein does the modern American man recover his sense of worth, not as dogged breadwinner and economic integer, but as romantic minister and phallic knight, as personage, embodiment, and hero? In adultery" (*Month*, 46).

More than anything, a comparison of *Couples* with Updike's later trilogy reveals how Updike has resolved the spirit-flesh conflict. The characters who are most blissfully happy, except during times when external circumstances or agents intercede, are those like Marshfield and Rabbit Angstrom, who gleefully elevate sex to an exalted, spiritual act. Those like Ned Bork, who is crass about his cheating, and to whom "in indolent footnote to his vows, fornication was a bodily incident no more crucial than spitting" (86), are the heathens or disbelievers in Updike's world of unified flesh and spirit. In this respect Updike's *Scarlet Letter* trilogy and Hawthorne-influenced novels point the way to understanding other Updike heroes better. If, as Marshfield claims, "what is the body but a swamp in which the spirit drowns?" (46), Updike's protagonists treat those drownings like baptisms, with forays into the flesh leading, inevitably, to an orgasm of the spirit as well.

Marshfield's emotional arc can be traced through his prose, which begins with sarcasm over his plight and the process of writing that he has apparently been instructed to go through at the curative retreat for wayward ministers to which he is sent, and moves quickly to defiance and subversion as he creates elaborate fictionalized recollections of his indiscretions – aimed more as a gentle shock to his "gentle reader" than the self-reflection for which the exercise has been intended (6). A creature of habit, Marshfield sermonizes on Sundays, but the effect of the journal is such that it inspires him to the point where he begins to sermonize, to a degree, each day – hence the book's title. There are footnotes throughout, the glib reverend punning suggestively and talking about his sexual exploits, using the footnotes to explain what he excuses as Freudian slips (5).[26]

More than Marshfield's sermonizing is inspired by his literary endeavors. *A Month of Sundays* opens with an epigraph from Psalm 45, "my tongue is the pen of a ready writer," and Marshfield is a ready writer whose pen is equally as mighty as his phallic sword. Indeed, it is the mighty pen that reinvigorates the mighty sword from the uncharacteristic impotence that Marshfield discovers himself experiencing over the course of the novel. Echoing de Rougemont, Updike suggests that sex without seduction can be detrimental to passion, that women, "deprived of shame and given the pill, had created a generation of impotent lads" (59). Yet the same process of journal writing that enables Marshfield to regain his ability to preach also enables him to succeed in his attempts to seduce the motel's manager, Ms. Prynne. His limp penis, which formerly had gotten such a workout among his parishioners, returns "into its ideal shape" after he presumably makes love to Ms. Prynne at the novel's end (228). That his spirits also "rise" is ironically reflected in the one honest prayer he offers in gratitude: "I pray my own face, a stranger to me, saluted in turn," just as Ms. Prynne apparently has during their lovemaking (228).

In *Roger's Version* this dynamic proposed by Updike – that sexual arousal can lead to spiritual renewal – is evident even in his Chillingworth figure. Although Dale wants to prove the existence of God and seems, on the surface, more of a pilgrim than his aged mentor, Roger Lambert is hardly the cold villain from Hawthorne's novel. He shows signs of discovering passion, and to that degree he is, in Updike's world, heroic. Roger happens to be married to a woman fourteen years his junior, "an age difference that has grown, not shrunk," to the point where they have little to talk about and perfunctory relations (*Roger's*, 35). But just as Marshfield's language changes throughout *A Month of Sundays*, becoming gradually more passionate, so does Roger's in the later novel. Because of his suspicions about Dale having an affair with his wife, Roger rediscovers dynamism and sexual passion through his appropriation of porn-speak, which seeps into his narrative and coexists alongside heady discussions of Karl Barth, Paul Tillich, Tertullian, Coptic Christians, Pascal, and Albert Einstein. Of this Roger is fully conscious, remarking, as he fantasizes about Dale and Esther, that "the willing wench, as porn novels say, takes note of his revived erection and puts aside her wine to bend her lips to its inviting hard-softness, its tacit standing homage to her" (153). By having Roger speak with a blend of technical, philosophical, and gutter language, Updike again reinforces his sense of the spirit-flesh conflict as being resolved through language, through passion, and through unification, even as the dualism is blurred by Roger's and Dale's mutually prying into each other, so that neither is clearly the victim. "Maybe *he's* using *you*," Esther tells Roger (161).

Updike underscores such uncertainties and ambiguities by addressing "the reader" directly, as did Hawthorne, and also uses footnotes, letters, tapes, and diary entries to call into question the reliability of his characters' narrations. Just as Hawthorne has Surveyor Pue leave behind artifacts from the scarlet letter incident for the narrator to discover, Updike has Marshfield leave his diary open for Ms. Prynne to find and for readers voyeuristically to experience. Just as Hawthorne's narrator bases his account not on the scarlet letter that inspires his imagination when he holds it, but on a "small roll of dingy paper, around which it had been twisted" that bears gossipy testimony from those who claimed to have witnessed the event,[27] Updike relies on narrative methods that call into question their reliability. Marshfield's accounts of his sexual escapades may or may not be true, because his stories are aimed at a specific reader, an ideal "insatiable" reader whom he hopes to seduce. His footnotes begin as asides and explanations, then betray ulterior motives and game-playing. Likewise, Roger's entire narrative is speculative (male) fantasy. And because Sarah in S. writes for different audiences using different voices, her own sincerity and attitudes toward the ashram for which she has left her doctor husband are called into question.

More than anything, these narrative techniques reinforce and magnify the voyeurism of Hawthorne's novel because of their level of intimacy. Diaries are highly personal, especially ones which divulge sexual escapades and masturbatory episodes, and so the reader becomes as much a voyeur as the wayward minister. As Marshfield seduces Ms. Prynne, readers vicariously "watch." As Roger offers up his erotic, neurotic, and highly speculative and voyeuristic narrative, he pulls the reader into his own twisted vision to peer in on Dale and Esther. As Sarah's personal letters are read, and she and the crooked guru Art/Arhat are caught on tape in an unrehearsed moment, the reader is there again to observe guiltily. Through language and narrative Updike is able to capture the prying essence of *The Scarlet Letter* as it strives to capture the interior of a human heart and imply at the same time that America itself has become a much more gossip-oriented and voyeuristic nation, even more so than in Hawthorne's time. In this respect Updike comments not only on *The Scarlet Letter* as myth, but on American morality still experiencing the curious aftershocks of Puritanism.

Newton Arvin wrote that Hawthorne is "one of those writers who have said too much, who have had too serious an insight into human experience, ever to be ignored or forgotten."[28] With these rich and revelatory novels that redress Hawthorne's complicated themes and symbols, the same ultimately holds true for Updike, who admitted, with characteristic candor and simplicity, that he has "never quite escaped the Christian church."[29] His alter ego Henry Bech "wants to be lifted out of flux, the way that literary immortals are" (*Picked-Up*, 507), and with Updike's dramatic intertextual dialogues with Hawthorne, his place in American literary history is all but assured.

NOTES

1. James Plath, ed., *Conversations with John Updike* (Jackson: University Press of Mississippi, 1994), p. 32.
2. Henry James, *Hawthorne* (1879; Ithaca, NY: Cornell University Press, 1967), p. 88.
3. Plath, *Conversations*, pp. 129, 120.
4. Richard H. Brodhead's *The School of Hawthorne* (Oxford: Oxford University Press, 1986) offers a broad discussion of Hawthorne's stylistic and aesthetic elements that are echoed in the fiction of later American writers. In another excellent study, *In Hawthorne's Shadow: American Romance from Melville to Mailer* (Lexington: University Press of Kentucky, 1985), Samuel Chase Coale explores Hawthorne's influence on the genre of American romance. For an expanded discussion of adultery in Hawthorne, James, and Updike, see Donald J. Greiner, *Adultery in the American Novel: Updike, James, and Hawthorne* (Columbia: University of South Carolina Press, 1985).
5. Alice and Kenneth Hamilton, *The Elements of John Updike* (Grand Rapids, MI: Eerdmans, 1970), p. 200.
6. Plath, *Conversations*, pp. 11, 267.
7. Ibid., pp. 178, 129.
8. Ibid., p. 178.
9. Ibid., p. 34.
10. Nicholson Baker, *U and I* (New York: Random House, 1991), p. 18.
11. See "More Love in the Western World," Updike's 1963 review of de Rougemont's sequel (*Assorted*, 283–300).
12. D. H. Lawrence, *Studies in Classic American Literature* (1923; New York: Viking, 1964), pp. 84–85.
13. Nathaniel Hawthorne, *The Scarlet Letter* (1850), ed. Fredson Bowers and Matthew J. Bruccoli (Columbus: Ohio State University Press, 1962), pp. 47, 52.
14. Newton Arvin, *Hawthorne* (1929; New York: Russell and Russell, 1961), p. 190.
15. Plath, *Conversations*, p. 184.
16. Lawrence, *Studies*, pp. 85, 87.
17. Plath, *Conversations*, p. 34.
18. For a full discussion of Judge John Hawthorne, see James R. Mellow, *Nathaniel Hawthorne in His Times* (Boston: Houghton Mifflin, 1980), p. 11.
19. James, *Hawthorne*, p. 91.
20. Chillingworth's having been "dropped down, as it were, out of the sky" to tend to the ailing Dimmesdale is likewise deemed "an absolute miracle" that "Heaven had wrought." See Hawthorne, *The Scarlet Letter*, p. 121.
21. Ibid., p. 50.
22. James A. Schiff, *John Updike Revisited* (New York: Twayne, 1998), p. 79.

23. Donald J. Greiner, "Updike on Hawthorne," *Nathaniel Hawthorne Review* 13 (1987), p. 3.

24. Denis de Rougemont, *Love in the Western World* (1939, 1954), trans. Montgomery Belgion (New York: Pantheon, 1956), p. 24.

25. Lawrence, *Studies*, p. 63; Hawthorne, *The Scarlet Letter*, p. 199.

26. Although he never mentions Freud, Lawrence's reading of *The Scarlet Letter* is highly psychoanalytic and perfectly suggests the functions of the id, the ego, and the superego. Dimmesdale, an agent of society who flagellates himself for not living up to the standards he preaches, is dominated by the superego. Chillingworth, the man of science whose intellectual curiosity supersedes even his cuckold's desire for vengeance, is dominated by the ego. Hester, the least tormented of the three, arguably by virtue of her having no sin to hide but also because she is inclined more to instinctive behavior, is dominated by the id, that part of the psyche which is prone to seek immediate gratification, and where there are no values or conflicts. In the id, contradictions exist side by side, without any need for resolution – which, of course, perfectly suits Updike's protagonists who are themselves walking contradictions, both spiritual and carnal.

27. Hawthorne, *The Scarlet Letter*, p. 32.

28. Arvin, *Hawthorne*, p. 220.

29. Plath, *Conversations*, p. 208.

GUIDE TO FURTHER READING

Greiner, Donald J. "Body and Soul: John Updike and *The Scarlet Letter*." *Journal of Modern Literature* 15 (1989), pp. 475–495.

Plath, James. "Giving the Devil His Due: Leeching and Edification of Spirit in *The Scarlet Letter* and *The Witches of Eastwick*." *John Updike and Religion: The Sense of the Sacred and the Motions of Grace.* Ed. James Yerkes. Grand Rapids, MI: Eerdmans, 1999, pp. 208–227.

Schiff, James A. *Updike's Version: Rewriting The Scarlet Letter.* Columbia: University of Missouri Press, 1992.

9

Updike, film, and American popular culture

Because movies these days are most often viewed at home, on relatively small though continually expanding screens, some may have difficulty understanding what it was like to watch movies during the 1930s, 1940s, and 1950s, particularly in a small town such as Shillington, Pennsylvania, where John Updike grew up. The author, who from the age of six attended movies alone, as often as three times a week, describes the communal nature as well as the grandeur of the experience:

> You had to get out of your house to go to the movies. It was, in the darkened theatre, a shared experience and social event. The very décor of the theatre, in its mirrored and gilded extravagance, its Arabian-nights fantasy and palatial scale, lifted the men and women of drab American towns and cities up from their ordinary lives onto a supernatural level . . . For Americans, it was our native opera, bastard and sublime. (*More*, 643)[1]

Although film continues to lift and inspire, the experience is somehow different in one's family room where the telephone may ring, or even in a mega-Cineplex where movies, listed like flavors in an ice-cream shop, are screened simultaneously in a dozen identical box-theaters. Further, during Updike's youth the projected visual image was relatively new, and the movie theater, along with the movies it presented, offered a radically innovative experience. Today projected visual images – via television, home video centers, computer screens, video games, digital cameras, and megascreens posted on disco walls and suspended above sports arenas – dominate our lives, to the extent that excess dilutes intensity. Whereas "[t]he major sexual experience" of Updike's boyhood was watching a newsreel showing women wrestling in a pit of mud ("The mud covered their bathing suits so they seemed naked"), today's children are each day likely to observe scores of images that possess far greater, or at least more graphic, sexuality (*Assorted*, 180).

My objective, however, is not to compare moviegoing today with moviegoing during Updike's youth, since such exercises usually tend toward nostalgia.

Rather, my purpose is to demonstrate how cinema as well as other popular culture operates in Updike's work. Given his literary ambition, his accomplished *oeuvre*, and his role as a "man of letters," in which he has composed thousands of pages of essays and reviews of world authors as well as American masters, Updike has been viewed by critics primarily through the lens of literature and "high culture" rather than popular culture. In addition, his stated influences generally reflect "high culture" modernism: Proust, Joyce, Nabokov, Henry Green. Further, when critics discuss the visual aspects of his writing, particularly his pictorial and highly descriptive style, it is again largely in terms of "high culture" and fine art. Allusion is often made to the year he spent at Oxford on a fellowship studying drawing, his longtime admiration for the paintings of Vermeer, and the considerable energy he has spent reviewing the work of Modigliani, Degas, John Singer Sargent, Egon Schiele, and many others.

While there is no denying the influence of literary modernism or fine art on Updike, one should recall that the author grew up in a small town where his early interests were primarily popular: "Like many another would-be practitioner in the arts, I caught the bug from popular culture: coloring books, animated cartoons, comic books, songs on the radio, radio drama and comedy, the so-called slick magazines, and the movies" (*Odd*, 87). The movies, of course, had a profound impact on Updike as a child, fueling his ambition and imagination as well as teaching him forms of behavior, including "kissing and smoking: at least we saw how these oral exercises were conducted by giant black-and-white lips on the screen" (*More*, 642). In addition to movies, Updike was profoundly affected by cartoons. One of his early ambitions was to become a cartoonist, more specifically an animator for Disney: "Spread out on the floor with my crayons and colored pencils, I taught myself to copy cartoons – I can still do a serviceable Mickey Mouse – and by the age of six or so was copying many of the syndicated comic strips of the day" (788). This interest in drawing and cartoons continued: "I copied comic-strip characters on plywood and cut them out with a coping saw; I scissored the strips out of the daily newspaper and made little books of them; I drew caricatures of my classmates; I became the class poster-maker. I sent fan letters to comic-strip artists and sometimes got back original strips in return" (788). Updike went on to contribute scores of cartoons to the Shillington High School *Chatterbox* and the Harvard *Lampoon*; however, he eventually realized that his more significant gifts were in writing, so abandoned his hope of becoming a cartoonist.[2]

Given Updike's early interest in the popular arts, it is no surprise, then, that they figure significantly in his work. Film, in particular, is a presence throughout Updike's *oeuvre*. Whether as cultural reference, narrative influence, subject matter, or inspiration for formal experimentation, film is present in Updike's writing, beginning with his first novel, *The Poorhouse Fair* (1959), and culminating in his seventeenth novel, *In the Beauty of the Lilies* (1996). Jack De Bellis has compiled a list of the hundreds of references to movies and movie personalities in Updike's writings, and he has pointed out that the only significant works in the author's *oeuvre* which fail to contain such references are his historical works set before the twentieth century, *Buchanan Dying* (1974) and *Gertrude and Claudius* (2000).[3] Many of these film references work either to heighten the verisimilitude or to provide a topic of conversation for the characters. In *Rabbit Is Rich* (1981), for instance, Harry and his son Nelson drive past a four-theater movie complex advertising "AGATHA MANHATTAN MEATBALLS AMITYVILLE HORROR," which prompts a conversation about *The Amityville Horror*, Satanism, and religion, which then reveals generational differences between father and son along with the father's fear of the "invisible" (161–162).

Elsewhere, these film references can be more substantial and integral to the text. For instance, in *Rabbit at Rest* (1990), Janice Angstrom, a late middle-aged housewife, decides to alter her life, and the inspiration, at least in part, is the movie *Working Girl*. Emerging from the theater, Janice announces: "I think I need a job. Wouldn't you like me better, Harry, if I was a working girl?" (*Rest*, 107). Subsequently, she begins a career as a real estate broker, acquiring a businesswoman's efficiency and confidence, and picking up the pieces when her husband's health fails and her son falls into drug addiction. Serving as more than simply a cultural reference, the movie provides the impetus for Janice's self-reinvention and reflects cultural trends in the air, such as the empowerment of women in business.

Film has also figured as a narrative influence on Updike's writing. Although it is difficult to determine precisely how much Updike's visual style and storytelling emanate from film, it would seem likely, given the hundreds of movies he watched during his youth, that his sense of scene, narrative, and character has in some significant way been shaped by film. Consider, for instance, the opening passage from *Rabbit, Run* (1960), a novel which Updike initially subtitled "A Movie":

> Boys are playing basketball around a telephone pole with a backboard bolted to it. Legs, shouts. The scrape and snap of Keds on loose alley pebbles seems to catapult their voices high into the moist March air blue above the wires. Rabbit Angstrom, coming up the alley in a business suit, stops and watches, though he's twenty-six and six three. So tall, he seems an unlikely rabbit, but the breadth of white face, the pallor of his blue irises, and a nervous flutter under his brief nose as he stabs a cigarette into his mouth partially explain the nickname, which was given to him when he too was a boy . . .

His standing there makes the real boys feel strange. Eyeballs slide . . . there are six of them and one of him.

The ball, rocketing off the crotch of the rim, leaps over the heads of the six and lands at the feet of the one. (3–4)

As Updike writes, "The opening bit of the boys playing basketball was visualized to be taking place under the titles and credits," and its present tense was meant to be "an equivalent of the cinematic mode of narration."[4] With its alliteration, sounds and scrapes, and focus on the visual – eyes turn to watch the arrival of a stranger – the scene *feels* cinematic, a quality which will persist throughout Updike's *oeuvre*.

This appropriation of film in *Rabbit, Run* is hardly unique. As critics have pointed out, Updike's early novels, in particular, experiment with cinematic technique: *The Poorhouse Fair* concludes with an extended montage sequence that feels cinematic in scope, and *The Centaur* (1963) employs a similar montage sequence in one of its chapters.[5] The example of *Ulysses* (1922) may have been fueling the early Updike, who in 1967 referred to Joyce's masterwork as one of the first and "noblest" attempts to "appropriate to prose fiction some of [film's] properties – the simultaneous intimacy and impersonality, the abrupt shifts from close-up to boom shot, the electric shuttle of scenes" (*Picked-Up*, 356–357). Yet in the same essay Updike suggests that subsequent experimental efforts to employ cinematic elements, such as in the fiction of the French novelist Alain Robbe-Grillet, have failed, and that the novel, perhaps, can only move so far toward film. Updike's own attempts at more experimental appropriation of cinematic techniques for the novel seem to subside by the mid-1960s.

What one begins to see in *Rabbit, Run*, however, and what evolves into a hallmark of Updike's fiction a decade later in *Rabbit Redux* (1971), is his appropriation and employment of popular culture and media. Updike turns his focus toward the ways in which contemporary songs, slogans, headlines, movies, television programs, products, and information, via media, enter the consciousness of an individual living in a small town and connect him or her to a larger, collective American experience. This technique, it would seem, begins almost accidentally. While composing *Rabbit, Run*, Updike left several blank spaces in his manuscript at points in which Harry "Rabbit" Angstrom is in his automobile listening to the radio. He later filled these blank spaces with references to popular songs, commercials, sports, and political news:

On the radio he hears "No Other Arms, No Other Lips," "Stagger Lee," a commercial for Raiko Clear Plastic Seat Covers, "If I Didn't Care" by Connie Francis, a commercial for Radio-Controlled Garage Door Operators, "I Ran

All the Way Home Just to Say I'm Sorry," . . . a commercial for Tame Cream Rinse, "Let's Stroll," news (President Eisenhower and Prime Minister Harold Macmillan began a series of talks in Gettysburg, Tibetans battle Chinese Communists in Lhasa, the whereabouts of the Dalai Lama, spiritual ruler of this remote and backward land, are unknown, a $250,000 trust fund has been left to a Park Avenue maid, Spring scheduled to arrive tomorrow), sports news . . . , weather . . . , a commercial for Speed-Shine Wax and Lanolin Clay, "Venus," and then the same news again. Where is the Dalai Lama? (*Run*, 30–31)

This catalogue of contemporary references, which consumes an entire page, is not so much integrated as it is pasted into the text. Although there is relatively little popular culture in *Rabbit, Run* compared with subsequent Rabbit novels, the seed for this narrative technique was ostensibly planted here, and as this technique evolves in Updike's fiction, it becomes more significant as well as seamlessly integrated.

When Updike began writing *Rabbit Redux* at the end of the 1960s, a time in which political and cultural events were particularly visible and pressing, he utilized popular culture far more liberally. *Rabbit Redux* alludes to and engages in dialogue with television (*The Carol Burnett Show*, *Laugh-In*), film (*2001: A Space Odyssey*, *Butch Cassidy and the Sundance Kid*), and other media and popular culture. More significantly, the Apollo 11 moon mission, experienced through television, becomes the novel's central metaphor, linking thematically as well as linguistically to the lives of Updike's characters. The novel begins with the moon blast-off, which Harry and his father watch from a bar: "The bar television is running, with the sound turned off. For the twentieth time that day the rocket blasts off, the numbers pouring backwards in tenths of seconds faster than the eye until zero is reached . . . The men dark along the bar murmur among themselves. They have not been lifted, they are left here" (*Redux*, 7). The moon shot is paralleled by another launch and expedition of discovery which takes place simultaneously: Janice Angstrom's domestic departure, in which she leaves her husband and son to live with another man.

The moon shot also colors Updike's language. Words such as *launch*, *drift*, *link*, *lunar*, and *crater* are applied to events, movements, and places in the characters' lives, and the metaphor of docking and redocking, which describes the connections between spacecraft, also applies to the sexual and personal couplings in the novel, including the split between Harry and Janice, who eventually drift back toward one another. In *Rabbit Redux* Updike makes Harry a receptacle for the headlines, stories, and information which popular culture was churning out and distributing, and in the process he enlarges his canvas, telling the story not just of a single individual but of a national culture as well.

Updike's engagement with popular culture in his fiction continues through-out the 1970s, 1980s, and 1990s. A scene in *Rabbit Is Rich*, in which Rabbit's drive home from his office in his 1978 Toyota Corona consumes nine pages, demonstrates the kind of dialogue Updike is suggesting takes place between American popular culture and a single interior consciousness. Here Updike constructs an extended stream-of-consciousness passage in which Rabbit's thoughts and personal history are interwoven with material from the radio as well as with his observations of the town through which he passes:

> The radio is what he enjoys, gliding through Brewer with the windows up and locked and the power-boosted ventilation flowing through and the four corners of the car dinging out disco music as from the four corners of the mind's ballroom. Peppy and gentle, the music reminds Rabbit of the music played on radios when he was in high school, "How High the Moon" with the clarinet breaking away, the licorice stick they used to call it . . . (*Rich*, 30)

Throughout the extended passage Rabbit's thoughts move freely and asso-ciatively (for example, from Toyota's array of automobile colors to Second World War depictions of the Japanese to the music from his youth to black girls singing in Detroit); and his thoughts shift according to what he hears on the radio (news reports, disco music) or observes on the familiar streets of Brewer (a four-theater movie complex, the neighborhood where he once lived with Ruth). The pop culture references – the Bee Gees singing "Stayin' Alive"; John Travolta starring as a Sweathog on the television program *Wel-come Back Kotter*; news items dealing with the gasoline crunch, Three-Mile Island, and Skylab – are no longer simply catalogued but woven carefully into Rabbit's stream of thoughts.

Further, Updike interweaves actual text from other media and genres: a newspaper headline and article concerning the death of Skeeter Johnson, a black militant whom Rabbit had once known; lyrics from the Donna Summer disco song "Hot Stuff." Despite the interior nature of these nine pages, the extended passage has a visual, even cinematic quality: "As he sits snug in his sealed and well-assembled car the venerable city of Brewer unrolls like a silent sideways movie past his closed windows" (32).

This extended passage, in which Rabbit becomes the receptacle for var-ious cultural materials which are then interwoven with the thoughts and experiences of his own quotidian life, is quintessential Updike. Similar pas-sages, occurring when Rabbit is watching television or listening to the radio, can be found throughout the later Rabbit texts and in other Updike nov-els. Through this technique Updike, whose novels are often set in small towns in Pennsylvania and New England, demonstrates how national news

stories, songs, television shows, movies, ideas, and trends are relayed and distributed, entering the lives and thoughts of individuals who are far removed
from the heights of Hollywood, Washington, or Manhattan. Popular culture becomes a crucial and influential part of Rabbit's daily experience. He
sings along with and is turned on by the songs he hears; his thoughts and
actions are driven by the television programs, movies, and consumer articles
he absorbs.

Because the Rabbit sequence is set between 1959 and 2000, a period during
which movies had a less profound impact on Updike than in his childhood,
film becomes secondary to the television programs and radio news reports
that Rabbit consumes. However, in his novel *In the Beauty of the Lilies*,
which chronicles America from 1910 until 1990, Updike found a way to
write about movies and the kinds of moviegoing experiences he had during
his youth in Shillington. What emerges is his finest and most extended exploration of how the American experience has been affected by film, and how
visual images have not only shaped culture but become part of our interior
experience.

In the Beauty of the Lilies is a large, ambitious novel which traces
the evolution of the Wilmot family through four generations, beginning
at the moment in 1910 in which Clarence Wilmot, a minister, loses
his faith, and concluding in 1990 with the death of his great-grandson,
Clark, who dies heroically during a Waco-like siege of an Adventist cult
compound. Unlike the Rabbit novels, which privilege a single character,
Lilies devotes equal time and attention to four generations: Clarence, who
falls from grace, abandoning his religious calling and becoming a door-
to-door encyclopedia salesman; Teddy, his withdrawn and sensitive son,
who works as a mailman; Essie, Teddy's confident and energetic daughter, who becomes a movie star; and Clark, Essie's neglected son, who
joins a religious cult just before its apocalyptic confrontation with the US
government. The Wilmot family functions as the novel's main character,
evolving through each successive generation despite the recurrence of various
traits, situations, and problems.

Much like his approach in the Rabbit novels, Updike simultaneously tells
the story of America, its popular culture (music, films, fashions, and trends)
as well as its history (labor strikes, wars), through what has been dubbed the
"American Century." The novel's title, which emanates from what Updike
refers to as that "odd and uplifting line" from "The Battle Hymn of the
Republic" – "In the beauty of the lilies Christ was born across the sea" –
had long been associated in the author's mind with "the hymning of this great
roughly rectangular country severed from Christ by the breadth of the sea"
(*Self-Consciousness*, 103). *Lilies*, then, which works on an immense canvas

and deals with significant themes, chronicles America, and demonstrates how cinema and religion figure in that history.

Film is pervasive throughout the novel, beginning with the opening scene. D. W. Griffith has come to the Wilmots' home town of Paterson, New Jersey, to shoot *The Call to Arms*, a movie set in medieval times which centers on "a lost jewel beyond price" and stars Mary Pickford (*Lilies*, 3). As the film crew prepares for her close-up, Pickford, suffering from the summer heat, loses consciousness. At this very same moment, the Reverend Clarence Arthur Wilmot, residing a few blocks away, "felt the last particles of his faith leave him" (5). The single moment which yields these two synchronous events is highly symbolic and points to a dominant theme in the novel: the rise of cinema, which through its powerful projection of images has inspired faith and devotion, and the related decline of religious faith. That Pickford loses consciousness at the moment of the "facial close-up," a technique of which Griffith was the "first great master,"[6] suggests that the human face, divinely enlarged on the big screen, replaces the face of God in the eyes of the worshiping public.

Upon leaving his ministry, Clarence becomes a salesman and spends his spare time in the movie theater, where he feels "lifted" and "released from accusation" (104). For Updike, the movie theater, where the "worshippers within these catacombs s[i]t scattered and silent" (103), resembles a church:

> [The projectionist's] little square windows emitted unscheduled blue flashes and whiffs of smoke that testified to the dangerous spark at the root of his sorcery. Then the projector, turned by hand, began to spin overhead its chuckling whir. There were splinters of daylight at the back of the building which Clarence ceased to see once the great screen came alive. This was a church with its mysteries looming brilliantly, undeniably above the expectant rows . . . the piano player in the corner, huddled beneath his sallow lamp like a monk at his candlelit prayers, sought to inscribe the silent images with thunders and tinklings that channeled the unified emotions of the audience into surging indignation, distress, suspense, and a relief that verged upon the comic in the violence of its discharge. (105)

Updike has spoken of how, in his youth, the movie theater and church, two of the central institutions of his small town, were situated "almost side by side," competing for his attention (the former usually won) and, interestingly, resembling one another.[7] Designed as grand spaces with elegant and extravagant architectural details, each attempted to lift, inspire, and transport its audience/congregation to another world. With its larger-than-life gods and goddesses, emanating as images of light which move across and conquer the darkness, the movie theater, Updike suggests in

Lilies, replaces the church as the dominant locus of yearning, passion, mystery, and transcendence.[8] In addition, film, like religion (which posits an all-seeing God), provides a new way of seeing: "[T]he camera had grown in cunning and flexibility, finding its vocabulary of cut, dissolve, close-up, tracking and dolly shot. Eyes had never before seen in this manner; impossibilities of connection and disjunction formed a magic, glittering sequence that left real time and its three rigid dimensions behind" (106).

For the Wilmots, however, the advent of cinema contributes to or is at least synchronous with their fall from grace. Clarence's loss of faith stands as the primal event in the novel, the one from which the family, which views itself as "somehow special, with a destiny that stretched above and beyond [the town of] Basingstoke" (261), must recover. Clarence's son Teddy, who inherits his father's tendency toward withdrawal, refuses to attend church or pray, since either would be an act of disloyalty to his father, and although he attends movies, he is "not quite the betranced moviegoer his father had been": the movies seem "menacing" and "embraced the chaos that sensible men and women in their ordinary lives plotted to avoid" (146). While the movies provide a courtship vehicle for Teddy and his wife Emily, offering an occasion for their first date as well as validation for their sexual impulses – "She began to kiss with an open mouth, like Greta Garbo with John Gilbert in *Flesh and the Devil*" (181) – the family remains wounded because of Clarence's fall.

It is Essie, the daughter of Teddy and Emily and the character in the novel whose experiences most closely align with Updike's, who plunges most intensely into the movies and strives to renew the Wilmot destiny. This boldly confident child of relatively timid parents becomes an active moviegoer who is immeasurably influenced by what she sees on the screen: "When she got older, she promised herself, she would paint her toenails so she could wear open-toed shoes with slinky slacks like Marlene Dietrich and Dolores Del Rio" (236). Essie not only imitates the movies but feels them internally: "[S]he sat upright, imitating Deanna Durbin's nice fearless posture, and let *One Hundred Men and a Girl* flow through her" (245). Full of talent and ambition, Essie is energized and lifted by the movies, finding in them what some discover in religion, a parallel world of beauty and grace which answers to her inner yearnings. Increasingly yielding herself to the movies, Essie soon discovers that the world inhabited by family and friends pales sadly and feels insubstantial beside "the light of the silvery movie world whose beautiful smooth people rattled all those words at each other and moved through their enormous ceilingless rooms with such swiftness and electric purpose" (252).

The movies become such a central part of her existence that Essie imagines real-life situations as if scenes from a film. She arrives at her cousin Patrick's exquisite Park Avenue apartment with "visions of a movie right here, in this lovely quiet set" (302); a few hours later, while lying in the bathtub, she anticipates (unaware her cousin is gay) that Patrick will seduce her – "All her nerves were tensed against the click of the door opening, as it would have in any movie" (303). Because her imagination and desires have been so profoundly shaped by the movies, Essie cannot help but imagine herself playing a role before a camera and audience. Further, the sensation of being watched, whether by an audience or God, is a familiar and deeply satisfying experience for her: "A cosmic attention beat on her skin as when she was a child God had watched her every move, recorded her every prayer and yearning, nothing unnoticed, the very hairs on her head numbered" (335). Becoming a movie star lifts Essie to a "heavenly realm" which she associates with Hollywood, her dead grandfather, and God:

> [I]t was the dead, unearthly grandfather she aspired to. In his unreality he held a promise of lifting her up toward the heavenly realm where movie stars flickered and glowed and from which radio shows, with movie stars as guests, emanated. When Essie prayed to God, she felt she was broadcasting a beam of pleading upward to a brown cathedral-shaped radio and her shadowy grandfather was sitting in a chair beside it listening. (270–271)

Once she begins appearing in movies, Essie discovers there is "something mystical in the way the camera lapped up her inner states through the thin skin of her face" (280), and on occasion she feels as if "something from God would flow into her face from behind" (336). Light, which she associates with God as well as with the movies, figures crucially for Essie. Always conscious of where light is coming from and whether it is "defining the good side of her face" (346), she is eager to submit to it and allow it to transform her face and soul. Whether as an indication of God's presence or as the vehicle which transmits her to millions of moviegoers, light is what makes Essie shine, and it stands as a sign of her personal election.

The novel's final section deals with Essie's neglected son (and Clarence's great-grandson) Clark, a young drifter who shares his mother's ambition but lacks her confidence and self-worth. Having worked most recently as a chair-loader at a Colorado ski resort owned by his great-uncle, Clark has wasted time by consuming a steady diet of television, movies, and drugs. He discovers his purpose, however, almost accidentally at the Temple of True and Actual Faith, an Adventist cult in the Colorado hills led by Jesse Smith, a David Koresh figure who proclaims himself the new American messiah. There at the cult compound Clark, who eventually assumes the role of communications coordinator, alters his identity as well as his name, which Jesse changes to Esau.

In Clark's section we see the degree to which film and television have been internalized in American culture at large. Clark's interior life is described on multiple occasions as a movie which runs in his head: "Clark had these irritating memory blanks, more and more of them lately; but then the break in the film was mended and the inner movie resumed" (382). As Updike explains, cinema, which began as an "oddity" early in the twentieth century, evolved to where it "has entered our innermost selves, so that we all sort of think we're on TV all the time."[9] This is literally what happens to Clark when Updike takes us inside the compound and depicts the siege as a great American television performance with cameras, helicopters, and a media circus. As Temple spokesman, Clark broadcasts its message to the world and, to his delight, becomes a fifteen-minute celebrity: "He didn't believe all of what he was saying, but he loved the sensation of saying it into the little coffee-colored Panasonic phone and feeling the words being drunk up by a thirsty world" (451). This sensation closely parallels Updike's own experience the first time he appeared on television: "They were feeding on me; I was being lapped up and broadcast into thousands and thousands of sets. *I was on TV*. The feeling was scary and delicious" (*Odd*, 31).

Indeed, just as film allows Essie to reinvent herself (she changes her name from Essie Wilmot to Alma DeMott), television allows Clark, once again, to reinvent himself (from Esau to Slick), and then distribute that self, multiplied and scattered, to millions who consume him with their eyes and ears. Such distribution of the self, whether through film, television, or print, has been important to Updike throughout his life, beginning in his childhood when he watched his ambitious, literary-minded mother send off her short stories to magazines: "I knew she was trying to reach beyond the street outside, where cars and people moved toward their local destinies as if underwater, toward a world we couldn't see, where magazines and books came from" (*Odd*, 834). Although his mother failed for many years to have her work accepted into print (eventually her fiction appeared in the *New Yorker* and in two published books), Updike pursued a similar objective and, perhaps fueled by her early failure, succeeded on a grand scale. This process of seeing his own mental musings and "marks on paper" transformed "handsomely" into reproduced books has been described by Updike as a "magical act" and a "delightful technical process": "To distribute oneself thus, as a kind of confetti shower falling upon the heads and shoulders of mankind out of bookstores and the pages of magazines, is surely a great privilege and a defiance of the usual earthbound laws whereby human beings make themselves known to one another" (835).

It is in pursuing a path that involves the distribution of the self or, perhaps, the delivery of "messages" that Clark finally aligns himself with the Wilmots who have preceded him, each of whom, as Stacey Olster notes, "deliberately opts for a career that fosters spiritual and/or national unification."[10] As a minister, Clarence delivers God's word to his congregation; later, as a door-to-door salesman of *The Popular Encyclopedia*, he peddles the people's word. Teddy, who once had a paper route, serves as his community's mailman, delivering magazines and letters to his neighbors. Essie, a movie star, delivers herself as emanations of light to moviegoers. And Clark broadcasts the Temple's message to millions via telephone. In writing of the Wilmots, who serve as vehicles through which God, art, and culture are communicated to the people, Updike is writing a personal and familiar story, one which underscores his interest in the relationship between the small-town individual and the heavenly realm of culture and art.

Untouched by God's grace, however, such distributed "messages" offer little in the way of revelation. Clark's section builds toward a fiery conclusion, in which his final act of heroism is delivered live to the world via television. The boy known to his stepfather as "*Superguy*" (362), who subsequently worked for a production unit hoping to "cash in on the Superman craze" (*Lilies*, 410), assumes the role of Superman, killing Jesse, saving the Temple's women and children, and sacrificing his own life. Clark has been so influenced by movies and television that he cannot help but imagine his life as a movie which, at the end, offers him a starring heroic opportunity. While this self-sacrificial act is redemptive and demonstrates, on Clark's part, a volition and desire which his great-grandfather abandoned, it can also be read as a misguided young man's mindless attempt to imitate "action movies." Whichever way one views it, *Lilies* ends in massive, violent destruction, and although the final image of the saved children is redemptive, sadness and waste lie in its wake.

As *Lilies* demonstrates, a profound symbiosis exists between America, democracy, and the movies. Not only did America emerge as "the unrivaled center of world filmmaking by 1920,"[11] a fact which holds true to this day, but, as Walter Benjamin and others have argued, cinema, through its mechanical reproduction, its ability to reach the masses, and its distance from traditional and higher forms of art, possessed the potential to become an instrument in the emancipation of the masses.[12] Further, by transferring power from artist to spectator, thereby making the latter a vital participant, cinema generated a democratic and audience-based aesthetic.[13] Consistent with this movement toward democracy and emancipation via the emergence of film, *Lilies* depicts, during the early part of the twentieth century, an America moving toward increased liberation: Paterson workers strike to free themselves from the bondage of mill owners; women struggle for freedom from patriarchal oppression; and clergymen like Clarence free themselves, through the writings of Ingersoll and others, from the enslavement of belief.

Unfortunately, the onslaught of freedom does not necessarily bring what is anticipated. For Clarence, liberation, which also means freedom from God, brings horrific emptiness. For Clark and other members of the Temple, liberation leads to self-absorption and self-destruction. For the movies, which signaled such hope and inspiration during Updike's youth, there is only, during the second half of the century, decline. Downtown movie theaters close, and the grandeur of cinema's large screen, as Essie explains in a fit of stuttering, is reduced to the small box of television: "It seems cheap and ugly . . . It's l-like r-reality, only it's in a box and has commercials" (322). Further, as Updike writes in 1996, the same year he published *Lilies*: "The Hollywood films of today, with their mechanical violence and computer-driven spectacle, seem made, most of them, for adolescent males" (*More*, 651).

Updike is hardly alone in his assessment of cinema's decline. Although Susan Sontag is less interested in popular film than Updike, she, too, has observed the fall of cinema (and cinephelia) during recent decades: "Cinema, once heralded as *the* art of the 20th century, seems now, as the century closes numerically, to be a decadent art."[14] Although both Updike and Sontag write persuasively, one could argue that these two prominent authors may be conflating, however unintentionally, the rise and fall of cinema with the arc of their own lives. What is significant, however, in regard to Updike's work is that the diminution of cinema's large screen to the small box of television mirrors a similar diminution of the country's grandeur. As early as *The Poorhouse Fair*, Updike began hinting at what he perceived to be America's decline, and by the 1990s this theme becomes prominent in novels like *Rabbit at Rest*, *Lilies*, and *Toward the End of Time* (1997). The impulse toward freedom in America leads, it would appear, to the laziness and moral detachment of Clark's generation as well as the fiery demise of the Temple. Although *Lilies* begins with film's early promise as well as its supplanting of religion in American culture, it concludes with television images of a radical and violent brand of religious fundamentalism spinning out of control. *Lilies*, thus, depicts the decline of the two significant institutions which have sustained Updike during his life, the church and the movies, and it offers nothing more in the way of hope than its final words, "The children" (491).

Whether one writes fiction (like Updike), is a screen actor (like Essie), or simply consumes cultural material (like Rabbit), there is a desire in each endeavor or situation to connect to something larger, something more powerful than oneself. By performing before a camera and transmitting her best self to millions, Essie realizes a transcendence in which God moves through her and helps her to shine. Although Rabbit does not experience transcendence by simply turning on his radio or television, he nevertheless connects to something larger than himself – namely, American culture, which through its grandiose scale, promise, and omnipresence, figures as godlike. In giving themselves over to the stories, images, faces, and news reports that they experience through various popular arts and media, Updike's characters experience a sense of connection which is both national and spiritual in nature.

Few writers have made as great an effort as John Updike to capture what it feels like to be an American living in the twentieth century. Through his dedication to portraying the surfaces of daily life, particularly the small domestic moments and events, he brings attention not only to our gestures, dress, manners, observations, moods, and hopes, but also to the ways in which we receive news, hear songs, make purchases, and watch television and movies. As Updike clearly demonstrates, film and popular culture have worked their way into the fabric of our everyday lives, refashioning our conceptions of our ideal selves as well as altering the ways we think, dream, and behave. Although a sense of decline and moral decay often flavors Updike's depiction of America, including his portrayal of the popular arts, the author's keen attention to its surfaces and details, as well as his feeling that this is a "land of promise where yearning never stops short at a particular satisfaction but keeps moving on" (*Lilies*, 333), provide both hope and drama. For the boy from Shillington who attended movies regularly, spent many hours drawing cartoons, and eventually became a distinguished novelist, the popular arts have long been an integral source of inspiration, serving to lift, educate, delight, and engage the author while connecting him to a higher, more heavenly realm.

NOTES

1. Updike has written considerably on cinema, including essays on movies and movie theaters, and reviews of biographies of movie stars. In particular, see the section in *More Matter* titled "Movies" (641–666), which contains the essay "The Old Movie Houses" as well as pieces on Lana Turner, Marilyn Monroe, Gene Kelly, and others. Also, see the section in *Odd Jobs* titled "Media" (31–45), which contains five brief essays dealing with television and film.
2. For further discussion of this early interest in illustration, see Updike's three brief pieces on cartooning (*More*, 787–796) and his 1991 introduction to a volume on Mickey Mouse (*More*, 202–210).
3. Jack De Bellis, *The John Updike Encyclopedia* (Westport, CT: Greenwood, 2000), pp. 501–511, 173–175.

4. James Plath, ed., *Conversations with John Updike* (Jackson: University Press of Mississippi, 1994), p. 40.

5. Jack De Bellis, "'It Captivates . . . It Hypnotizes': Updike Goes to the Movies," *Literature/Film Quarterly* 23 (1995), p. 171.

6. Paula Marantz Cohen, *Silent Film and the Triumph of the American Myth* (Oxford: Oxford University Press, 2001), p. 115.

7. Charles Gibson, "John Updike Interview," *Good Morning America*, WABC, 16 February 1996 (Show #2526), p. 9 (transcript).

8. Ironically, as Updike writes in "The Old Movie Houses," many of the old theaters from his youth, which have closed and been replaced by suburban multiplex theaters, are now being used as churches: "The newer brand of Protestant churches, indeed, are among the few customers for these deserted theatres of dreams, whose spaciousness and elegant details were designed to inculcate a religious mood" (*More*, 641).

9. Jack Ford, "John Updike Interview," *Sunday Today*, WNBC, 25 February 1996, p. 15 (transcript).

10. Stacey Olster, *The Trash Phenomenon: Contemporary Literature, Popular Culture, and the Making of the American Century* (Athens, GA: University of Georgia Press, 2003), p. 206.

11. Cohen, *Silent Film*, p. 5

12. See Walter Benjamin, "The Work of Art in the Age of Mechanical Reproduction" (1936), in Benjamin, *Illuminations*, ed. Hannah Arendt, trans. Harry Zohn (1968; New York: Schocken, 1969), pp. 217–251.

13. Cohen, *Silent Film*, p. 9

14. Susan Sontag, "The Decay of Cinema," *New York Times Magazine*, 25 February 1996, p. 60.

GUIDE TO FURTHER READING

De Bellis, Jack. "'The Awful Power': John Updike's Use of Kubrick's *2001: A Space Odyssey* in *Rabbit Redux*." *Literature/Film Quarterly* 21 (1993), pp. 209–217.

Olster, Stacey. *The Trash Phenomenon: Contemporary Literature, Popular Culture, and the Making of the American Century*. Athens, GA: University of Georgia Press, 2003.

Schiff, James A. *John Updike Revisited*. New York: Twayne, 1998.

Sontag, Susan. "The Decay of Cinema." *New York Times Magazine*, 25 February 1996, pp. 60–61.

Updike, John. "High Art Versus Popular Culture." *Odd Jobs: Essays and Criticism*. New York: Knopf, 1991, pp. 87–88.

10

DONALD J. GREINER

Updike, Rabbit, and the myth of American exceptionalism

He had thought . . . that from shore to shore all America was the same.
– Rabbit, Run (1960)

America is a vast conspiracy to make you happy.
– "How to Love America and Leave It at the Same Time" (1972)

the American way . . .
– "Americana" (2001)

[M]y only duty was to describe reality as it had come to me – to give the mundane its beautiful due.
– Foreword, The Early Stories, 1953–1975 (2003)

When, at the beginning of his career, John Updike published the first, preliminary characterizations of Rabbit Angstrom – the short story "Ace in the Hole" (1955; *Same,* 14–26) and the poem "Ex-Basketball Player" (1957; *Carpentered,* 2–3) – he did not know that he was committing himself to a long meditation on America. The meditation has lasted a lifetime. At its center sit the four novels that trace Rabbit Angstrom's anguished run, but surrounding this core and giving it resonance are the tales and essays in which Updike probes the national character, seeking to define America itself. The definition has changed during the course of his distinguished career. Rather than a straight line toward confirmation of an ideal, it is a receding curve toward questioning of a once-assured certainty.

Updike's United States is predominantly a culture of the middle class, but this does not mean that the "middle" or his sense of America remains static. To the consternation of his negative – usually ideologically committed – critics, he prefers posing problems to preaching answers. Read as a whole, his canon reveals a changing, darkening, increasingly skeptical view of Americanness: the middle is still beautiful, as he once argued in "The Dogwood Tree: A Boyhood" (1962; *Assorted,* 151–187), but the quest for happiness is today more problematical, more tenuous. Like most great authors, he is under no obligation to be consistent in either the perspective toward his subject matter or the technique used to express it. His short stories frame the curve that the Rabbit novels illustrate. To read the tales along with the saga of Rabbit's search is to understand how Updike's view of American exceptionalism becomes less assured as the 1950s fade in the glare of the dying century.

I

Updike's religious faith, albeit intellectually honed by the arcane arguments of Søren Kierkegaard and Karl Barth, informs his understanding of American exceptionalism. Forged by Enlightenment principles, the United States offered the world an astonishingly new model of nationhood in the late eighteenth century: the proposition that citizens are guaranteed certain self-evident, inalienable rights ordained by God, and that, consequently, the purpose of elected government is to protect those rights. Spiritual values and civic duty merge, with the assumption that the people support the government, which in turn ensures the rights. The good and the just become one. Revolutionary in nature, inspiring in concept, this definition of a country is nevertheless particularly difficult to implement when moved from the abstract to the daily. To resist a government elected according to these Enlightenment standards is somehow to reject the God who decreed the inalienable rights the government was formed to guarantee. Rabbit eventually intuits the dilemma but cannot adequately articulate it. Updike, however, dissects the problem in such closely argued though divergent essays as "Faith in Search of Understanding" (1963; about Karl Barth) and "On Not Being a Dove" (1989; about government protests).

In his foreword to *The Early Stories, 1953–1975* (2003), Updike asks, "But when has happiness ever been the subject of fiction?" (xiv). The tension in much of his lifelong investigation of middle America comes from the fact that Rabbit and his counterparts in the stories believe – and believe fervently – in what Thomas Jefferson memorably called Americans' right to "the pursuit of happiness." Unfortunately, however, they mistake the grail for the quest. That is, they misread Jefferson's words to promise happiness rather than the pursuit of it. Thus they are always running toward an ever-receding goal. As Updike notes, "What is possessed is devalued by what is coveted" (*Early*, xiv). When the Reverend Eccles (*Rabbit, Run* [1960]), for example, asks him to clarify what he is searching for, all the inarticulate but deeply feeling Rabbit can reply is, "*it*" (134). Like America, Updike's characters seek recurring confirmation of their innocence. The fragility of happiness that Rabbit suffers is, writes Updike, a "worthy, inevitable" subject (*Early*, xiv).

If, as seems likely, historians in this century will continue to label the previous one hundred years the "American Century," then it is also likely that Updike will be the primary novelist to read for an understanding of the enormous complexity of American society after 1950. Drawn to thesis/antithesis (for example, domesticity/freedom, America/Other) but leery of synthesis, he continues to disturb politically minded readers who insist that he offer solutions to issues he sees as always in conflict, always in tension, always dialectical. The American historical context has shaped his work from the moment he published his first professional story ("Friends from Philadelphia"; *Same*, 3–13) in 1954 to the collapse of the Soviet Union in 1989, and beyond. Born in 1932 and thus a child of the Great Depression and Second World War, he matured during two decades of unremitting national hardship, years when most Americans could readily agree on the identification of a pair of frightening enemies: economic disaster inside the borders, Fascist aggression outside. Updike explains:

My generation, once called Silent, was, in a considerable fraction of its white majority, a fortunate one . . . we included many only children given, by penny-pinching parents, piano lessons and a confining sense of shelter. We acquired in hard times a habit of work and came to adulthood in times when work paid off; we experienced when young the patriotic cohesion of World War II without having to fight the war . . . Yet, though spared many of the material deprivations and religious terrors that had dogged our parents, and awash in a disproportionate share of the world's resources, we continued prey to what Freud called "normal human unhappiness." (*Early*, xiv)

The abiding irony in the second half of the American Century is that total victory in war did not bring sustained calm in peace. Prosperity flourished after 1945, but fear held because, beginning with the Berlin Airlift, the Cold War took sudden shape as the latest in an apparently ceaseless series of national crises. One can only imagine the shiver that adults in the late 1940s and early 1950s must have felt each day despite the economic boom that funded the GI Bill and a move to the suburbs. Many of these adults first endured the Depression and then survived the Second World War, only to face an imposing new threat across the ocean.

Updike lived the shiver. The unusual union of optimism and anxiety that marks his canon reflects what most Americans suffered during the Cold War. His fictionalizing of his small-town roots in the early novels and stories sets the foundation for the ironic tone in his later accounts of adult aspiration and inevitable unhappiness. What Updike calls "a more expansive post-war sense of American reality" is the America that Rabbit yearns for yet cannot find (x). Leaving New York, where he lived for twenty months in the middle 1950s, Updike believed that "[t]he real America seemed to me 'out there,' too homogenous and electrified by now to pose much threat of the provinciality that people used to come to New York to escape. Out there was where I belonged, immersed in the ordinary, which careful explication would reveal to be extraordinary" (x). Thus, unlike, say, Saul Bellow, whose Augie March also personifies America but who is proud of being big-city "Chicago born," or J. D. Salinger, whose Holden Caulfield is on a quest to return to his home in New York, Rabbit looks for the national culture in the American middle. In other words, Updike's American heroes are not Sherwood Anderson's George Willard, itching to escape Winesburg, Ohio, for the alluring lights of the bustling city. Updike's protagonists learn early on what F. Scott Fitzgerald's Nick Carraway understands only at the conclusion of *The Great Gatsby* (1925), that the truth of America is back there, in the mundane middle beyond the metropolis, where the snow is "real" and where the challenge to American exceptionalism is less dramatic.

Three stories, published almost thirty-five years apart, set the context for examination of the Rabbit tetralogy. In "The Witnesses" (1966) – a tale that mentions the Second World War, which his generation was too young to fight – the narrator muses, "[O]ur task had been to bring a society across a chasm and set it down safely on the other side, unchanged. That it changed later was not our affair" (*Museums*, 70). Alluding to a famous Western movie from the 1950s to confirm the readily assumed, stark differences between good and evil that obtained then, Updike describes the fearful first years of the Cold War as "the high noon of the Eisenhower era" – that is, white-hatted America against black-hatted bad guys (71). Yet in "The Witnesses" Updike also laments the gradual release of the tension despite the perils of high noon. External threat enhances cultural cohesiveness, a faith in national unity. The lessening of both anticipates by a half-decade the situation in *Rabbit Redux* (1971), in which Rabbit stumbles through the late 1960s trying, like many another citizen, to make sense of race riots, drugs, and violent protests against an elected government engaged in another war.

Had he been more expressive, more intelligent, Rabbit might have joined the first person narrator of "When Everyone Was Pregnant" (1972), a companion to "The Witnesses" and a pivotal story in Updike's consideration of American exceptionalism. A love song to the 1950s, the tale follows the unspoken thoughts of a man riding in a train – a symbol of passing time – as he regrets the change in America from the early 1950s to the mid-to-late 1960s that "The Witnesses" mentions and that Rabbit lives while scampering from *Rabbit, Run* to *Rabbit Redux*. The narrator contrasts his generation with the youth of "today": "The world's skin of fear shivered but held . . . Young people now are many things but they aren't afraid, and aren't grateful" (*Museums*, 93). He fondly recalls "the years when everyone was pregnant. Not only kind but beautiful years," and traces his nostalgia to the "smug conviction that the world was doomed. Beyond the sparkling horizon, an absolute enemy" (91, 93). The enemy is, of course, the Soviet Union, a non-American Other. Still, for all its horror, the Cold War solidified the concept of America's ordained destiny for the narrator, for Rabbit, and for Updike. Yet it is to Updike's credit that he nudges the narrator to doubt the accuracy of the backward glance. When the narrator poignantly asks, "Did the Fifties exist?," he concedes his uncertainty, his fallibility, his guilt (97). Is he merely nostalgic or strictly accurate? Significantly, he echoes one of Rabbit's final comments in *Redux*: "I feel so guilty" (406). The story ends with a revealing confession: "I am still afraid. Still grateful" (*Museums*, 97). His gratitude is not for "today" but for the America that shaped him.

Twenty-eight years later, Updike added another companion piece to "The Witnesses" when he published "Scenes from the Fifties" (2000). Returning to the defining moment in his canon, the era of *Rabbit, Run*, he nevertheless signals a pointed alteration in his understanding of the United States at mid-century. Rather than lament the absence of gratitude for the country in today's Americans, the narrator recalls not the high noon of the Eisenhower presidency but a nation that now seems exotic: "the breadfruit island of Eisenhower's America" (*Licks*, 152). Still longing for the decade's "kind but beautiful years," he gently mocks the man he thinks he was: "We were full of peacetime's rarefied ambitions and uncurtailed egos" (153). Like the Harry Angstrom of *Rabbit at Rest* (1990), the narrator's confidence in both himself and the American way slips as the Cold War eases. Instead of loudly defending the nation against the nay-sayers, he now unexpectedly remembers the Cold War as a half-century of relative calm, "a blessed interim, a Metternichian remission of the usual savageries" (154). The irony is clear, although only Updike and the narrator – not Rabbit – see it: instead of the monolithic enemy of "When Everyone Was Pregnant," the Soviet Union is today perceived as contributing to the half-century peace. Mutual threats by superpowers enhance the fear but douse the fire.

In 1995, five years after *Rabbit at Rest*, Updike wrote to D. Quentin Miller, "The thing about the Cold War was you ignored it if you could."[1] For Updike and Rabbit, of course, the critical word is "if" – and both know you could not. Thus while the myth of American exceptionalism remains a lure, Updike shows that the thawing of the Cold War had the unforeseen result of hurtling the dreams of cultural harmony in the 1950s into the cynical fragmentation of the 1990s. The decades of this declension are those of the Rabbit tetralogy. Global politics and Updike's art join, with Rabbit both intuiting and illustrating the juncture. Just before his death in *Rabbit at Rest* (1990), Rabbit confesses, "I miss it . . . The cold war. It gave you a reason to get up in the morning" (353). Ever the defender of American rightness, he dresses as Uncle Sam for a Fourth of July parade and proclaims the "truth" of the national myth: "Without the cold war, what's the point of being an American? Still, we held out. We held off the oafs for forty years. History will remember that" (*Rest*, 442–443). History will indeed; but, unlike Harry, Updike knows that identifying the father with Uncle Sam today means that the patriarch, the personification of the American way, is near to toppling on the verge of disaster. America in *Rabbit at Rest* is not the America that Rabbit idealizes.

Rabbit dies as the Cold War concludes, a coincidence that Updike planned, for this patriot and proponent of American power needs the comfort of cultural unity that the Soviet threat once nurtured in order to justify himself to himself. He even links death and Russia: "The thing about the afterlife, it kept this life within bounds somehow, like the Russians" (272). Responding to a critic who in 1968 carelessly charged Updike with ignoring history in his writing, Updike retorted, "Not so . . . My fiction about the daily doings of ordinary people has more history in it than history books."[2] He describes his fiction as illustrating a "yes, but" quality, a tension that sustains the dialectical perspective of the Rabbit novels as they dissect the historical conflict between the longing for exceptionalism and the fading of the dream. Updike's position is clear: "I feel that to be a person is to be in a situation of tension, is to be in a dialectical situation. A truly adjusted person is not a person at all."[3] The same could be said of a nation. Thus the irony of Rabbit's run: as he "rises" from blue-collar status to middle-class suburbs, comically demonstrated in the change from eating peanuts to affording cashews, his certainty in the rightness of the American myth holds firm, but Updike's falters. Updike's refusal to resolve the tension between the character's faith and the author's doubt requires readers to confront the ambiguity. "Yes, but" is always more potent than "yes, no."

II

That the complexity of Harry Angstrom's relationship to his country continues to intrigue Updike is illustrated by four short introductions that he published in special editions of the Rabbit novels. Writing in 1977, for example, an essay for the Franklin Library limited edition of *Rabbit, Run*, he initiated a series of explanations to both his readers and himself. American literary heroes typically reflect the complexity of the culture, a culture that tries to ignore time by venerating not the wisdom of age but the assurance of youth. Deerslayer, Ishmael, Huck, Nick Adams, Augie March, Holden Caulfield – all are young, and all are vital to the nation's sense of itself. America is always refashioning its image in terms of its Enlightenment ideals, and thus it tends to focus on the attraction of the present rather than the weight of the past or the uncertainty of the future. For the 1950s, the time of *Rabbit, Run*, the past is the terror of economic collapse and world war, while the future is fear of the Soviet Union. Creating in Harry Angstrom a quintessential average American as nurtured by the 1950s, Updike linked character to culture when he decided to write *Rabbit, Run* in the present tense: "To emphasize how thoroughly the zigzagging hero lived in the present, it was written in the present tense – a piece of technical daring in 1959" (*Hugging*, 850). Rabbit may be the hero, yet Updike asks a key question that echoes throughout his investigation of the nature of America: "but is he a good man? The question is meant to lead to another – What is goodness?" (850). Moral ambiguity shadows both Rabbit and the country he embraces in *Run*, and Updike knows that, despite seismic changes in the way Americans view America, Rabbit and his country continue to mirror each other: "wild and timid, harmful and loving, hard-hearted and open to the motions of Grace" – in other words, a classic definition of unresolved tension (851). The clash between Eccles's humanistic religion that stresses a social definition of goodness and Kruppenbach's conservative theology that features a Barthian reliance on faith is a critical illustration of the moral dilemma that Updike senses in his native land.

The short stories "Home" (1960) and "My Father on the Verge of Disgrace" (1997) offer a perspective on Rabbit's fate after *Rabbit, Run*. Published in the same year as *Run*, "Home" details how much the United States means to an American returning from abroad. (Having studied at Oxford after graduation from Harvard, Updike based the story on his trip back to the United States.) As Rabbit would surely agree, the narrator finds the Statue of Liberty "genuinely awesome," recalls crying when he watches an American movie in England, and names America "his fatherland" (*Pigeon*, 152). Significantly, then, Updike equates devotion to country and commitment to family: "His father was always so conspicuous. He was so tall that he had been chosen, on the occasion of another return from Europe, to be Uncle Sam and lead their town's Victory Parade in the autumn of 1945" (155). Victory, father, and country merge to become an idealized United States, worthy of the veneration that Rabbit gives it throughout the conflicted moments of the tetralogy.

Almost forty years after "Home," Updike revisited the once-comforting equation of father and Uncle Sam. Titling the story "My Father on the Verge of Disgrace," he indirectly plots the very curve from veneration to uncertainty that troubles Rabbit in the course of his long run through and with America. Updike's second look at the father/Uncle Sam identification is instructive: "it was this sense of his height that led, perhaps, to my fear that he would somehow topple" (*Licks*, 45). The point is not that the country will crumble but that what the narrator calls the "power of righteousness and enforcement" might diminish (45). The merger of righteousness and power defines America's confidence in its Enlightenment uniqueness, a confidence made all the more potent when the tall father calls the narrator "young America" (47). Each generation passes the "truth" of exceptionalism on to the next in what the nation's founders believed would be an ever active cycle of renewal. At the conclusion of the tale, faith in father and fatherland holds, but by merely hinting that it could "topple," Updike suggests a hesitation, a questioning, a doubt – the very doubt that momentarily buffets Rabbit just before he dies and the Cold War ends.

Ten years after *Rabbit Redux*, Updike wrote for the Franklin Library edition of *Redux* (1981) the second of his four introductions, in which he reveals his sense of how far America has toppled from the remembered moment in "When Everyone Was Pregnant." *Redux* describes what he now calls – and what Rabbit miserably lives – "the interminable Sixties" (*Hugging*, 858). A barometer for his culture but shaken by the challenge to what he believes are the nation's inalienable truths, Rabbit witnesses, in Updike's words, "all the oppressive, distressing, overstimulating developments of the most dissentious American decade since the Civil War – anti-war protest, black power and rhetoric, teach-ins, middle-class runaways, drugs, and . . . the moon shot" (858).

Redux tells the tale of an American determined to honor the Enlightenment myth but finding fellow countrymen tarnishing it at every turn. Updike explicitly identifies Rabbit with the United States when he writes of the 1960s, "America and Harry suffered, marvelled, listened, and endured. Not without cost, of course" (858). The cost is the shattering of cohesiveness, the nation's naïve but strongly held faith in its special status. Tracing the separation of the Angstrom family in *Redux* and Harry's failure to create a substitute family with Skeeter and Jill, Updike suggests that disintegration of home inevitably follows break-up of country. The dissolution of the unity that sustained America through the twin tragedies of depression and war shook both author and character. As Updike correctly points out, the question that concludes *Redux* – "O.K.?" (407) – is not meant to have an easy answer. Two passages from *Redux* will illustrate Rabbit's bafflement: "He has gotten loud again; it makes him rigid, the thoughts of the treachery and ingratitude befouling the flag, befouling him"; "America is beyond power, it acts as in a dream, as a face of God . . . Beneath her patient bombers, paradise is possible" (45, 47). This is not Updike speaking but Rabbit, yet the thoughts eerily recall the linking of ordained rights and just country that the Enlightenment founders articulated.

Nearly two decades after *Redux*, Updike published a revelatory personal essay about his reaction to the 1960s. His response to the questionnaire that eventuated in *Authors Take Sides on Vietnam* (1967)[4] is the catalyst for "On Not Being a Dove" (1989). The Rabbit of *Redux* would not understand Updike's sophisticated argument, but he would appreciate his creator's assumption of America's essential good will. A key comment in "Dove" suggests the tension: "A war was going on, and political differences, however shrill, were submerged in our common identity as young Americans doing our bit to defeat Hitler and Mussolini and Hirohito" (*Self-Consciousness*, 118). In other words, America should always be America, be it the 1940s with the Second World War or the 1960s with Vietnam. The requirements of cultural solidarity outweigh the privileges of personal protest. The irony, which Rabbit would not recognize, is that Updike voted for Lyndon Johnson against Barry Goldwater, marched in civil rights demonstrations, and contributed to the NAACP. Yet Rabbit would surely nod when Updike confesses he "thought it sad that our patriotic myth of invincible virtue was crashing, and shocking that so many Americans were gleeful at the crash" (124). By the end of the tetralogy, the myth is not so invincible. Questions engender skepticism, and skepticism challenges myth. As Updike remarks, "As for my patriotic debt to my country, I feel, as I age, less anxious about that" (163). So, alas, does Rabbit. He would rather die than face an America that no longer believes.

For the Franklin Library *Rabbit at Rest* (1990), Updike wrote his third introduction to clarify that in creating Harry Angstrom he was imagining America: "America – its news items, its popular entertainment, its economic emanations – is always a character" (*Odd*, 870–871), adding, "I wanted, in *Rabbit at Rest*," to portray "a specimen American male's evolution" (872). Significantly, then, when he composed the fourth introduction, a retrospective of the entire tetralogy (1995), five years after publication of the final Rabbit novel, he began by emphasizing not the hero but the nation: "The United States, democratic and various though it is, is not an easy country for a fiction-writer to enter: the slot between the fantastic and the drab seems too narrow" (*Tetralogy*, ix). Even more important, he uses the introduction specifically to define Rabbit as *the* character providing a key for the entry: "Harry 'Rabbit' Angstrom was for me a way in – a ticket to the America all around me. What I saw through Rabbit's eyes was more worth telling than what I saw through my own" (ix).

Committed to conveying the bedrock beneath the lovingly described American details, Updike refuses to offer solutions to the cultural problems he depicts – refuses, in short, to preach: "Rather than arrive at a verdict and a directive, I sought to present sides of an unresolvable tension intrinsic to being human" (xiii). The tension is bordered on the one hand by what Pascal calls "the motions of Grace" and on the other hand by "the hardness of the heart," a paradox that defines America. The rending of culture that shattered the United States in the 1960s confused Rabbit and startled Updike. The Rabbit of *Redux* is much less exuberant, much more hesitant, than the Rabbit of *Run*, and the radical diminishment of his confidence directly reflects the sudden astonishment in Updike.

Admitting that civil disobedience was "antithetical" to the way he was reared, Updike recalls that "the rhetoric of social protest and revolt which roiled the Sixties alarmed and, even, disoriented me" (xiv). He was unprepared for what he calls the "savagery" of the attacks on the government, and thus he depicts a bewildered Rabbit trying to hunker down behind the pregnable walls of his house in *Redux* while the Other, personified by Skeeter (race riots) and Jill (drug culture), slips in under the door. The house fire and death that conclude *Redux* signal an American Armageddon, a betrayal of the beliefs that had once made America unique. The point is, of course, that not only Rabbit and Updike but also the idea of the United States itself was overwhelmed. Unlike the 1940s and 1950s, the circumstances of the 1960s countered the promise of the nation, and in Rabbit's and Updike's eyes, at least, the country suffered another fall. Yet character and creator are reluctant to abandon their abstract idealism for trendy naysaying. Generally tolerant, usually adaptable, "America survives its chronic apocalypses" (xvii).

No wonder that despite Rabbit's thwarted longing, *Rabbit Is Rich* (1981) is the happiest of the four novels. Even he himself brags, "So who says he's running out of gas?" (*Rich*, 55). True to the equation of family and nation in the tetralogy, Updike confirms the return to relative normalcy when he details the reintegration of the Angstrom nuclear family and the birth of a granddaughter. Rebounding from the contentious 1960s, the United States in the 1970s faces a crisis of no more magnitude than a prolonged fuel shortage. A more cynical author might seize the moment to pontificate about how America is winding down, but Updike is no cynic. His curiosity is too insistent, his joy in quotidian details too intense for him to abandon the pursuit of happiness. The key difference, the notable shift in his perspective, is that the curve of his canon reveals increased questioning of the American ideal. Rabbit may be middle-aged and happy for the moment – he describes his life in *Rich* as "sweet" (6) – but Updike's bemused touch is clear: being able to play golf instead of basketball is a long, disheartening way from the fulfillment of Jefferson's resounding words. The city on a hill that the Puritans envisioned becomes a home in the suburbs that encloses a rabbit. Updike can only laud the potential and lament the decline.

Rabbit senses the diminishment. Rather than a shining light, he and the country have settled for material comfort. He muses, "He sees his life as just beginning, on clear ground at last, now that he has a margin of resources, and the stifled terror that always made him restless has dulled down. He wants less. Freedom, that he always thought was outward motion, turns out to be this inner dwindling" (97). Dwindling presages death. The reader is not surprised, then, that Rabbit holds on to the moral certainty that has conditioned America's understanding of its righteous action since the founding: "Laugh at ministers all you want, they have the words we need to hear, the ones the dead have spoken" (243).

Not until *Rabbit at Rest*, however, does Updike push Rabbit toward death. Overweight, undermotivated, and mortal, the 56-year-old Rabbit remains inextricably bound to an America that relies on goodness laced with might to confirm its special destiny. By 1989, the time of *Rest*, Rabbit is back on the road, restlessly moving from Pennsylvania to Florida, just as he once sought to drive to the sunny South in *Run*. In the first of the Rabbit novels, he has no place to go and nowhere to hide, and thus he turns back momentarily to renew his dingy life with Janice. In the final novel, he gets as far as the Sunshine State, only to find the paradise he seeks populated with retirees like himself, drifting toward the end. Yet America's historical faith in its ability to renew itself, to promise rebirth, to jettison the mistakes of the past no longer applies to Rabbit. In *Rabbit at Rest*, Harry may save a female child from drowning as he cannot do in *Rabbit, Run*, but when Updike shrewdly sends him back to the basketball court, the reader knows that the heart-impaired American hero will never succeed in duplicating the dazzling dash toward graceful motion that he demonstrates in the very first pages of the tetralogy. In *Rabbit, Run*, Harry wants to tell the kids playing sandlot basketball that there is nothing to growing old. In *Rabbit at Rest* the age of both his heart and his mid-century understanding of America brings him down.

Rabbit cannot express the complexity in such terms, but he can feel that a redefined America signals a displaced self. As Updike writes in the introduction to the tetralogy: "[H]e senses the coming collapse of the Soviet Union and its empire, whose opposition to the free world has shadowed and shaped his entire adult life. Freedom has had its hazards for him, and capitalist enterprise its surfeit, but he was ever the loyal citizen. God he can doubt, but not America" (*Tetralogy*, xxi). The conclusion of the Cold War means the end of both Rabbit and the nation as he knew it, a nation forever united in confronting belligerent, threatening aggressors. He dies with the word "enough" on his lips. Still, America is always falling from grace but always reinventing itself in the image of its Enlightenment foundation. Updike regrets the change but recalls the promise: "We forget most of our past but embody all of it" (xxiii).

A decade after Rabbit's death, the Angstrom family revisits his reluctance to abandon allegiance to a duly elected government. Passed from generation to generation, in much the same way that the father figure always remains Uncle Sam despite verging on disgrace, the equation of government with goodness lingers in *Rabbit Remembered* (2000). Note the reaction of Rabbit's adult son: "Nelson's father within him winces when anyone threatens to disparage Clinton or any sitting President" (*Licks*, 323). And yet, Rabbit's survivors intuit that their patriarch – a perplexed but earnest Uncle Sam – felt less and less threatened by the disparagers as the Cold War ended. Anything Other, anything non-American, remained puzzling to him except, ironically, the Japanese cars he sold for a living. Despite the inevitable interconnectedness of the so-called global community, Harry would have rejected an invitation to join. His son concedes that the little details of the *American* moment confirmed his father's faith: "His father had been a rebel of a sort, and a daredevil, but as he got older and tame he radiated happiness at just the simplest American things, driving along in an automobile, the radio giving off music" (252). Not a ringing endorsement of exceptionalism exactly, but a welcome calm filtered through a diminished sense of inalienable rights.

Rabbit is now part of the honor roll of American literary heroes, characters who reflect the culture. The differences between, say, Natty Bumppo's purity and Harry Angstrom's paradoxes are immense, but both embody the dreams of the society of their time. The honor roll calls the names of the American identity – Natty, Hester, Uncle Tom, Ahab and Ishmael, Huck and Jim, Maggie Verver, Antonia, Jake Barnes, Gatsby, Tom Joad, Ike McCaslin, Holden Caulfield, Invisible Man, Augie March, Dean Moriarty, Yossarian, Rabbit. The list goes on. Yet the list also confirms the changing nature of the country's sense of its own individuality, its own greatness, its own destiny.

All through the Rabbit saga, Updike's subject is the puzzle of America. It always was.

NOTES

1. D. Quentin Miller, *John Updike and the Cold War: Drawing the Iron Curtain* (Columbia: University of Missouri Press, 2001), p. 52.
2. Charles Thomas Samuels, "The Art of Fiction XLIII: John Updike," *Paris Review* 45 (1968), pp. 105–106.
3. Ibid., pp. 100, 101.

4. See Cecil Woolf and John Bagguley, eds., *Authors Take Sides on Vietnam: Two Questions on the War in Vietnam Answered by the Authors of Several Nations* (London: Peter Owen, 1967), pp. 50–51.

GUIDE TO FURTHER READING

Boswell, Marshall. *John Updike's Rabbit Tetralogy: Mastered Irony in Motion.* Columbia: University of Missouri Press, 2001.

Broer, Lawrence R., ed. *Rabbit Tales: Poetry and Politics in John Updike's Rabbit Novels.* Tuscaloosa: University of Alabama Press, 1998.

Greiner, Donald J. *John Updike's Novels.* Athens, OH: Ohio University Press, 1984.

"No Place to Run: Rabbit Angstrom as Adamic Hero." *Rabbit Tales: Poetry and Politics in John Updike's Rabbit Novels.* Ed. Lawrence R. Broer. Tuscaloosa: University of Alabama Press, 1998, pp. 8–16.

"The World as Host: John Updike and the Cultural Affirmation of Faith." *John Updike and Religion: The Sense of the Sacred and the Motions of Grace.* Ed. James Yerkes. Grand Rapids, MI: Eerdmans, 1999, pp. 257–266.

Schiff, James A. *John Updike Revisited.* New York: Twayne, 1998, pp. 28–65.

Yerkes, James, ed. *John Updike and Religion: The Sense of the Sacred and the Motions of Grace.* Grand Rapids, MI: Eerdmans, 1999.

CONCLUSION: U(PDIKE) & P(OSTMODERNISM)

JOHN N. DUVALL

A mall had sprung up between Nashua and Pierce Junction, on the site of a dairy farm whose silver-tipped silos I still expected to see gleaming at that particular turn of the highway. Instead, there was this explosively fragmented glitter – chain stores in postmodern glass skins, and a vast asphalt meadow paved with cars.

– John Updike, *Licks of Love* (2000)

ENGLISH CRITIC, TEACHER DEAD / IN WEST SIDE SUBWAY MISHAP, the headline read . . . *according to witnesses appeared to fling himself under the subway train as it approached the platform . . . colleagues at CUNY puzzled but agreed he had been under significant stress compiling permissions for his textbook of postmodern narrative strategies . . .*

– John Updike, *Bech at Bay* (1998)

My title doubtless will strike many readers as odd, since criticism on John Updike almost never mentions postmodernism. His fiction is most often identified as realist; occasionally, as modernist. And yet as the two epigraphs I begin with reveal, Updike is not unaware of the cultural phenomenon of postmodernism. Updike's relation to postmodernism, however, goes well beyond such passing references. In fact, much of Updike's fiction since *A Month of Sundays* (1975) reveals a novelist who, if not exactly a postmodernist, has read a number of key poststructuralist texts that inform postmodern poetics and has experimented with postmodern narrative strategies as he chronicles contemporary America. Updike has written novels in the past three decades that intertextually play with the aesthetic past, that are often highly metafictional, and that draw on genres ranging from magic realism (*Brazil* [1994]) to science fiction (*Toward the End of Time* [1997]). What one finds is a reflexive relation between U & P, one in which postmodern theory and poetics problematize Updike's status as latter-day realist, while Updike's deployment of postmodern narrative strategies poses a challenge to certain definitions of postmodernism. And although like his alter ego, the Jewish novelist Henry Bech, Updike comes to bury postmodernism, not to praise it, postmodern theory often provides an illuminating purchase from which to read Updike's fiction. After all, by knowingly poking fun at postmodern theory, Updike implicitly invites readers to speculate on what such theory might have to say about his own work.

Postmodernism and postmodernity

If modernism represents the arts' critical response to the alienation of modernization, the relation of postmodernism to postmodernity is more contested. The first problem of postmodernism resides in the variety of dates that have been suggested as its beginning. For some, postmodernism begins with the advent of the nuclear age in 1945. The Marxist critic Fredric Jameson, while finally settling on the Arab oil embargo of 1973 as the economic advent of postmodernism, sees the beginning of postmodernism in the canonization of modernist literature in anthologies and modernist art in museums during the late 1950s and early 1960s. Whatever radical formal or political urges such art may have had are contained by such institutional contexts. Pop Art for Jameson initially represents a hopeful moment of critique but one that too quickly points to what he identifies as the central problem of postmodernism, the commodification of aesthetics, best illustrated by the phenomenon of Andy Warhol's reproducible art.[1] In April 2004 Campbell's announced a limited edition of its tomato soup. This special edition replaced the traditional red and white label (the target of Warhol's Pop treatment forty years earlier) with a number of alternative labels featuring Warholesque defamiliarizing colors, such as yellows, greens, and pinks. Pop ultimately, according to Jameson, only points to the way that in contemporary America there is no distance between postmodernity and postmodernism; that is, there is no art that can effectively critique the conditions of postmodernity because all aesthetic production is finally absorbed by commodity production.

The French sociologist Jean Baudrillard, on whom Jameson frequently draws in characterizing postmodernism, has written of the fundamental mutation of lived experience in first-world culture brought about by the proliferation of the electronic media and consumer society.[2] To a degree, one could say that, like Jameson and Baudrillard, Updike has always been critical of American cultural postmodernism. In *Rabbit, Run* (1960), for example, Rabbit Angstrom's immersion in the voices of his car radio or his absorption of television's "lessons" on ethics and salesmanship as imaged forth by the Mickey Mouse Club are instances of Updike's awareness of the power of the electronic media both to turn everything into a schizophrenic space of celebrity (in which there is really no difference between Connie

Francis and the Dali Lama) and to model and shape human behavior. In short, Updike's depiction of contemporary America has never been far from what Baudrillard terms hyperreality.[3]

Turning from cultural to aesthetic postmodernism provides a different purchase for understanding the relationship between U & P. In his essay "The Literature of Exhaustion" (1967), the metafictional novelist John Barth speaks of the "felt ultimacy" of modernist aesthetics and distinguishes between the "technically old-fashioned artist" and the technically "up-to-date artist." Barth's disdain for "those novelists who for better or worse write not as if the twentieth century didn't exist, but as if the great writers of the last sixty years or so hadn't existed" seems directed at writers such as the early Updike, whose realism seemed to overlook modernism.[4] Barth marks 1961 as a key year in which Samuel Beckett and Jorge Louis Borges shared the International Publishers' Prize. Beckett in his late fiction represents for Barth the "used-upness" of the modernist thematic of alienation. Beckett takes modernism to its limit, so far as to make it seem untranscendable – until Borges turns to metafiction, fiction that calls attention to its production and status as fiction. As Barth clarifies in "The Literature of Replenishment" (1980), what was exhausted was not literature but modernism, and through metafiction the novel finds new life.[5] While Barth's position now seems overstated (many contemporary novels are published that are not metafictional), his claim does provide an interesting point of departure for exploring Updike's more recent fictional production.

Updike as metafictionist

One can begin to understand Updike's engagement with postmodern narrative theory by turning to *A Month of Sundays*, the first of three novels that feature a directed intertextual relationship with Nathaniel Hawthorne's *The Scarlet Letter* (1850). Updike's use of the aesthetic past is hardly the same as the modernists' use of what T. S. Eliot termed "mythological method." Joyce's use of Homer's *Odyssey* to structure *Ulysses* (1922) or Faulkner's structuring *Light in August* (1932) on the Gospel of John allowed these authors to measure the disruptions of modernity against an imagined stability of a mythic past. Updike participates in a much more ludic use of the aesthetic past. Reverend Thomas Marshfield may figure the position of Hawthorne's Reverend Arthur Dimmesdale, but Updike's fallen minister, rather than wallowing in guilt and self-recrimination, becomes an advocate for the "sacrament" of adultery. When forced to spend a month at a desert retreat for disgraced clergy, his goal becomes in part the seduction of the woman who runs the facility, Ms. Prynne.

While some work has been done on Updike and Barth, the Barth in question always refers to one of Updike's favorite theologians, Karl Barth. But in *A Month of Sundays* when Reverend Thomas Marshfield's father-in-law-to-be, Augustus Chillingworth, asks, "What is it . . . that you find so heartening in Barth?" (55), readers might be forgiven if they think John rather than Karl. The reason is that much of the pleasure of the text resides in its metafictionality. What one ostensibly reads are the thirty-one entries that constitute the journal Marshfield wrote during his month-long therapeutic regimen at the recovery center. Marshfield insistently calls attention to his production of the written word. The journal reveals a Marshfield who seeks control and mastery: in the story it is mastery over his curate, Ned Bork, whom Marshfield assumes to be a latent homosexual; and in the discourse, over the troubling and elusive figure of the reader. Marshfield objects to Bork because of the curate's "limp-wristed" theology (*Month*, 13), Marshfield's way of naming a theology of good works. In the story, though, Bork wins the day. As a result of his multiple adulteries, Marshfield will never be allowed to return to his New England congregation.

Since mastery is not possible in history, writing offers a different field for asserting mastery, this time over the reader. Marshfield's problem as a writer, however, is that he has no tangible proof that there is a reader for his confessions. The writing is apparently an end unto itself, since no therapist reads his daily word production. So Marshfield is forced to construct the figure of the Ideal Reader. Eventually, Marshfield finds a way to complete the reader-writer circuit by imaging his ideal reader as Ms. Prynne, the proprietor of the institution, a relationship he increasingly eroticizes. But before this "discovery," one flesh-and-blood reader already exists – Marshfield himself, because he meticulously reads over what he has written and often provides a metacommentary on his text. Traces of Marshfield's reading appear as his text's footnotes, which interpret his typos before another reader might be tempted to interrogate his Freudian slips. Marshfield's urge to control the reader's response recalls that of another amateur novelist, Todd Andrews in John Barth's *The Floating Opera* (1956), who similarly anticipates moments when the reader might be tempted to interpret such "innocent" things as the meaning of his name.

Marshfield increasingly attempts to shape how his text might be read. Speaking about his conversation with his wife, Jane, after his mistress, Alicia, has told Jane of the affair, Marshfield writes, "not only was I fascinating to her [Jane], as I spilled out the details and near-misses on the other side of the looking glass,* but she to me." At the bottom of the page, the asterisk expands the moment: "*FYI: I swear, Alicia's name is real, not contrived to fit Wonderland. And the last 'm' wanted to be a 'k.' 'Near-Mrs.' occurs to me as a homonym of Alicia's plight" (97). Not content merely to read his actual typos, Marshfield begins to identify gaffes that he has not actually made, essentially performing the kind of playful, postmodern reading that denies authority to the text, turning "near-misses" to "near-kisses" and drawing out the homonym.

Marshfield's hyperclose reading of his own text, I believe, points to Updike's reading of poststructuralist literary theory. In the 1970s Updike reviewed several translations of the work of Roland Barthes. Updike's review of *S/Z* (1970) and *The Pleasure of the Text* (1973) appeared in the 24 November 1975 issue of the *New Yorker*, at a time when reviews of *A Month of Sundays* were appearing. Resonances between Updike's novel and Barthes's *The Pleasure of the Text* are uncanny; indeed, it often seems as though Updike were writing a fictionalized meditation on Barthes. Barthes's short book speaks in erotic metaphors of the relationship between writer and reader. In one of Barthes's early aphorisms, he asserts, "Does writing in pleasure guarantee – guarantee me, the writer – my reader's pleasure? Not at all. I musk seek out this reader (must 'cruise' him) *without knowing where he is*. A site of bliss is then created. It is not the reader's 'person' that is necessary to me, it is this site: the possibility of a dialectics of desire, of an unpredictability of bliss . . ."[6] The text, wherein the collective processes of reading and writing merge, is always a space of desire. Neither reader nor writer is *in* the text; rather, they are fictive constructs necessarily made by particular writers and readers, and whether one's readerly texts of pleasure occasion the writerly moment of bliss, one thing is certain – the writer is always inescapably a reader.

In *A Month of Sundays* Marshfield literalizes what for Barthes is metaphoric. Over the course of the novel, Marshfield apparently comes to believe that Ms. Prynne is the embodied reader of his text and seeks to "cruise" or seduce her. And, if one takes the ending literally, his successful seduction of Ms. Prynne ironically undercuts the salutary effects of the progress he exhibits in the four sermons he writes each Sunday of his confinement, which move from heresy to an apparent return to doctrine. But as critics have pointed out, the honorific "Ms." is also the abbreviation for manuscript.[7] If we look separately at her honorific and patronymic, we are pointed to two intertextual possibilities – Barthes's textuality and Hawthorne's character; although, if we consider her full designation (Ms. Prynne), her name suggests the "mis-print," those textual aporias that become the very sites where Marshfield's own doubled status as reader and writer meet.

Throughout the novel Marshfield's textual production is linked to sexual pleasure. If the erotic novel is sometimes referred to as "one-handed literature," Marshfield's journal reports directly on such masturbatory moments that temporarily halt his textual production. All these "handy" moments speak to the ending of Chapter 27, which seems to provide proof of Ms. Prynne's corporeal existence. At the conclusion of Marshfield's last sermon, the following words appear: "[*in pencil, in the slant hand of another:*] Yes – at last, a sermon that could be preached" (212). But because Marshfield's journal is typed, *any* holographic editorial mark on the manuscript would be the "hand of another," which serves as a curious instantiation of Derrida's famous claim that "*[t]here is nothing outside of the text.*"[8]

If the story Marshfield tells of his adulterous heterosexual exploits also recounts his theological struggles with (and subliminal attraction to) the curate whom he assumes to be at least a latent homosexual, in his discursive presentation of himself Marshfield provides ample evidence that he is at least bitextual. To write his sermons, for example, Marshfield turns his texts of readerly pleasure into the stuff of writerly bliss. His reading of scripture cannot be separated from (indeed is already a form of) his writing his sermons. Updike claims in his *New Yorker* review that "Barthes's critical approach seems specifically manly – insisting on readerly activity rather than passivity" (*Hugging*, 580).

Associating masculinity with activity and femininity with passivity is one of the oldest conventions in both Western and Eastern thought, although it takes on an ironic cast when the novelist who has drawn so many homophobic male characters locates "manly" reading in a homosexual critic. But while, taken literally, the novel may conclude with the active male writer repeatedly penetrating his Ideal (female) Reader, the telling of the story works in the opposite direction by problematizing any urge to prioritize the writer (or the masculine) over the reader (or the feminine).

Updike as historiographic metafictionist

If *A Month of Sundays* represents Updike's foray into postmodern metafiction, *Memories of the Ford Administration* (1992) takes another step that enables us to see his fiction as an important site to refine debates about postmodernism. The Canadian theorist of postmodernism Linda Hutcheon takes exception with Fredric Jameson's pessimistic view of the possibilities for a critical postmodernism. If Jameson sees a degraded historicism in the present caused by the ubiquity of consumer culture, Hutcheon posits instead a critical role for postmodern fiction, which she identifies as historiographic metafiction. Blending the reflexivity of metafiction with an ironized sense of history, historiographic metafiction draws one's attention to the problematic status of historical representation. Speaking of two novels that reimagine the Rosenberg executions, Robert Coover's *The Public Burning* (1977) and E. L. Doctorow's *The Book of Daniel* (1971), Hutcheon argues that "they juxtapose what we think we know of the past (from official archival sources and personal memory) with an alternate representation that foregrounds the postmodern epistemological questioning of the nature of historical knowledge."[9] Unlike Jameson's sense of the cooptation of all aesthetic forms, Hutcheon's historiographic metafiction remains a vehicle for parodic cultural critique, albeit a paradoxical one inasmuch as it "depends upon and draws its power from that which it contests."[10]

Working from a variety of Marxist and post-Marxist theoretical contexts, Hutcheon is able to expand the discussion of postmodern narrative, which formerly had been limited to a small set of white male writers, to include a large number of feminist, minority, and postcolonial novelists. Not surprisingly, Hutcheon's politics of postmodernism, as reflected by such historiographic metafictionists as Toni Morrison, Salmon Rushdie, Angela Carter, Ishmael Reed, and Maxine Hong Kingston, are well left of center, as if these novelists' historiographic relation to their materials ensured leftist politics.

Where does that leave *Memories of the Ford Administration*? This novel playfully blurs the boundary between history and fiction through the narration of Alfred Clayton, a history professor at a third-tier liberal arts college. Asked by a minor journal, *Retrospect*, for his brief impressions of the Ford administration for a forthcoming special issue, Clayton submits a book-length manuscript, full of bracketed asides to the journal editors commenting on what they might wish to trim. The manuscript, which he claims is what he remembers of the Ford administration, mixes an account of his extramarital affairs with a never-completed book on President James Buchanan that he had been writing during that time. Updike's fictional premise seems to make his novel a paradigmatic instance of historiographic metafiction. According to Hutcheon's poetics of postmodernism, *Memories of the Ford Administration* could only be historiographic metafiction. But according to Hutcheon's politics of postmodernism, Updike's novel could never be mistaken for historiographic metafiction because his politics are too conservative for Hutcheon's category. Rather than using historiographic metafiction to dedoxify the order of things, Updike wishes to lead his readers to a different orthodoxy involving his version of Christianity.

Over and above this challenge to Hutcheon's definition of postmodern narrative, *Memories of the Ford Administration* illustrates Updike's continuing engagement with poststructuralist theory. If *A Month of Sundays* serves as Updike's intertextual play with Barthes, *Memories of the Ford Administration* directly parodies deconstruction. In the story Alf tells of his past, the partner in his adultery, Genevieve, is the wife of the new deconstructionist, Brent Mueller, hired by the English Department. Alf despises Brent for both his disrespect for canonical literature and his popularity with students, who then ape his theoretical interests. What Alf does not register is the extent to which he, too, becomes one of Brent's students. His research on Buchanan going nowhere, he is seduced by Brent's claim that "there is no Platonically ideal history apart from texts, and texts are inevitably indefinite, self-contradictory, and doomed to final aporia" (*Memories*, 35). Alf begins to see his self-interest in such a perspective, recalling that he began "to overcome [his] mistaken reverence for the knowable actual versus supposition or fiction, [his] illusory distinction between fact and fancy" (35). From this new perspective, Alf is able to produce more pages.

If Alf's manuscript reveals the pretense of Brent's deconstruction, Updike's construction of his authority to represent deconstruction is similarly doubled in the novel's epigraphs from Rousseau and Heidegger, two authors Derrida famously deconstructs in *Of Grammatology* (1967). The Heidegger quotation is footnoted, an academic touch suggesting that we may already be in Alf's manuscript; the footnote points out that Gayatri Chakravorty Spivak's translation coincides, "but not everywhere," with that of another published translation of Heidegger. The authorizing gesture is twofold, claiming simultaneously that "I not only have read Derrida but also am familiar with the philosophical texts he deconstructs" and "I know when Derrida's translator has taken shortcuts in her work." This academic context introduced at the outset is completed by the "Brief Bibliography" that follows Alf's manuscript.

Alf's narrative reveals Brent to be a poseur, someone for whom deconstruction was merely a means of career enhancement. When threatened by the prospect of Genevieve's leaving him, Brent will go to almost any extreme to save his bourgeois marriage and family. The flaming deconstructionist turns out to be closet traditionalist. But what of the conservative Alf? The novel concludes with Alf's memory of a ski trip some fifteen years earlier during which his wife, along with some colleagues and their spouses (two of whom were his mistresses), witnesses Alf display a moment of masterful skiing. But when he tries to fix the date of this memory, he cannot, which leads to a series of questions about his memory's specificity that ultimately casts doubt on whether any such event ever happened:

> But what mountain could it have been? Gunstock and Sunapee don't have outdoor tables, and Cranmore and Wildcat don't have run-out slopes the way I remember this one. Could it have been Pleasant Mountain, across the state line in Bridgton, Maine? How could Norma and Genevieve, rivals

for my hand, have been there both at once, beaming at me from above the Chardinesque tumble of welcoming food? Perhaps my vivid mental picture derives from the winter before our *crise* began. Or perhaps we had all patched things up for appearances' sake, for this holiday outing, one big falsely happy family. (369)

Memory, the conclusion seems to assert (as have so many other postmodern novelists and theorists), cannot ground personal identity and is, much like Brent's characterization of deconstruction, "inevitably indefinite, self-contradictory, and doomed to final aporia." To the extent that the only self available is a textual construct, Alf becomes an ungrounded character, one left finally in the realm of *écriture* that he mocks in this text. While his deconstructionist rival wins back Genevieve and goes on to a career at Yale, Alf fails to complete his Buchanan book and returns to his family. He becomes the embodiment of deconstructed subjectivity, stuck in the present in a career and marriage with a nearly complete absence of affect and possessed of a fully delusional relationship to the publishability of the manuscript he submits to *Retrospect*.

Updike and feminism: pastiche and self-parody

More recently, in *Gertrude and Claudius* (2000) and *Seek My Face* (2002), Updike has written novels that can be taken as further problematizing instances of historiographic metafiction. Both novels are remarkable for an almost self-parodying revision of one of Updike's most significant paradigms – the married man who tries to stabilize his masculine identity through adultery. With some of the novelist's most complexly developed women characters, these two recent novels almost seem to respond to that strain of Updike criticism that identifies the author as a misogynist.

Gertrude and Claudius explores the back story to Shakespeare's *Hamlet*. Secondary figures to Hamlet's introspective attempt to avenge his father's death, King Hamlet, his wife Gertrude, and his brother Claudius come to the foreground as Updike imagines the conditions that lead to adultery and murder. The metafictionality of the novel resides in its playing with the most canonical text of Western literature's most canonical author, and its historiography comes from its self-conscious blurring of the boundaries between the historical and the literary figures of the Hamlet saga. The foreword promises something like scholarly rigor, explaining that the names in each of the novel's three sections change to reflect borrowings from different versions of the Hamlet story, including such source texts as Saxo Grammaticus's twelfth-century *Historia Danica* and François de Belleforest's *Histoires tragiques* of 1576.

Despite this promise, and while the novel does offer some superficial verisimilitude of setting, it falls prey to a charge of presentism, a kind of anachronistic imposition of contemporary psychology on the characters. For Jameson, such presentism typifies the degraded historicism of postmodernism in which intertextuality serves "as a deliberate, built-in feature of the aesthetic effect and as the operator of a new connotation of 'pastness,'" a situation "in which we are condemned to seek History by way of our own pop images and simulacra of that history, which itself remains forever out of reach."[11] Laura Elena Savu is undoubtedly correct in claiming that Updike reimagines Gertrude "as a desiring subject," a move that reveals some of the "patriarchal assumptions behind Shakespeare's delineation of female characters in *Hamlet*."[12] But in doing so, Updike has to imagine a female subjectivity unlike any available in the twelfth century. From the outset Updike's Gertrude has a feminist perspective on the patriarchal social order of kingship and warriors. Updike is hardly the first author to time-travel in such a fashion, and given his interest in *The Scarlet Letter*, one wonders if he did not learn this lesson from Hawthorne, who takes a Transcendentalist feminist of mid-nineteenth-century New England and transports her in the figure of Hester Prynne to the Puritan past of the 1640s.

But despite the historiographic expectations engendered by the foreword, Updike's purpose in *Gertrude and Claudius* is not to rewrite history but to rewrite literary history, and this is actually aided by the playful textual anachronisms; not satisfied to borrow only images and lines from *Hamlet*, Updike alludes to the history of *Hamlet* criticism. (At one point Claudius even advances the psychoanalytic reading of the play, explaining to his new wife that Hamlet "blames himself, I believe, for his father's death . . . He feels he willed it, in desiring you" [*Gertrude*, 199].) By writing the prequel to *Hamlet*, Updike is also writing an interpretation of Shakespeare's play. This is made clear in the afterword: "Putting aside the murder being covered up, Claudius seems a capable king, Gertrude a novel queen, Ophelia a treasure of sweetness, Polonius a tedious but not evil counsellor, Laertes a generic young man. Hamlet pulls them all into death" (212). As Stephen Greenblatt argues, Updike deflects us from Hamlet's nauseated, disgusted view of the flesh to reveal "a carnality that heals, not imprisons, the soul" in the sexual passion of Gertrude and Claudius.[13]

Updike's story makes this passion visible from the outset. Seventeen-year-old Gerutha/Gertrude is attracted to Feng/Claudius but her father, King Rorik, has selected Claudius's older brother, Horwendil/Hamlet, to be her husband. Updike renders the difference between the brothers by their very different courtships of Gertrude and the gifts they present to her. Hamlet's is open and public, and involves the offering of two pied linnets; oblivious to the irony of his gift, the unsubtle warrior clearly does not know why the caged birds sing. Claudius's is secretive and symbolic; after roving the world in the service of various princes, he returns at age forty-seven and invites the 35-year-old Gertrude to his estate, ostensibly to share with her his passion for falconry, a sport that uses only female birds. In their coded conversations about the way the falcons' eyes are sewn during training and the relation of the falconer to the falcon, the two speak to one another of the constraints in which they find themselves. Aware that his passion may lead to transgression, Claudius leaves Denmark again but has his servant take the falcon Bathsheba to the queen as a parting gift.

Claudius absents himself for another twelve years before returning to the Danish court. The Gertrude he finds, even at forty-seven, is still as desirable as ever. Updike clearly constructs his readers' sympathies for the adulterous couple, who consummate a passion they have repressed for thirty years. Clearly a sexual awakening for Gertrude, it is also figured as a spiritual renewal. Claudius may be her redeemer, but the affair also grants her a newfound sexual pleasure from old Hamlet, the husband who had fallen asleep on their wedding night before the marriage was consummated. It is her ability to act duplicitously toward both men that is the final mark of her renewal: "she felt the thrill of deception between her legs, where two men contended, one the world's anointed and the other her own anointed" (131). Only when old Hamlet discovers the adultery and tells Claudius that he will be banished and the queen shamed does Claudius commit the murder that leads to his kingship.

Despite Updike's ability to imagine the sexually desiring woman in Gertrude, such characterization in and of itself does not overthrow patriarchal social organization. From beginning to end, Gertrude remains subject to the will of father/husband/king. Each of the novel's three parts begins with the same line: "The king was irate" (3, 79, 163). To be sure, it is a different king each time – first Rorik, her father; then her first husband, Hamlet; and finally her second husband, Claudius – but in each instance the king's anger is occasioned by a perceived failing of Gertrude's performance of her role as daughter, wife, or mother. Even her romantic lover Claudius succumbs to the public role of kingship and, once crowned, is scarcely distinguishable from old Hamlet, not simply in the performance of this public role but more significantly in his relationship to his wife. As the novel's title makes clear, the focus is on both Gertrude and Claudius, and the novel's concluding pages are entirely from the angle of vision of Claudius, who now views his wife as an appropriate ornament to his kingly state. While *Gertrude and Claudius* is a tour de force performance, one that works simultaneously as a novel and as a piece of literary criticism, one must turn to *Seek My Face* to find Updike's fullest exploration of female subjectivity.

Seek My Face directly thematizes the turn from late modernism to postmodernism in the post-Second World War American art scene in ways that resonate with John Barth's discussion of poetics in "The Literature of Exhaustion" and the "The Literature of Replenishment." The novel allows this portrait of the turn from Abstract Expressionism to Pop Art to emerge through an interview that the aging painter Hope Chafetz grants to the young aspiring art critic Kathryn D'Angelo. Taking place in Hope's Vermont home and studio, the day-long interview ranges over the artist's personal and professional life. Despite the recognition her art has earned late in life, what makes Hope a particularly significant figure is her first two marriages to artists, both of whom confront the "felt ultimacy" of the end of representational art. Her first husband was Zack McCoy, whose drip paintings represent the zenith of Abstract Expressionism; her second, Guy Holloway, whose embrace of commercialism and cool epitomized Pop Art.

Updike's novel, then, is a kind of *roman à clef*: Zack is based largely on Jackson Pollock, while Guy is an amalgam – although primarily based on Andy Warhol and his art, Guy is also credited with work done by Jasper Johns, Roy Lichtenstein, and Claes Oldenburg. (McCoy/Pollock and Holloway/Warhol, then, serve as the painterly analogs to Barth's sense of the difference between Beckett and Borges that I discussed earlier.) Updike's use of history again blends fact and fiction in the fashion of historiographic metafiction. The novel's metafictionality lies in the fact that we are reading a novel, the explicit matter of which is the production of art. This leads to a self-reflexivity in the discourse, as when Kathryn complains about the pointlessness of some of Guy's films. Hope explains that "there isn't a story because there *shouldn't* be a story, because there aren't any stories any more, just as painting . . . had to give up anecdote . . . A story presupposes an author, moving the characters about from above, moving *us* about from above, to some morally intelligible end, and who believed that any more, after the Holocaust, after the A-bomb –" (*Seek*, 216). Hope's defense of the absence of stories, which seems to gesture simultaneously to Lyotard's sense of the end of master narratives and Adorno's concern about the possibility of making art after the Holocaust, of course, takes place in a narrative that still firmly believes in story.

The version of story that *Seek My Face* still believes in leads us again to pastiche, although not Jameson's sense of castrated parody; rather, it is pastiche as a form of homage directly signaled by the text. At one point Kathryn compares Zack's three huge canvases to "the three last novels by Henry James," a comparison that Hope interprets as a sign of the younger woman's good taste (107). Later, Hope comments on what she learned from touring Europe with her third husband, the art collector Jerry Chafetz; it allowed her to see "at last what Henry James was saying" (237). These references to James are more than passing allusions. They in fact suggest the way that *Seek My Face* serves as a pastiche of James's limited third-person narration and his use of painting as a way to speak about his aesthetic concerns regarding the novel, something one finds in his essay "The Art of Fiction" (1884), in which he identifies fiction as one of the fine arts, and his story "The Real Thing" (1892), with its artist narrator obsessing about type and character.

Like James, Updike writes a story of a finely nuanced consciousness in which very little happens. In one sense, all of Hope's stories of the rise and fall of Abstract Expressionism are an extended piece of character delineation. Everything Hope reveals to (or decides to conceal from) Kathryn underscores the centrality of the thrust and parry relationship between interviewer and interviewee. The relationship that develops is, ultimately, one with an erotic subtext. Throughout, Hope gives loving descriptions of Kathryn's clothes and physical appearance, even the "beauty to the underside of the other woman's nose"; at the end of these reveries, "Hope sees the other woman as one a man could adore, go sick in love of, sink his seed into the groin of as if his life's work would be thereby accomplished" (226). What Hope, who has been discussing her life's work, fails to realize is how much her own observations turn back on her own apparently heterosexual life. The unacknowledged in Hope's sexual life emerges when Kathryn asks whether the artist was shocked to learn that her daughter Dorothy was a lesbian. At this point Hope asks that the tape recorder be turned off. She speaks candidly of her estrangement from Dot, who did not turn out to be the "tall, elegant, womanly woman" that Hope assumed she and Guy would produce (180). In speaking to Kathryn, who is tall and elegant, Hope reveals her own attraction to Dot's first lover and speaks of Dot's accusation that Hope had "seduc[ed] Guy away from his real orientation" (182). This accusation doubles an assertion Kathryn makes earlier in the day when she tells Hope that she "made [Zack] into a heterosexual" (84). Such doubling serves to show the ways in which Kathryn comes to stand in for Dot, and the intimacy that develops between the two women at one level allows Hope an imaginative way to try to correct the mistakes she made with Dot in withholding affection.

When Hope allows Kathryn to turn the tape recorder back on to answer the charge that she forced her first two husbands into unnatural heterosexuality, Hope speaks in a fashion that unconsciously comments on the relationship between interviewer and interviewee: "Within your experience, Kathryn, does one person seduce another? Or is it that two people give off signals – surround themselves with atomic auras – which bring them closer? People are drawn together by the instinct that their lives can benefit, that there will be – how do physicists talk – a net gain of order" (183–184). What the interviewer gains, clearly, is a piece that may help make her critical career. For Hope, the gain is more nebulous, but Kathryn's line of questioning makes Hope realize that Dot may have been right, that her penchant for the sexually passive Guy may speak something about her own desire.

The climactic moment of the novel occurs when Hope, "her face flood[ed] with an excited warmth," accompanies Kathryn out to her car in the rain. At this point Updike literalizes the religious seeking from Psalm 27 that serves as one of the novel's epigraphs, through a kiss that denotes a mother-daughter relation, but that more covertly connotes the erotic: "Hope . . . embraces her, though being so much shorter she lands her lips not on the other woman's cheek but on the bony curve of her jaw. Still she hangs on, relishing this muffled, impatient other body, naked and savory beneath its clothes, warmer than the air" (261). Hope warns Kathryn not to allow heterosexual relations to subsume her work and the younger woman self-consciously returns the kiss with thanks for Hope's generosity; Hope in turn thanks Kathryn for allowing her to make her life real to herself.

In the aftermath of the narrative climax, however, Kathryn's kiss (which holds nothing of the erotic from the young woman's perspective) is no more sustaining for Hope than sex with a woman is for Updike's male protagonists. Relieved to be alone again, "Hope feels a weight rolled away, the tall dark girl gone, swallowed by the storm, lost in the vortex now that the damp moment is past when she felt her solid in her arms, like Dot in those faraway days when the infant lay wriggling in her lonely cot on the floor dying to be plucked up and held" (268).

Ultimately, Hope is a more complex representation of the desiring woman than Gertrude. What makes this the case is that in *Seek My Face* Updike, whose earlier representations of homosexuality have often depended on stereotypes, is able to imagine the sexual multiplicities that lie behind Hope's ostensibly heterosexual desire. Rather than marginalize non-normative desire, Updike portrays it as a constitutive feature of Hope's identity.

What I have only been able to suggest in this brief survey of some of Updike's more recent fiction is that U & P remains open for further exploration. One almost wonders whether some of the fiction Updike has published in the past thirty years, had it appeared under some other name than "John Updike," might have been hailed as postmodern. But I am not (simply) claiming that Updike is (simply) a postmodernist. Updike has too often openly attacked the antihumanist implications of postmodern theory to make such an easy identification; the deconstructed subject and the transcendent soul are, finally, unlikely bedfellows. However, Updike's interrogation of the possibilities of faith, which seems to find increasingly narrow grounds for belief, means that he often stands much closer to postmodern conceptions of narrative, writing, and identity than has previously been suspected.

NOTES

1. Fredric Jameson, *Postmodernism, or, The Cultural Logic of Late Capitalism* (Durham: Duke University Press, 1991), p. 9.
2. See the excerpt from *Consumer Society* (1970), in *Jean Baudrillard: Selected Writings*, ed. Mark Poster, trans. Jacques Mourrain (Stanford: Stanford University Press, 1988), pp. 29–56.
3. Jean Baudrillard, "The Orders of Simulacra," in *Simulations*, trans. Paul Foss, Paul Patton, and Philip Beitchman (New York: Semiotext[e], 1983), pp. 141–142.
4. John Barth, "The Literature of Exhaustion" (1967), in Barth, *The Friday Book: Essays and Other Nonfiction* (Baltimore: Johns Hopkins University Press, 1984), p. 66.
5. John Barth, "The Literature of Replenishment" (1980), in Barth, *The Friday Book*, p. 206.
6. Roland Barthes, *The Pleasure of the Text* (1973), trans. Richard Miller (New York: Hill and Wang, 1975), p. 4.
7. John T. Matthews, "The Word as Scandal: Updike's *A Month of Sundays*," *Arizona Quarterly* 39 (1983), p. 380.
8. Jacques Derrida, *Of Grammatology* (1967), trans. Gayatri Chakravorty Spivak (Baltimore: Johns Hopkins University Press, 1976), p. 158.
9. Linda Hutcheon, *The Politics of Postmodernism* (London: Routledge, 1989), p. 71.
10. Linda Hutcheon, *A Poetics of Postmodernism: History, Theory, Fiction* (New York: Routledge, 1988), p. 120.
11. Jameson, *Postmodernism*, pp. 20, 25.
12. Laura Elena Savu, "In Desire's Grip: Gender, Politics, and Intertextual Games in Updike's *Gertrude and Claudius*," *Papers on Language and Literature* 39 (2003), pp. 22, 24.
13. Stephen Greenblatt, "With Dirge in Marriage," *New Republic*, 21 February 2000, p. 36.

GUIDE TO FURTHER READING

Updike, John. "Ecolalia." 1986. *Odd Jobs: Essays and Criticism*. New York: Knopf, 1991, pp. 680–685.
   "Elusive Evil." 1996. *More Matter: Essays and Criticism*. New York: Knopf, 1999, pp. 464–480.

"Modernist, Postmodernist, What Will They Think of Next?" 1984. *Odd Jobs: Essays and Criticism.* New York: Knopf, 1991, pp. 694–702.
"Novel Thoughts." 1995. *More Matter: Essays and Criticism.* New York: Knopf, 1999, pp. 453–464.
"On the Edge of the Post-Human." 1997. *More Matter: Essays and Criticism.* New York: Knopf, 1999, pp. 363–365.

SELECT BIBLIOGRAPHY

UPDIKE'S WRITINGS

Novels

Brazil. New York: Knopf, 1994.
The Centaur. New York: Knopf, 1963.
The Coup. New York: Knopf, 1978.
Couples. New York: Knopf, 1968.
Gertrude and Claudius. New York: Knopf, 2000.
In the Beauty of the Lilies. New York: Knopf, 1996.
Marry Me: A Romance. New York: Knopf, 1976.
Memories of the Ford Administration: A Novel. New York: Knopf, 1992.
A Month of Sundays. New York: Knopf, 1975.
Of the Farm. New York: Knopf, 1965.
The Poorhouse Fair. New York: Knopf, 1959.
Rabbit Angstrom: A Tetralogy. New York: Everyman's Library-Knopf, 1995.
Rabbit at Rest. New York: Knopf, 1990.
Rabbit Is Rich. New York: Knopf, 1981.
Rabbit Redux. New York: Knopf, 1971.
Rabbit, Run. New York: Knopf, 1960.
Roger's Version. New York: Knopf, 1986.
S. New York: Knopf, 1988.
Seek My Face. New York: Knopf, 2002.
Toward the End of Time. New York: Knopf, 1997.
Villages. New York: Knopf, 2004.
The Witches of Eastwick. New York: Knopf, 1984.

Short stories

The Afterlife and Other Stories. New York: Knopf, 1994.
Bech: A Book. New York: Knopf, 1970.
Bech at Bay: A Quasi-Novel. New York: Knopf, 1998.
Bech Is Back. New York: Knopf, 1982.
The Complete Henry Beck: Twenty Stories. New York: Everyman's Library-Knopf, 2001.

The Early Stories, 1953–1975. New York: Knopf, 2003.
Licks of Love: Short Stories and a Sequel. New York: Knopf, 2000.
Museums and Women and Other Stories. New York: Knopf, 1972.
The Music School: Short Stories. New York: Knopf, 1966.
Olinger Stories: A Selection. New York: Vintage, 1964.
Pigeon Feathers and Other Stories. New York: Knopf, 1962.
Problems and Other Stories. New York: Knopf, 1979.
The Same Door: Short Stories. New York: Knopf, 1959.
Too Far to Go: The Maples Stories. New York: Fawcett Crest, 1979.
Trust Me: Short Stories. New York: Knopf, 1987.

Poetry

Americana and Other Poems. New York: Knopf, 2001.
The Carpentered Hen and Other Tame Creatures. New York: Harper and Brothers,
    1958.
Collected Poems 1953–1993. New York: Knopf, 1993.
Facing Nature: Poems. New York: Knopf, 1985.
Midpoint and Other Poems. New York: Knopf, 1969.
Telephone Poles and Other Poems. New York: Knopf, 1963.
Tossing and Turning: Poems. New York: Knopf, 1977.

Play

Buchanan Dying: A Play. New York: Knopf, 1974.

Essays and criticism

Assorted Prose. New York: Knopf, 1965.
Golf Dreams: Writings on Golf. New York: Knopf, 1996.
Hugging the Shore: Essays and Criticism. New York: Knopf, 1983.
Just Looking: Essays on Art. New York: Knopf, 1989.
More Matter: Essays and Criticism. New York: Knopf, 1999.
Odd Jobs: Essays and Criticism. New York: Knopf, 1991.
Picked-Up Pieces. New York: Knopf, 1975.

Memoir

Self-Consciousness: Memoirs. New York: Knopf, 1989.

Children's books

Bottom's Dream. New York: Knopf, 1969.
A Child's Calendar. New York: Knopf, 1965.
A Helpful Alphabet of Friendly Objects: Poems. New York: Knopf, 1995.
The Magic Flute. New York: Knopf, 1962.
The Ring. New York: Knopf, 1964.

SECONDARY SOURCES

Bibliographies, encyclopedias, and related resources

In addition to the texts listed below, bibliographical information on Updike is published annually in *American Literary Scholarship: An Annual* (Durham: Duke University Press) and in the *MLA Bibliography*. Updike's papers can be viewed at the Houghton Library, Harvard University.

De Bellis, Jack, comp. *John Updike: A Bibliography, 1967–1993*. Westport, CT: Greenwood, 1994.

The John Updike Encyclopedia. Westport, CT: Greenwood, 2000.

Gearhart, Elizabeth A. *John Updike: A Comprehensive Bibliography with Selected Annotations*. Norwood, PA: Norwood, 1978.

Olivas, Michael A. *An Annotated Bibliography of John Updike Criticism 1967–1973, and A Checklist of His Works*. New York: Garland, 1975.

Sokoloff, B. A., and David E. Arnason. *John Updike: A Comprehensive Bibliography*. Folcroft, PA: Folcroft, 1971.

Taylor, C. Clarke. *John Updike: A Bibliography*. Kent, OH: Kent State University Press, 1968.

Yerkes, James. *The Centaurian Website*. http://userpages.prexar.com/joyerkes/index. html

Essay collections, collected interviews, and journal special issues

Bloom, Harold, ed. *John Updike*. New York: Chelsea House, 1987.

Broer, Lawrence R., ed. *Rabbit Tales: Poetry and Politics in John Updike's Rabbit Novels*. Tuscaloosa: University of Alabama Press, 1998.

De Bellis, Jack, ed. *John Updike: The Critical Responses to the "Rabbit" Saga*. Westport, CT: Greenwood, 2005.

Mcnaughton, William R., ed. *Critical Essays on John Updike*. Boston: G. K. Hall, 1982.

Plath, James, ed. *Conversations with John Updike*. Jackson: University Press of Mississippi, 1994.

Stafford, William T., ed. *John Updike Number. Modern Fiction Studies* 20 (1974).

Stuckey, William J., ed. *John Updike Special Issue. Modern Fiction Studies* 37 (1991).

Thorburn, David, and Howard Eiland, eds. *John Updike: A Collection of Critical Essays*. Englewood Cliffs, NJ: Prentice-Hall, 1979.

Trachtenberg, Stanley, ed. *New Essays on Rabbit, Run*. Cambridge: Cambridge University Press, 1993.

Yerkes, James, ed. *John Updike and Religion: The Sense of the Sacred and the Motions of Grace*. Grand Rapids, MI: Eerdmans, 1999.

Book-length studies of John Updike

Boswell, Marshall. *John Updike's Rabbit Tetralogy: Mastered Irony in Motion*. Columbia: University of Missouri Press, 2001.

Burchard, Rachael C. *John Updike: Yea Sayings*. Carbondale: Southern Illinois University Press, 1971.

Campbell, Jeff H. *Updike's Novels: Thorns Spell a Word*. Wichita Falls, TX: Midwestern State University Press, 1987.

Detweiler, Robert. *John Updike*. New York: Twayne, 1972; rev. ed. Boston: Twayne, 1984.

Greiner, Donald J. *Adultery in the American Novel: Updike, James, and Hawthorne*. Columbia: University of South Carolina Press, 1985.

John Updike's Novels. Athens, OH: Ohio University Press, 1984.

The Other John Updike: Poems/Short Stories/Prose/Play. Athens, OH: Ohio University Press, 1981.

Hamilton, Alice and Kenneth. *The Elements of John Updike*. Grand Rapids, MI: Eerdmans, 1970.

Hunt, George W. *John Updike and the Three Great Secret Things: Sex, Religion, and Art*. Grand Rapids, MI: Eerdmans, 1980.

Luscher, Robert M. *John Updike: A Study of the Short Fiction*. New York: Twayne, 1993.

Markle, Joyce B. *Fighters and Lovers: Theme in the Novels of John Updike*. New York: New York University Press, 1973.

Miller, D. Quentin. *John Updike and the Cold War: Drawing the Iron Curtain*. Columbia: University of Missouri Press, 2001.

Neary, John. *Something and Nothingness: The Fiction of John Updike and John Fowles*. Carbondale: Southern Illinois University Press, 1992.

Newman, Judie. *John Updike*. New York: St. Martin's Press, 1988.

O'Connell, Mary. *Updike and the Patriarchal Dilemma: Masculinity in the Rabbit Novels*. Carbondale: Southern Illinois University Press, 1996.

Pritchard, William H. *Updike: America's Man of Letters*. South Royalton, VT: Steerforth, 2000.

Ristoff, Dilvo I. *John Updike's Rabbit at Rest: Appropriating History*. New York: Peter Lang, 1998.

Updike's America: The Presence of Contemporary American History in John Updike's Rabbit Trilogy. New York: Peter Lang, 1988.

Samuels, Charles Thomas. *John Updike*. Minneapolis: University of Minnesota Press, 1969.

Schiff, James A. *John Updike Revisited*. New York: Twayne, 1998.

Updike's Version: Rewriting The Scarlet Letter. Columbia: University of Missouri Press, 1992.

Searles, George J. *The Fiction of Philip Roth and John Updike*. Carbondale: Southern Illinois University Press, 1985.

Tallent, Elizabeth. *Married Men and Magic Tricks: John Updike's Erotic Heroes*. Berkeley, CA: Creative Arts, 1982.

Taylor, Larry E. *Pastoral and Anti-Pastoral Patterns in John Updike's Fiction*. Carbondale: Southern Illinois University Press, 1971.

Uphaus, Suzanne Henning. *John Updike*. New York: Ungar, 1980.

Vargo, Edward P. *Rainstorms and Fire: Ritual in the Novels of John Updike*. Port Washington, NY: Kennikat, 1973.

Vaughan, Philip H. *John Updike's Images of America*. Reseda, CA: Mojave, 1981.

Book chapters and articles on John Updike

Ahearn, Kerry. "Family and Adultery: Images and Ideas in Updike's Rabbit Novels." *Twentieth Century Literature* 34 (1988), pp. 62–83.

Alonso-Gallo, Laura P. "*Brazil*: John Updike's Contemporary Rendition of Romance and Medieval Myth." *Grove* 2 (1997), pp. 7–17.

Alter, Robert. "Updike, Malamud, and the Fire This Time." *Commentary*, October 1972, pp. 68–74.

Bailey, Peter. "Notes on the Novel-as-Autobiography." *Genre* 14 (1981), pp. 79–93.

Balbert, Peter. "A Panoply of Metaphor: Exuberances of Style in Pynchon and Updike." *Studies in the Novel* 15 (1983), pp. 265–276.

Berryman, Charles. "The Education of Harry Angstrom: Rabbit and the Moon." *Literary Review* 27 (1983), pp. 117–126.

Boswell, Marshall. "The Black Jesus: Racism and Redemption in John Updike's *Rabbit Redux*." *Contemporary Literature* 39 (1998), pp. 99–132.

Boyer, Paul. "Notes of a Disillusioned Lover: John Updike's *Memories of the Ford Administration*." *American Literary History* 13 (2001), pp. 67–78.

Brenner, Gerry. "*Rabbit, Run*: John Updike's Criticism of the 'Return to Nature.'" *Twentieth Century Literature* 12 (1966), pp. 3–14.

Burhans Jr., Clinton S. "Things Falling Apart: Structure and Theme in *Rabbit, Run*." *Studies in the Novel* 5 (1973), pp. 336–351.

Caesar, Terry. "'So That's the Flag': The Representation of Brazil and the Politics of Nation in American Literature." *Criticism* 41 (1999), pp. 365–384.

Calinescu, Matei. "Secrecy in Fiction: Textual and Intertextual Secrets in Hawthorne and Updike." *Poetics Today* 15 (1994), pp. 443–465.

Chanley, Steven M. "Quest for Order in 'Pigeon Feathers': Updike's Use of Christian Mythology." *Arizona Quarterly* 43 (1987), pp. 251–263.

Clausen, Jan. "Native Fathers." *Kenyon Review* 14.2 (1992), pp. 44–55.

Coale, Samuel C. "Marriage in Contemporary American Literature: The Mismatched Marriages of Manichean Minds." *Thought* 58 (1983), pp. 111–121.

Corbellari, Alain, and Catherine Müller. "John Updike's Tristanian Passion." *Tristania* 19 (1999), pp. 115–125.

Crews, Frederick. "Mr. Updike's Planet." *The Critics Bear It Away: American Fiction and the Academy*. New York: Random House, 1992, pp. 168–186.

Crowley, Sue Mitchell. "John Updike and Kierkegaard's Negative Way: Irony and Indirect Communication in *A Month of Sundays*." *Soundings* 68 (1985), pp. 212–228.

De Bellis, Jack. "'The Awful Power': John Updike's Use of Kubrick's *2001: A Space Odyssey* in *Rabbit Redux*." *Literature/Film Quarterly* 21 (1993), pp. 209–217.

"'It Captivates . . . It Hypnotizes': Updike Goes to the Movies." *Literature/Film Quarterly* 23 (1995), pp. 169–187.

Detweiler, Robert. "Updike's *Couples*: Eros Demythologized." *Twentieth Century Literature* 17 (1971), pp. 235–246.

Doody, Terrence A. "Updike's Idea of Reification." *Contemporary Literature* 20 (1979), pp. 204–220.

Duvall, John N. "Cross-Confessing: Updike's Erect Faith in *A Month of Sundays*." *Straight with a Twist: Queer Theory and the Subject of Heterosexuality*. Ed. Calvin Thomas. Urbana: University of Illinois Press, 2000, pp. 122–145.

"The Pleasure of Textual/Sexual Wrestling: Pornography and Heresy in *Roger's Version*." *Modern Fiction Studies* 37 (1991), pp. 81–95.

Eiland, Howard. "Updike's Womanly Man." *Centennial Review* 26 (1982), pp. 312–323.

El Moncef, Salah. "Sounding the Black Box: Linear Reproduction and Chance Bifurcations in *Rabbit at Rest.*" *Arizona Quarterly* 51.4 (1995), pp. 69–108.

Fleischauer, John F. "John Updike's Prose Style: Definition at the Periphery of Meaning." *Critique* 30 (1989), pp. 277–290.

Galloway, David D. "The Absurd Man as Saint: The Novels of John Updike." *Modern Fiction Studies* 10 (1964), pp. 111–127.

Gindin, James. "Megalotopia and the WASP Backlash: The Fiction of Mailer and Updike." *Centennial Review* 15 (1971), pp. 38–52.

Gordon, Mary. "Good Boys and Dead Girls." *Good Boys and Dead Girls and Other Essays*. New York: Viking Penguin, 1991, pp. 3–23.

Greiner, Donald J. "Body and Soul: John Updike and *The Scarlet Letter.*" *Journal of Modern Literature* 15 (1989), pp. 475–495.

Hallissy, Margaret M. "Marriage, Morality and Maturity in Updike's *Marry Me.*" *Renascence* 37 (1985), pp. 96–106.

Hamilton, Alice and Kenneth. "Metamorphosis Through Art: John Updike's *Bech: A Book.*" *Queen's Quarterly* 77 (1970), pp. 624–636.

"Theme and Technique in John Updike's *Midpoint.*" *Mosaic* 4.1 (1970), pp. 79–106.

Harper Jr., Howard M. "John Updike: The Intrinsic Problem of Human Existence." *Desperate Faith: A Study of Bellow, Salinger, Mailer, Baldwin, and Updike.* Chapel Hill: University of North Carolina Press, 1967, pp. 162–190.

Held, George. "Men on the Moon: American Novelists Explore Lunar Space." *Michigan Quarterly Review* 18 (1979), pp. 318–342.

Horton, Andrew S. "Ken Kesey, John Updike and the Lone Ranger." *Journal of Popular Culture* 8 (1974), pp. 570–578.

Horvath, Brooke. "The Failure of Erotic Questing in John Updike's Rabbit Novels." *Denver Quarterly* 23 (1988), pp. 70–89.

Hunt, George W. "Updike's Pilgrims in a World of Nothingness." *Thought* 53 (1978), pp. 384–400.

Jackson, Edward M. "Rabbit Is Racist." *College Language Association Journal* 28 (1985), pp. 444–451.

Keskinen, Mikko. "Bech Signing: Repetition, Identity, and Signature in John Updike's 'Three Illuminations in the Life of an American Author.'" *Imaginaires* 9 (2003), pp. 287–301.

Klinkowitz, Jerome. "John Updike's America." *North American Review*, September 1980, pp. 68–71.

"Toward a New American Mainstream: John Updike and Kurt Vonnegut." *Traditions, Voices, and Dreams: The American Novel since the 1960s.* Ed. Melvin J. Friedman and Ben Siegel. Newark: University of Delaware Press, 1995, pp. 150–167.

Lasseter, Victor K. "*Rabbit Is Rich* as a Naturalistic Novel." *American Literature* 61 (1989), pp. 429–445.

Lathrop, Kathleen. "*The Coup:* John Updike's Modernist Masterpiece." *Modern Fiction Studies* 31 (1985), pp. 249–262.

Leckie, Barbara. "'The Adulterous Society': John Updike's *Marry Me.*" *Modern Fiction Studies* 37 (1991), pp. 61–79.

Leigh, David. "Ironic Apocalypse in John Updike's *Toward the End of Time.*" *Religion and Literature* 34 (2002), pp. 51–65.

Le Pellec, Yves. "Rabbit Underground." *Les Américanistes: New French Criticism on Modern American Fiction.* Ed. Ira D. Johnson and Christiane Johnson. Port Washington, NY: Kennikat, 1978, pp. 94–109.

Luscher, Robert M. "John Updike's *Olinger Stories*: New Light Among the Shadows." *Journal of the Short Story in English* 11 (1988), pp. 99–117.

Matthews, John T. "The Word as Scandal: Updike's *A Month of Sundays.*" *Arizona Quarterly* 39 (1983), pp. 351–380.

Mazurek, Raymond A. "'Bringing the Corners Forward': Ideology and Representation in Updike's Rabbit Trilogy." *Politics and the Muse: Studies in the Politics of Recent American Literature.* Ed. Adam J. Sorkin. Bowling Green, OH: Bowling Green State University Popular Press, 1989, pp. 142–160.

Mellard, James M. "The Novel as Lyric Elegy: The Mode of Updike's *The Centaur.*" *Texas Studies in Literature and Language* 21 (1979), pp. 112–127.

Miller, D. Quentin. "Updike's Rabbit Novels and the Tragedy of Parenthood." *Family Matters in the British and American Novel.* Ed. Andrea O'Reilly Herrera, Elizabeth Mahn Nollen, and Sheila Reitzel Foor. Bowling Green, OH: Bowling Green State University Popular Press, 1997, pp. 195–215.

Miller, Miriam Youngerman. "A Land Too Ripe for Enigma: John Updike as Regionalist." *Arizona Quarterly* 40 (1984), pp. 197–218.

Moran, Joe. "John Updike's *Self-Consciousness* and Literary Fame." *A/B: Auto/Biography Studies* 15 (2000), pp. 298–309.

Neary, John M. "'Ah, Runs': Updike, Rabbit, and Repetition." *Religion and Literature* 21 (1989), pp. 89–110.

Oates, Joyce Carol. "Updike's American Comedies." *Modern Fiction Studies* 21 (1975), pp. 459–472.

Olster, Stacey. "Rabbit Is Redundant: Updike's End of an American Epoch." *Neo-Realism in Contemporary American Fiction.* Ed. Kristiaan Versluys. Amsterdam: Rodopi, 1992, pp. 111–129.

"Rabbit Rerun: Updike's Replay of Popular Culture in *Rabbit at Rest.*" *Modern Fiction Studies* 37 (1991), pp. 45–59.

Ozick, Cynthia. "Bech, Passing." *Art & Ardor.* New York: Knopf, 1983, pp. 114–129.

Pasewark, Kyle A. "The Troubles with Harry: Freedom, America, and God in John Updike's Rabbit Novels." *Religion and American Culture* 6 (1996), pp. 1–33.

Pinsker, Sanford. "Joyce's Poldy/Updike's Rabbit: Popular Culture and the Problem of Consciousness." *Cimarron Review* 110 (1995), pp. 92–101.

Plagman, Linda M. "*Eros* and *Agape*: The Opposition in Updike's *Couples.*" *Renascence* 28 (1976), pp. 83–93.

Porter, M. Gilbert. "From Babbitt to Rabbit: The American Materialist in Search of a Soul." *American Literature in Belgium.* Ed. Gilbert Debusscher and Marc Maufort. Amsterdam: Rodopi, 1988, pp. 185–198.

Powers, Peter Kerry. "Scribbling for a Life: Masculinity, Doctrine, and Style in the Work of John Updike." *Christianity and Literature* 43 (1994), pp. 329–346.

Prosser, Jay. "The Thick-Skinned Art of John Updike: 'From the Journal of a Leper.'" *Yearbook of English Studies* 31 (2001), pp. 182–191.

"Under the Skin of John Updike: Self-Consciousness and the Racial Unconscious." *PMLA* 116 (2001), pp. 579–593.

Regan, Robert Alton. "Updike's Symbol of the Center." *Modern Fiction Studies* 20 (1974), pp. 77–96.

Robinson, Sally. "'Unyoung, Unpoor, Unblack': John Updike and the Construction of Middle American Masculinity." *Modern Fiction Studies* 44 (1998), pp. 331–363.

Royal, Derek Parker. "An Absent Presence: The Rewriting of Hawthorne's Narratology in John Updike's *S.*" *Critique* 44 (2002), pp. 73–85.

Saldívar, Toni. "The Art of John Updike's 'A & P.'" *Studies in Short Fiction* 34 (1997), pp. 215–225.

Savu, Laura Elena. "In Desire's Grip: Gender, Politics, and Intertextual Games in Updike's *Gertrude and Claudius.*" *Papers on Language and Literature* 39 (2003), pp. 22–48.

Schiff, James A. "Updike Ignored: The Contemporary Independent Critic." *American Literature* 67 (1995), pp. 531–552.

Schopen, Bernard A. "Faith, Morality, and the Novels of John Updike." *Twentieth Century Literature* 24 (1978), pp. 523–535.

Schueller, Malini. "Containing the Third World: John Updike's *The Coup.*" *Modern Fiction Studies* 37 (1991), pp. 113–128.

Sethuraman, Ramchandran. "Updike's *The Centaur*: On Aphanisis, Gaze, Eyes, and the Death Drive." *Literature and Psychology* 39.3 (1993), pp. 38–65.

Siegel, Gary. "Rabbit Runs Down." *The Modern American Novel and the Movies.* Ed. Gerald Peary and Roger Shatzkin. New York: Ungar, 1978, pp. 247–255.

Strandberg, Victor. "John Updike and the Changing of the Gods." *Mosaic* 12.1 (1978), pp. 157–175.

Tracy, Bruce H. "The Habit of Confession: Recovery of the Self in Updike's 'The Music School.'" *Studies in Short Fiction* 21 (1984), pp. 339–355.

Uphaus, Suzanne. "*The Centaur*: Updike's Mock Epic." *Journal of Narrative Technique* 7 (1977), pp. 24–36.

Vargo, Edward P. "The Necessity of Myth in Updike's *The Centaur.*" *PMLA* 88 (1973), pp. 452–460.

"Tempering the Darkness: John Updike's Light Verse." *Fu Jen Studies* 22 (1989), pp. 33–52.

Verduin, Kathleen. "Sex, Nature, and Dualism in *The Witches of Eastwick.*" *Modern Language Quarterly* 46 (1985), pp. 293–315.

Waldron, Randall H. "Rabbit Revised." *American Literature* 56 (1984), pp. 51–67.

Wang, An-chi. "The American Dream Ideology in John Updike's Rabbit Tetralogy." *Studies in Language and Literature* 9 (2000), pp. 227–268.

Wilson III, Raymond J. "*Roger's Version*: Updike's Negative-Solid Model of *The Scarlet Letter.*" *Modern Fiction Studies* 35 (1989), pp. 241–250.

INDEX

CAMBRIDGE COMPANIONS TO LITERATURE

CAMBRIDGE COMPANIONS TO CULTURE

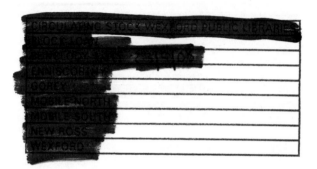